Farewell to Arabia

Omani Tribesmen

FAREWELL TO ARABIA

by

DAVID HOLDEN

Walker and Company

New York

First published in the United States of America in 1966 by Walker and Company, a division of Publications Development Corporation.

Printed in the United States of America from type set in Great Britain.

Contents

7

Illustrations

9

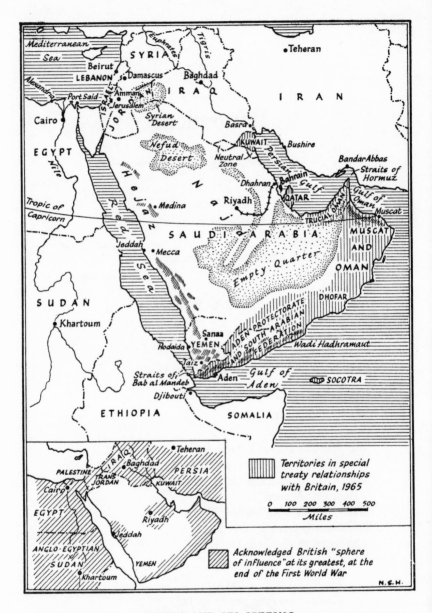

Territories in special
treaty relationships
with Britain, 1965

0   100 200 300 400 500
Miles

Acknowledged British "sphere
of influence" at its greatest, at the
end of the First World War

N.S.H.

ARABIA AND ITS SETTING

Introduction

Arabia. The name has always evoked an exotic image. Because it signified for so long a land so desolate, isolated and unknown, it conveys even now a ring of loneliness and a promise of escape calculated to stir in all of us some flicker of romance. The names and deeds of its great explorers surge vaguely and nostalgically in the memory at its utterance. Burckhardt and Palgrave, Burton and Doughty — their lean and bearded faces, hooded in the secretive, disguising robes of the desert, peer at us from the lithographs of dusty Victorian texts. Lawrence, with the name itself attached to him forever like a golden cloak, raises schoolboy ghosts of valour and derring-do. Down to our own day the roll-call of remembered names continues, through St. John Philby, Bertram Thomas, and Wilfred Thesiger — all of them wrapped in the spell of the sere peninsula. Their names are the record of a love affair, between mortal men and the immortal image of mystery that Arabia represented.

This book writes goodbye to all that, in a story of change so swift and embracing as to merit the title of revolution. It is only a couple of generations, after all, since the romantic image of Arabia was still essentially the true one, at least as far as the outside world was concerned. As recently as thirty or forty years ago much of the peninsula was still the forbidden land. A tract of desert as big as western Europe, relieved only by a few hidden corners of fertility, it had survived in inbred isolation to become one of the last substantial *terrae incognitae* of the inhabited world. Its harsh periphery had defeated nearly every attempt at prolonged foreign conquest or penetration. The Romans sent an army into the rain-tipped mountains of the Yemen, and thought them green enough to earn the title of *Arabia Felix*, but not all their vast imperial energy was enough to enable them to stay. The Egyptians followed them, 1,800 years later, when Mehemet Ali tried to assert his hegemony over the heartland of Islam, but they, too, were defeated by

Arabia's grim defences. The Turks occupied parts of the peninsula after a fashion, but their rule was unorganised and their peace sporadic, and they left no lasting impression upon the vast majority of its people. The Persians sent their soldiers to Arabia's eastern fringes, but could establish only a brief foothold; and the Portuguese, indefatigable in the pursuit of trade four centuries ago, built forts and factories in Muscat and Oman but withdrew after a century of local hostility bequeathing nothing to Arabia but crumbling walls and fading memories. Otherwise, scarcely a score of foreign travellers had got far beyond Arabia's coasts before this century opened, and until well after the Second World War some parts of its interior were still almost unknown.

Arabia's aspect was always daunting. The sand dunes and lava fields along most of its shores and the savage heat of the desert sun promised nothing but hardship, and although scientific curiosity or a love of adventure might impel some men to assault these barriers, few of them envisaged and none found any means of turning curiosity to commerce or adventure to material advantage. 'Here is a dead land,' wrote Charles Doughty, in that great classic of travel, *Arabia Deserta*, 'whence, if he die not, (the traveller) shall bring home nothing but a perpetual weariness in his bones. . . . In a parcel of earth great as an house floor, you shall not find many blades and hardly some one of the desert bushes, of which two thirds are no cattle-meat but quite waste and naught.' Among the scattered inhabitants of this desolation, war, xenophobia and religious bigotry flourished, to the further discouragement of all sensible travellers. The efforts of the explorers remained, therefore, purely personal affairs, unsupported as a rule by either governments or trade.

Behind their complementary barriers of man and nature, the tribes of Arabia sustained themselves in poverty and introspection, innocent of nationhood and ignorant of the world. Their governments were a function of individuals rather than institutions, and instability was endemic. Nomadism was usually essential in their desert life, and fixed frontiers accordingly were unknown. Few foreign flags were raised over them, and no empire-builders settled among them, even in the heyday of European expansion. Only Britain, among the later imperial powers, developed any lasting connexion with the peninsula, and for nearly 150 years that was little more than a maritime domination of its coastal fringe exercised exclusively in the interest of her Indian Empire.

As this curious relationship between Britain and Arabia will crop up repeatedly in the following pages, it is worth taking a brief, introductory look at its nature here. It was said of T. E. Lawrence that he had a genius for backing into the limelight; it might be said that his country has shown at least as great a talent for backing into Arabia. There has never been any British frontal assault upon Arabia — only a hesitant and remarkably recent encroachment inspired, almost against Britain's will and better judgement, by the logic of latter-day politics and economics which neither Britain nor Arabia could escape. In the first place, it was only the need to secure the approaches to India that induced Britain to sign her first Arabian treaty, when she obtained a promise of the Sultan of Muscat's help against the French during the Napoleonic wars. It was the same need to frustrate Napoleon's intentions in India that caused her to seize her first Arabian military base, when she occupied the island of Perim, west of Aden, during the French attack on Egypt. It was to subdue piracy upon her Indian trade that she imposed a maritime truce on the shaikhdoms of the Persian Gulf and annexed the port of Aden. And it was to exclude the other great powers from the back door to India that she later extended her sway along the Arabian coast by a series of agreements which gave her the right to conduct the foreign affairs of many of the local rulers in exchange for a commitment to defend them from their enemies.

The protection of India and its trade, however, required no British territorial sovereignty in Arabia. As long as the seas were free and the other powers were kept at arm's length, the mainland of Arabia could be left to look after itself. Only in the port of Aden — a paltry 75 square miles — did Britain assume the responsibility of direct rule, and even that was inspired chiefly by the desire of the East India Company to establish there a coaling station for its new steamships in the Indian trade. The rest of the thirty or forty separate territories between the Aden Protectorate and the shaikhdom of Kuwait remained more or less independent principalities in 'special treaty relationships' with Britain. The ambiguity of that phrase is deliberate, for it embraces many a varied and curious agreement, establishing many a different degree of shaikhly subordination to British power. In no case, however, was the subordination total. Every one of the treaties confirmed the rulers in some measure of independence by deliberately restricting Britain's right to interfere in their internal affairs. It was no part of the mission of the British Raj to accept entanglement in the barren wastes of Arabia, or to extend the *Pax Britannica* to its warlike tribes. Thus, while the railways and colonial officers were changing the face of the rest of the world in the nineteenth century, Arabia remained untouched. While the great powers drew their frontiers over the maps of Africa and Asia, Arabia remained a cartographic blank until the outbreak of the First World War.

Then, almost without anyone realising it, the contemporary Arabian revolution was conceived. Politically, it began through the collapse of Ottoman power and the turmoil of the Arab revolt, which created eventually the modern, independent Arabian states of the Yemen and Saudi Arabia that were to offer, in turn, the first, indigenous challenge to British authority around the fringes of the peninsula. Economically, it started with the signature of the first oil agreements between Britain and the rulers of the Gulf states, which gave the British — and the world — their first direct territorial interest in Arabia. Technically, it was heralded by the rapid development of the motor car, the aeroplane and the radio which were soon to transform the means of travel and communication and open Arabia to the world and the world to Arabia in a manner never before imagined.

Even so, the old Arabia was at first only marginally affected. When the First World War was over, much of the peninsula's interior was still unexplored, the oil industry was still a creature of the future, and the British connexion was still peripheral and governed more by the pre-conceptions of the Raj in India than by anything else. The next quarter-of-a-century was the revolution's period of gestation. While Arabia's life remained, apparently, almost as introspective, tribal and aloof as ever, the first embryonic changes of the new world were working invisibly within. Only when the Second World War was over did they break decisively through the mantle of Arabian tradition. Then, Britain's withdrawal from India and the swift rise of Arab nationalism accelerated the political changes that the fall of the Ottoman Empire had presaged; the new dimensions of the oil industry in the Persian Gulf swept much of the peninsula into an unprecedented economic boom; and the fresh technical advances in all the means of travel and communication not merely opened up the country but transformed the significance of government and frontiers alike.

This triple-fronted movement took a few more years to gather strength and speed, but since the middle 1950's it has brought every facet of the old Arabia under sustained attack. Rapid and widespread dissolution has resulted — in morals and society as much as in politics or economics. Only yesterday most of the people of Arabia enjoyed a life that was coherent and self-contained, and basically unchanged since the days of Abraham. Today they are in a state of schizophrenia as the twentieth century sucks them into its common maw. Revolutionary ideas of society have been imported through prosperity, education and the radio. The search for new kinds of political freedom has been inspired by the example of successful independence movements elsewhere and the pressures of the international cold war. The demands and opportunities of a wage economy have undermined the individualism of tribal life; and in territories where the resources are now measured in terms of oil reserves instead of date gardens, and where money is counted in millions of pounds instead of hundreds of rupees, shaikhs and sultans have needed technicians and civil servants more than slaves or concubines. Frontiers have had to be fixed, administrations organised and laws codified. The rulers have been set against the administrators, the old tribes against the new townsmen, the orthodox faithful against the secular reformists; while Britain has been forced to extend the *Pax Britannica* inland in defiance of her growing military weakness and her surrender of imperial responsibilities elsewhere.

Of course, this does not mean that the old Arabia has disappeared in the space of the last few years. On the contrary, both emotionally and physically, it maintains a fierce rearguard action against the encroachment of the new world. The townsmen have not yet subdued the tribes, nor have modern prosperity and techniques altered Arabia's fundamental aspect of desolation. Hour after hour, as you fly across the great plateaux of the centre, baked and cracked in the sun like mud, nothing but a black speckle of scrub hints at life from horizon to horizon. Hour after hour, the red ripples of the giant sand dunes pass beneath you in the Empty Quarter, as clean and burnished as a sheet of beaten copper; and hour after hour you may drone along deserted shores, sometimes jagged with red rocks plunging into a black-blue sea, sometimes smoothed into curves as frail and indeterminate as chiffon where the sandspits, lagoons and coral reefs blend the water into every shade of purple, green and yellow. This Arabia will not vanish or be transformed in a decade or two. It is too tough and its people are too individual to be forced at once into any new mould. All the same, the twentieth century in the end brooks no defaulters. Unlike any other era in history it has made us all members one of another even when we would rather not be, because there is no longer any real possibility anywhere of isolation or mutual forgetfulness. Not even in Arabia.

By the chance of professional assignment I made the first of many visits to Arabia just when this truism began to be pressed home in every corner of the peninsula — and when, therefore, its present conflicts and confusions began to force themselves irresistibly upon the world's attention. That was at the end of 1956 — the year of the Suez crisis — and I hope it will not seem too egocentric to suggest that the years since then, which provide most of the material for this book, have been particularly important in the development of what I call, for convenience' sake, the new Arabia. All the major events of the period have been, in some sense, revolutionary. The Yemen revolt and subsequent civil war; Kuwait's achievement of full independence and its critical aftermath; the first attempts to turn Saudi Arabia into a modern state; the formal ending of slavery throughout most of the peninsula; Britain's promise of independence to a new state of South Arabia; and the continuing growth of the oil industry along the shores of the Persian Gulf, all reflect or have created radically new relationships within Arabia and between Arabia and the rest of the world. The repercussions of the Suez crisis itself have left a profound mark upon many of these events. The mutual distrust of Britain and Egypt, which it so viciously inflamed; the sense of an emotional and political renaissance among the Arabs, which it greatly strengthened; the realisation that Britain could no longer go it alone as a world power, which it confirmed; and the intrusion of both America and Russia into the Middle East, which it accelerated, are all recurrent themes in Arabia today.

I do not hope, however, to offer either a comprehensive history or a political analysis of all these events and themes. The canvas is too big and the business is too unfinished for that. Before these words can appear in print it is likely that some of the situations they describe will have been overtaken by fresh events, so swiftly does the revolution now advance. All that this can be is an interim report — an attempt to picture the process of change in action, capturing and perhaps dissecting a little the forms it has taken and the forces of which it has been composed among the places and people I have seen in the last decade. As such it is the story, fitful maybe and certainly incomplete, of how the whole of this once-unknown peninsula is being made for the first time and presumably forever part of the common consciousness of the world. It contains, therefore, an involuntary welcome to a new Arabia as well as a farewell to the old.

I

The Town Insurgent

From the roof of the Crescent Hotel in Aden you may look out over one of the widest, finest and busiest harbours between London and Bombay. Behind you is a massive range of red and jagged cliffs, with a thin bracelet of buildings clinging to its base. Before you is a great sweep of sheltered water, filled with ships. A cluster of rocky peaks in the distance marks the peninsula of Little Aden, to the right there is a white glitter of salt pans, and off to the left, southwards, the Indian Ocean shimmers under a sun that in summer strikes upon Aden like an axe. From time to time a hot gust comes from the north to narrow your eyes and burn your cheeks, as if someone had opened a furnace door. There, under a layer of purple haze, topped sometimes by the cauliflower growth of thunderheads, is Arabia. Here, around the wide harbour of Aden, is that harsh peninsula's best and biggest port — one of those natural toll-gates of the world, to which caravans, ships and people are drawn in the course of commerce.

Bumboats, ocean liners, tramps and tankers churn up the water, and put ashore their passengers and crews to search for the duty-free luxuries of Hong-Kong, Germany and Japan in the rows of Indian shops behind the waterfront. Cameras, radios, watches and perfumes are the cargo they seek, while their vessels take on fuel. This is Steamer Point, where the ships of the world began to call when they acquired paddles, screws and coal-fired furnaces over a century ago. But other ships were calling at Aden long before that, to anchor in a smaller harbour two miles away on the other side of the red cliffs, close to an older settlement. Two thousand years ago, according to an anonymous Greek sea captain of the day who wrote a maritime guide called *Periplus of the Erythrean Sea*, that harbour was the site of 'Eudaemon Arabia, a village by the shore ... having convenient anchorages and watering places'. Far back even beyond the Greeks, Aden was an entrepôt on the

17

spice and silk route from the Indies, as the little sailing boats ventured out of the east with the annual monsoon, hugged the barren coasts of Arabia, and put in here for fresh supplies before attempting the burning passage of the Red Sea, or turning again for home. For thousands of years incense passed this way by both land and sea, from the green uplands of Dhofar and the hidden valley of the Hadhramaut to the east, northwards up the Red Sea coast to Mecca, Petra, Jerusalem and Byblos, and westwards to Egypt, Greece and Rome. To the Arabs of the interior, Aden was always 'the eye of the Yemen' — the principal port for the fertile valleys of the high Yemen, secreted behind the perpetual purple haze to the north, 100 miles away; and when Marco Polo got here nearly 700 years ago he found the 'Soldan of Aden' grown immensely rich, 'arising from the imposts he lays, as well upon the merchandise that comes from India, as upon that which is shipped in his port as the returning cargo; this being the most considerable mart in all that quarter for the exchange of commodities, and the place to which all trading vessels resort.'

Marco Polo, although he could not know it, was in almost at the death of the old Aden. In his day the best route from there to Europe lay up the Red Sea, then overland to the Nile and downstream to Alexandria. 'This,' said he, 'is the least difficult and the shortest route the merchants can take with their goods, the produce of India, from Aden to that city.' A century later Vasco da Gama rounded the Cape of Good Hope, opening a continuous sea passage between east and west, and Aden entered a long decline. Soon afterwards the Turks occupied the Yemen and sacked Aden, and for three centuries thereafter the town attracted neither international trade nor local commerce. By the beginning of the nineteenth century it was no more than a pirate village, preying on the routine traffic of the Indian Ocean. In the 1830's, however, it preyed once too often when an Indian ship under a British flag was wrecked nearby and its passengers and crew were held to ransom by the ragged successor of Marco Polo's wealthy 'Soldan' — the impoverished Sultan of the territory of Lahej. Captain Haines of the Indian Navy was dispatched forthwith from Bombay, in command of 700 troops, the ten-gun H.M.S. *Cruizer* and the 28-gun H.M.S. *Volage* to teach the presumptuous natives a lesson. As the British East India Company was also looking for coaling stations for its new steamships, the opportunity seemed too good to miss of acquiring a permanent lease on Aden, and at a cost of 15 British casualties Captain Haines secured his objective in 1839 and annexed Aden to the Bombay Presidency. It was the first British territorial acquisition of Queen Victoria's reign, and one destined to carry the flavour of the Victorian age far into the twentieth century, surviving in faded imperial glory even after the Bombay Presidency and the Vice-Regal Government in Delhi were dead and gone.

Captain Haines found a community of barely 500 people in 'a condition of most indigent poverty and neglect'. How lamentable a contrast, he remarked in his diary, to Aden's former 'unrivalled celebrity', its 'impenetrable fortifications,' its 'flourishing commerce'. As a coaling station, however, secure under British rule, Aden soon began to revive, and after the opening of the Suez Canal in 1869, when the route from the East that Marco Polo knew became once more a significant artery of world trade, its harbour was made famous again as the first place east of Suez on the highroad to imperial India. Even so, Aden remained uncomfortably neglected for the better part of a century — a hardship post for troops and officials, a responsibility that London wanted little to do with, and a distant appendage that the Bombay Presidency rarely bothered its head about. It was not until 1932 that the Indian Imperial Government in New Delhi took Aden under its own, more capacious, wing; and only in 1937 did the British Government in Whitehall decide that the shadow of the old Raj had fallen across Aden long enough. In that year, a full century after the arrival of Captain Haines, it declared Aden a Crown Colony and switched its administration from the fatigued and preoccupied offices of the Viceroy to the slightly more energetic desks of the Colonial Office in London.

Only once since then has Aden's prosperity faltered, and that was in the months after November 1956, when the Suez Canal was blocked and the world's shipping returned, willy-nilly, to Vasco da Gama's route. When I visited Aden then the wide waters of the harbour were a tranquil, empty mirror of the red volcanic cliffs behind. The laden oil tankers from the Persian Gulf were sailing 1,000 miles southwards, heading for the Cape, the P. & O. liners and the British India cargo boats were calling at Durban and Port Elizabeth, and the Aden bumboats that were usually clamouring at their sides were moored silently at the water's edge. The new British Petroleum oil refinery, glittering among the red pinnacles of Little Aden across the bay, had halved its output because the bunkering trade had vanished, and the shopkeepers of Steamer Point, accustomed to welcoming 500 tourists a day, watched their duty-free temptations gathering dust. It was as if four centuries of history were being relived in four months, as Aden's seaborne business was pared away by her temporary isolation to a score of dhows and a rusty assortment of misshapen coasters from the Red Sea trade.

But nobody then was much dismayed. Aden's Financial Secretary, introducing his annual budget to the Colony's Legislative Council, spoke confidently of Aden's bright future. The shipping agents cheerfully and correctly predicted that their trade would return as soon as the Canal was reopened, in spite of the jeremiahs in London who declared that since President Nasser had 'brought the Canal into politics' it would never be a safe shipping route again. A few of the local merchants took the chance of a holiday and thousands of port workers went back to their homes in the Yemen to wait until the ships returned. Aden seized the moment for a nap.

Among the British residents, life was surprisingly relaxed. Every noon the bar of the Crescent Hotel, newly air-conditioned, was a noisy men's club where gloomy prognostications of British retreat were decried in brave, imperial voices. 'Don't you worry, old boy,' they rumbled, over the pink gins, 'we'll be here for another 30 years.'

'Mustn't take too much notice of Nasser, old chap. Flash in the pan, that's all.'

'Pity we didn't finish the job at Suez — could've done, too, except for those bloody Yanks.'

'Of course, they don't understand the wogs like we do.'

To the visitor fresh from the political turmoil of Cairo, Damascus and Amman in those days, these were like voices from beyond the grave, pleading causes that were already dead. Britain had been flung out of Suez; in Jordan and Iraq her military bases were about to be 'negotiated' out of existence; and in Cyprus they were under both armed and diplomatic attack. Nor did the apparatus of defence in Aden look likely to withstand much pressure. A couple of blunt corvettes in the harbour, an elderly transport aircraft lumbering overhead, the occasional roar of a jet engine from Khormaksar airfield, five miles away — these were hardly the outward manifestations of a world power. In Aden, as elsewhere, military Britain was looking decidedly threadbare: smart but impoverished, like a country gentleman keeping up appearances after his estate had gone under the hammer.

The British residents in Aden, however, were still blessed with a sense of remoteness from the pressures and politics of the Arab world, as they had been throughout the previous century. Tucked away in their little corner, behind their cliffs and their cosy prejudices, facing outwards to the living sea rather than inwards to the barren Arabia at their backs, they knew little and seemed to care less of the revolution that had begun. There had been already some political agitation among the Arabs of the Colony, and some effective industrial strikes had been organised in the spring of 1956, but the old hands sniffed at such demonstrations. 'The Arabs will demonstrate for anything,' they said, 'if you only pay them enough.' Had any of them made an effort to talk or listen, to the leaders of the demonstrators, they might have been less complacent. But they were, after all, only human, and they heard and read only what was most comforting. Blinded by the mists of colonial narcissism they scarcely noticed how warped and shabby were the buildings of the Aden Government, and how much their surroundings spoke of neglect in the long and dusty years when the Colony was a mere provincial town in the Bombay Presidency. They saw only that the Union flag still flew above them as a sign of an ordered life which they wished to preserve; and on the engraved invitations that still issued from Government House they read, as much as ever, the imprint of power. The Governor assumed in all things the precedence of the Monarch, as befitted her representative on the spot. At his dinner parties he was served before all his guests, and at his cocktail parties he remained in one place while his perspiring *aides de camp* shuttled the visitors to and fro before him for the honour of a handshake and a polite inquiry about their business. By him and his small court the social customs of the British residents were established and from them the pecking order descended through the rigid hierarchies of military rank and civilian standing. There were clubs for officers and clubs for 'other ranks,' beaches patronised chiefly by 'foreigners', and beaches where only the British seemed to go. The sun-bleached daughters of bank managers and Air Commodores were properly squired by bronzed young subalterns to black tie dances on the roof of the Crescent Hotel; the privates cut loose in women-less drinking in the bars around the corner. The servants called their mistresses 'memsahib' and passed the cucumber sandwiches at afternoon tea parties; and social calls were announced — and returned — by visiting cards left on little silver trays. No doubt it all had some purpose once, when society in Britain, too, was ordered in such glassy patterns, but in 1956 it made Aden seem like a land of Nod, where time had gone to sleep. To the stalwart British community of the Colony, one felt, the Empire was still the old Empire, and the Royal Navy — God bless it — was still the biggest in the world.

To be fair, perhaps, one should reflect that in 1956 most of the Empire did still exist on paper; and although the Royal Navy was little more than a feeble adjunct of the American fleets, vaguely imperial attitudes were still deeply ingrained in Britain. Nobody in the British Government then spoke of a 'wind of change' in Africa, and the passionate, and often anti-American, reactions to the failure of the Suez landings, on both sides of the political fence, revealed how little was understood about the post-war change in Britain's power. The residents of Aden could scarcely be blamed for thinking that all would be well in their little world when they were supported by so much old-fashioned sentiment at home. Moreover, they had the words of a certain Lord Lloyd to reassure them. In May of that year, after the latest round of strikes in the Colony, Lord Lloyd arrived from London, in his capacity as Under-Secretary of State for the Colonies, to address the Aden Legislative Council. He did so in the bold, patrician tones of a true pro-consul. There had been, he noted disapprovingly, much harmful speculation recently about the political future of the Colony. If carried to undue lengths this might easily divert into unfruitful channels energies which might be better exerted in the pursuit of reasonable aspirations. Her Majesty's Government considered therefore that the time had come to state their own political intentions in respect of Aden, and he, Lord Lloyd, was there to do so. He had listened to the views of various bodies and individuals with interest and sympathy, but everyone must realise that the Colony's constitutional development must depend on the sense of responsibility displayed by its people and their leaders.

'Many of you,' he continued, 'have a perfectly legitimate desire to take a greater part in the affairs of Government, and there is no reason why this desire should not be realised. But I should like you to understand that for the foreseeable future it would not be reasonable or sensible, or indeed in the interests of the Colony's inhabitants, for them to aspire to any aim beyond that of a considerable degree of internal self-government. Therefore, whilst I have indicated the type of constitutional advance to which the people in this Colony may legitimately aspire, Her Majesty's Government wish to make it clear that the importance of Aden, both strategically and economically, within the Commonwealth is such that they cannot foresee the possibility of any fundamental relaxation of their responsibilities for the Colony. I feel confident that this assurance will be welcome to you and to the vast majority of the inhabitants of the Colony.'

But it was not. Time had not gone to sleep for everyone in Aden, and the reaction of the non-British community to Lord Lloyd's speech was predictable. The anti-British elements became more anti-British, and the pro-British groups were disappointed. The Aden Association, a right little, tight little, largely non-Arab collection of merchants and professional men who aspired to nothing more than self-government for Aden within the Commonwealth, had the ground cut from under them and retired in grumbling uncertainty. The South Arabian League, a more inflammatory organisation run from the neighbouring state of Lahej, that wanted an independent state comprising the Colony and the shaikhdoms of the Aden Protectorates, immediately increased its agitation. Its leader, Muhammad Ali al Jifri, a member of a powerful South Arabian family, was exiled by the British authorities in August of that year and chose, inevitably, to resort to Cairo where Nasser was by then dramatically at grips with the British over Suez. The Imam of Yemen, too, anxious to secure Aden for himself, increased his efforts to subvert both the large immigrant Yemeni population in the Colony and the tribesmen of the Aden Protectorate states bordering his kingdom. When, at the end of October, the British, French and Israeli armies descended upon Egypt in what appeared to every Arab a piece of deliberate and concerted sabotage and aggression in an attempt to overthrow Gamal Abdul Nasser and restore the Anglo-French position on the Suez Canal, there was no doubt whatever where the sympathies of most of Aden's people lay. And when — in spite of the laborious gathering of Anglo-French military strength and the swift successes of the Israeli Army in Sinai — President Nasser had the last word, the thrill of an Arab victory ran like an orgasm through the back streets of Aden, as it did through all the alleys of the Arab world.

To feel its visceral impact to the full you had to leave the imperial purlieus of Steamer Point and take a taxi through a gap in the red rock wall of Aden into Crater. This is the heart of the Colony — a great, irregular cup in the jagged mountains that once was literally a volcanic crater and that now houses 100,000 Aden settlers and conceals beneath its consequent shroud of squalor a great deal of money. Crater must have been known to Marco Polo as the heart of Aden; indeed, the anchorage where his sailing vessel probably moored is still used by occasional dhows, just half a mile from Crater's main streets. Now, in its modern re-incarnation, the names of Crater's important local merchants have the proper cosmopolitan ring of an eastern entrepôt: Cowasjee Dinshaw, the Parsee trader; Besse & Co., a firm of French origin, whose founder made enough money to endow St. Antony's College at Oxford with £1,000,000; Luke Thomas & Co., created by a sharp young British Captain who arrived in 1840 as agent for the Peninsular and Oriental Line; the Athanas Brothers, Alexandrian Greeks, with a flourishing import-export business and honorary collective identities as the Greek Consul and, for many years, local correspondent for *The Times*.

These are the financial lords of Aden; the serfs are in Crater's slums, a dusty, geometrical grid of streets where all the styles and faces of Arabia and the Indian Ocean have fetched up over the years of imperial rule. Arabs of the coast and Arabs from the Sudan, in long white dish-dashers and turbans. Arabs of the interior and the Yemen in printed cotton *futas*, or kilts, and bright, embroidered Kashmiri shawls wound round their heads. Somalis, proud of carriage and skinny of leg, stalking among the rest like black and glistening wading birds in a throng of chattering sparrows. Indians crouched in dark cubby holes with sewing machines and Pakistanis squatting sleepily among bales of cloth. None of them truly belongs here, except perhaps for a few of the coastal Arabs whose ancestors may have lived in Aden as fishermen and pirates before the days of Captain Haines. Yet if citizens of Aden can be defined at all (and the Aden Government has always had great difficulty with such a definition) these are they; and these rancid alleys are their home. Outside each house, rope and wood-frame beds are stacked on top of one another by day and laid end-to-end in the streets on summer nights, each with a family sprawled upon it seeking sleep in the sultry air. Goats rummage here for garbage, their udders wrapped protectively in bright satin brassières, and camels pad silently through the crowd with their characteristic look of sick disdain, as if they were always about to retch at the world's vulgarity. In spite of its sometimes suffocating lid of heat, Crater is always alive, a world removed from the colonial gentility of the British at Steamer Point; and a world removed, too, from colonialist sentiments in politics. When I was there at the end of 1956 I could see, in room after dark room, in shop after cramped shop, the familiar face of President Nasser gleaming from the walls, all teeth and self-confident bonhomie; and from somewhere in every street there came the sound of a harsh and crudely amplified Arabic voice in whose words and timbre even a novice could identify the *Voice of the Arabs* on Cairo Radio attacking British 'imperialism'.

Never again, I suspected, as I walked down these bustling, smelly lanes after the Suez crisis, would Lord Lloyd and his like be taken seriously here. The Indians and Pakistanis, fearful of their minority standing, might not like the new mood of nationalist politics; the Somalis, pre-occupied with their own independence efforts in Africa, across the water, might not care. But the Arabs were plainly conscious that they had found a leader, a new Saladin as their press and radio had christened him, and they were jubilant. 'Gamal Abdul Nasser!' shouted a small boy one morning as I went by. 'Gamal Abdul Nasser! Gamal Abdul Nasser!' he repeated, skipping along behind me, his eyes bright with mischief, his thumb metaphorically at his nose. It was his full vocabulary of insult for an Englishman; and though I might walk on loftily pretending not to hear, or turn and laugh gaily as if I shared the joke, he kept up the chant the length of a street, with many a silently approving glance from the Arabs we passed on the way.

In such ways did Aden Colony cross a political watershed during the months of the Suez crisis, from the firmly proclaimed imperial restrictions of Lord Lloyd in May to a dawning realisation in December that the old bonds could be broken after all. In those six months Arab nationalism found its feet in the Colony, standing up to do battle with its British imperialist enemy and tutor. For, of course, it was part of the paradox of nationalism in Aden — as elsewhere in the British Empire — that it was very much a British creation. It was not only a local reaction to the arrogance and complacency of some of the British, but also a natural result of the breakdown of tribalism in the successful urban environment that the British had created; and it was fostered by just those democratic institutions and orderly administration with which the British like to justify their colonial record. The Trade Union movement, for example, introduced to Aden in the early 1950's as part of Britain's standard colonial policy, rapidly became an effective instrument of political education and agitation and by 1956, as the strikes before Lord Lloyd's visit had shown, it was proving genuinely troublesome to the British authorities. The independence of the Aden courts enabled opposition spokesmen — who would have been detained without trial under similar circumstances in Cairo or Baghdad — to escape much of the retribution and many of the restrictions that the Colonial Government would have liked to impose upon them. The local press, enjoying a freedom unparalleled elsewhere in the Arab world, could attack the British with relish. The new schools financed by the Colonial Government had begun to produce a generation of students with a contemporary, secular education which was a fertile seed-bed for political discontent. To this extent, Arab nationalism in Aden was a mirror image of the colonial power, and the more the British intervened in Aden — with whatever goodwill and ostensibly democratic purpose — the more vigorous the image became. By 1956, as a result, Aden was easily the most politically sophisticated territory in Arabia. All that its new nationalist leaders lacked to enforce their growing demands for self-government was the sheer physical and diplomatic strength which, as it happened, the aftermath of Suez gave them. Behind them, thereafter, they had President Nasser and his Arab revolution and the Imam of Yemen as well; and however ill-assorted those two might be, they had a common aim in Aden. They simply wished to get the British out.

Luckily for Britain, however, her imperial rule had hardly been effectively extended in southern Arabia beyond the tiny confines of

Aden Colony. In the surrounding shaikhdoms of the Aden Protectorates her intervention had been comparatively recent and feeble, and nationalism was correspondingly weak. There, in quarrelsome indigence and traditional feudalism, the tribes and their rulers were still supreme. Neither politically nor materially, therefore, did the Colony and the Protectorates share each other's heritage or assumptions, and as 1957 opened they seemed to be set upon divergent courses. While the nationalist leaders of the Colony soon began to leap over the heads of the more moderate spokesmen, crying ever more boldly for the British to go, the rulers of the Protectorate shaikhdoms were urging the British to stay. In that division of the local leaders the pattern of South Arabian politics was set for the next decade.

2

The Tribes Intransigeant

One afternoon early in 1957 I sat on the floor of the white-washed mud palace of Sharif Husain of the State of Baihan and wrestled with a hunk of goat's meat. Only a couple of hours earlier the beast had been bleating in the courtyard outside and his flesh, so hastily committed to the fire, was tough. With my left hand held awkwardly behind me where it could not, by any accident, commit the solecism of touching the food (for the left hand is used for unclean purposes in the daily toilet of Islam), I pulled away a few strings of meat with my right hand and carried them to my mouth. No sooner was my right hand emptied than in was involuntarily filled again as my host, crying encouragement, lobbed a hard-boiled egg across the floor towards me, through a well-calculated parabola of some twenty feet. Throughout the meal, eggs flew like ping-pong balls to all the guests. '*Wallahi!*' the Sharif would exclaim whenever he glimpsed a momentarily empty hand around him, 'You English eat too little! Eat, my friends, eat!'

We ate. Goat's meat, chickens, rice, tinned peaches, custard, dark and fragrant wild honey, ping-pong balls and all. It was a considerable spread. But then, by Baihan standards in those days, we were a considerable company, including one British Political Adviser, one British Brigadier, several junior Army and Air Force officers, and some British and American journalists; and the Sharif had just had the satisfaction of reading us all a testy lecture on the responsibilities towards him of Her Britannic Majesty's Government. The Sharif just missed looking noble as he did so. There was something too crafty about his glancing eyes, perhaps, too much roguery in his frequent laughter to make him an entirely convincing advocate of his cause. But with his full black beard and a glitter of gold about his teeth, he cut an undeniably striking figure, like a wilder brother of Archbishop Makarios in a turban instead of a stovepipe hat. Unlike the Archbishop, however, who then was

SOUTH-WEST ARABIA

trying to kick the British out of Cyprus, the Sharif was intent on persuading the British to stay in Baihan.

For the last six or seven years, he said, his neighbours in the Yemen had offered money, ammunition, rifles and food to tribesmen everywhere in the Aden Protectorate, encouraging them to rebel against their lawful leaders who wished to remain friendly with the British. He had done what he could to keep his own men loyal and to help the British; now, he declared, it was time the British helped him, as they had undertaken to do by treaty. Was not the Queen of England called the Defender of the Faith? He gestured to a coloured photograph of the Queen and the Duke of Edinburgh on the wall behind him. That was indeed a noble title. 'But now,' he added, 'she must defend *me* and *my* faith or —' and he paused a moment for dramatic effect — '*I* will call *her* deceitful.'

We may argue with the Sharif's rhetorical interpretation of the Queen's role in relation to his faith, but there is no blinking the fact that by treaty, as binding as any that ever was signed, Her Majesty's Government was, and still is, committed to Baihan's protection. The obligation dates from 1903 when Sharif Ahmad-am-Mohsin, father of Sharif Husain, 'being desirous of maintaining and strengthening the relations of peace and friendship' with the British, signed a protectorate treaty with them through the Government of India. 'In the Name of God, the Merciful Compassionate,' it declared, and in compliance with the wish of the Sharif Ahmad, 'the British Government hereby undertakes to extend to the territory of Behan-al-Kasab and its dependencies, being under the authority and jurisdiction of the said Sharif, the gracious favour and protection of His Majesty, the King-Emperor.' In return, the Sharif undertook never to enter into any agreement with another foreign power. Forty years later his son signed another treaty, also nominally at his own request, agreeing to accept the advice of the Governor of Aden on the internal affairs of his state, so that the British then added to the duty of protection the doubtful privilege and inescapable responsibility of indirect rule as well.[1]

Not all the petty chieftains near the south Arabian coast were as eager to enjoy British protection and advice as Sharif Husain and his father. Some were cajoled, or had these benefits thrust upon them. Some refused all overtures, others were ignored. But one way or another what happened in Baihan was repeated in some thirty ill-defined tribal 'states' between the Red Sea and Dhofar in the nineteenth and twentieth centuries, to create that curious strip of pink on the old schoolroom

[1] See Appendices I and II.

maps of Empire known as the Aden Protectorate. By 1954, when the British signed their last protectorate treaty with an obscure tribe called the Busi in an equally obscure district known as Upper Yafai, ninety separate treaties had been signed and every one of them was still in force, to cover an area not much bigger than Great Britain with a total population of less than three-quarters-of-a-million.

No doubt the purpose of these remained clear enough to the British who saw the Protectorate simply as a *cordon sanitaire* for the port of Aden, protecting British commercial and strategic interests from the depredations of wild tribesmen, invading Turks, interfering Frenchmen, or even — in the early nineteenth century when it all began — from the Egyptians under Ibrahim Pasha who then had temporarily occupied the Yemen. But on the spot, such grand designs were apt to vanish among the petty and highly personal realities of tribal life, to which the treaties, drafted with such care and attention, often bore only the vaguest relation.

Consider, for example, the complex status of even so notable a figure as His Highness the Sultan of Lahej, ruler of the tribal area of Abdali, adjoining Aden Colony. He was, said a British Government record of twenty years ago, the 'Premier chief of the Western Aden Protectorate' and entitled to a salute of 11 guns.[1] He was also 'recognised to some degree as overlord by the Amir of Dhala' who was himself entitled, presumably in recognition of this imprecise degree of deference, to a salute of only nine guns. But further than this, the Sultan of Lahej was 'suzerain of the Subeihis and to a less extent of the Haushabis'. This had not, however, prevented the Haushabi Sultan and no less than eight shaikhs of the Subaihis from signing their own treaties of protection and advice with the British Government. Wherein, then, lay the Lahej Sultan's 'suzerainty' and 'overlordship'? Perhaps in the fact that neither the Haushabi nor the Subaihi chiefs appeared to be entitled to a salute of any guns at all.

Equally obfuscated by the dissimilarity between British treaties and Arab tradition are the powers and privileges of the so-called Sultan of Qishn and Socotra, at the farthest end of the Eastern Protectorate, who is not, in fact, recognised as a sultan by the tribesmen of Qishn. They prefer another branch of the family that has no treaty status at all; and although the net result of this confusion is that Qishn has been left to this day without any organised government whatever, its ostensible Sultan is still accorded the dignity of a nine-gun salute.

The British Government's record of these singular potentates weaves

[1] *Western Arabia and the Red Sea.* Geographical Handbook Series, Naval Intelligence Division, London, 1946, pp. 361–3.

its way over three pages of fine print, through thirty-eight shaikhs, sultans, amirs, sharifs, naibs and what-not, whose powers, territories, and allegiances one after another defy precise description. To most western minds such titles are apt to denote some sort of feudal autocrat, perhaps romantic, probably fierce, whose least word is law among his people. The eastern reality is rather different. A Sultan, to be sure, is in theory a kind of monarch, a ruler of absolute authority. But, as we have just seen, a man may even be a Sultan and possess no authority at all. A Sharif is officially a descendant of the Prophet, and by extension, therefore, some sort of holy man; but I should be surprised if anyone in Baihan today believed there was anything especially holy about their Sharif Husain.[1] An Amir, strictly speaking, is a commander, and a Naib is a kind of governor; but that is not to say that the one may command or the other govern without some rudimentary popular consent. A Shaikh is perhaps the most ambiguous creature of them all. He may be an old man whose years and wisdom entitle him to respect, a religious dignitary, a tribal leader, or a combination of all three; and his authority may amount to all or nothing.

What is common to all these resounding titles is a fairly strict relationship between power and performance. Few traditional rulers among the Arabs are simple hereditary monarchs. Such power as they possess in their tribal world comes less from heredity (although this is usually involved in some degree) than from personality. Their rule must be patriarchal, in the style of Abraham, but it can be despotic only, so to speak, by consent. A tribal ruler must nurse his position as well as assert it, through open consultation with his people in his *majlis*, or council, through bribery, favouritism, marriage and — most of all — through success. He must be ruthless; but if he is too severe he may be hated and possibly murdered. If he is not ruthless enough, he may be despised and overthrown. It is a narrow line that he must follow, and a difficult one among men who may accept without a murmur the removal of a hand for theft, but may rebel over the digging of a new water-hole because it offends some ancient custom.

Such a highly individualised form of government is bound to be unstable; yet it is coherent in its own terms, for in the wandering life of the desert and its fringes, individuals — far more than institutions — are the logical pivots of society. Unfortunately but inevitably, the

---

[1] In fact, it is generally accepted among South Arabian experts that the Sharif ought never to have acquired the status of a ruler. His father, it is said, bluffed the ignorant British into recognising him as one, and many tribesmen still insist that Sharif Husain is a fraud.

British imposed upon this fluid, semi-nomadic life the static patterns of western society. To them a Sultan was a Sultan was a Sultan, and a Shaikh became a Shaikh became a Shaikh. At an arbitrary point in time the system was suddenly fossilized, because local dignitaries who had the good fortune to sign a scrap of paper with a British agent became established powers in British eyes, apparently for evermore; while others who were ignored at the crucial moment of treaty signature became permanent outcasts.

As it happened, this ossification did not matter very much until after the First World War, for until then the treaties were honoured as much in the breach as the observance. Life among the tribes went on much as it always had done, in shifting patterns of loyalty, chicanery, poverty and violence. It was no concern of British policy to stop the tribal wars or to punish shaikhly murderers. As long as the flag was shown occasionally by some intrepid agent in the Aden hinterland, and as long as no rival powers gained any footing there, the officials of Whitehall and Delhi were content. They had enough to worry about elsewhere without having to pacify or patrol these remote and unrewarding frontiers of Arabia with any unnecessary zeal. So Aden's *cordon sanitaire* remained a thing of paper throughout the nineteenth century, and well into the twentieth — territorially undefined, militarily neglected and administratively almost virgin. It was only in 1915 that British complacency in Aden was shaken, when the Turks got an expeditionary force from the Yemen to within 20 miles of the Colony where, after a comically calamitous attempt to eject it by a British column, it was allowed to remain unmolested for the duration of the war. It was not until a further challenge came from the Yemen after the war was over that Britain was forced into active intervention in Protectorate affairs.

Until then she had achieved little more in the way of self-assertion than a convention signed in 1914 with the Turkish authorities in the Yemen, establishing an agreed but still uncharted frontier between the Yemen and the neighbouring western states of the Protectorate. The final destruction of Ottoman power during the war, however, enabled the Yemen to become independent again, and the Anglo-Turkish convention was rejected by the new Yemeni ruler, the Imam Yahia. He chose, instead, to pursue a traditional Yemeni claim to possession of the whole of south-western Arabia, including Aden and the Protectorate, and his forces promptly overran several of the western shaikhdoms. From then onwards the British were drawn irrevocably by their own treaties into the preservation of the territorial integrity of the shaikhdoms and, by a logical process, into their internal pacification and development.

Yahia's claim to sovereignty over Aden and the Protectorate was not new, but no-one before him during the British occupancy of Aden had enjoyed the power or the determination to press it. The Turks had maintained it in theory only — and, indeed, as it rested largely on the religious authority of the Yemeni Imams which they had diminished or replaced, they were perhaps in no position to be more than theoretical about it. Briefly the argument runs thus: '*al Yemen*' means the right, or the right hand, and in geographical matters it indicates to Arabs all that part of Arabia which lies to the right of Mecca (always provided you happen to be facing eastwards, as Arabs do by custom for the purpose of dividing the world into its four corners). The Prophet Muhammad sent his son-in-law, Ali, to rule *al Yemen*, and the Imams, being leaders of the Zaidi sect of the Shiite Muslims, claim direct descent from Ali and his wife, the Prophet's daughter, Fatima. Hence, it is argued, their right to rule throughout south-western Arabia, including Aden, was established from the beginning by God's messenger on earth. To this theological hypothesis a morsel of historical proof is added by the fact that for nearly a century, from 1636 to 1728, the Yemeni Imams, breaking loose from Turkish occupation, did achieve some ascendancy in the whole area.

Neither the British nor the Protectorate rulers, however, have ever been convinced. Historically, the British point out, slightly less than a century of suzerainty in the now fairly distant past is of no more significance in contemporary politics than the reign of the English kings in France. And theologically, so the Protectorate shaikhs would have us know, the Imamic claims are totally unacceptable. Most of the in-habitants of the Protectorates, as well as those of coastal and southern Yemen, belong to the Shafii sect of the Sunni Muslims, between whom and the Zaidi Shiites in the central highlands of the Yemen there is no love lost. Where the rule of the Zaidi Imams has extended over the Shafii of the west and south, even within the present boundaries of the Yemen, it has never been popular and has frequently been bitterly resented — a fact which explains much that is otherwise confusing about the aftermath of the Yemen revolution of 1962. That it should ever have been willingly accepted by the chiefs of the Aden Protectorates was unthinkable; or so the British were asked to believe.

Certainly, the vigour with which Yahia, the Zaidi Imam, pursued his claim to the Protectorate, or 'south Yemen', in the 1920's caused the Shafii rulers of the western shaikhdoms to invoke their British treaties of protection in the name of Allah as well as for the benefit of the British Raj; and the British, bound by their word as much as by their interest, duly responded with a mixture of force and diplomacy that compelled the Yemenis to withdraw from the areas they had occupied in the Protectorate and to accept a treaty, signed in Sanaa, the Yemeni capital, in 1934, by which both sides agreed to maintain the *status quo* for a period of forty years. At that point all seemed well. The *cordon sanitaire* had been restored and strengthened, the Yemenis had been shown that Britain was not to be trifled with, and the Protectorate rulers had learned that the British kept their word.

Alas, the real troubles in the Protectorate were only just beginning. In the first place, misunderstanding appeared to have been built into the Treaty of Sanaa. The British thought it referred to the *status quo* on the frontier line, roughly as established by the Anglo-Turkish convention of 1914. The Yemenis believed it covered the *status quo* in the whole area of 'south Yemen' that had been in dispute. The ambiguity lay in the meaning of the Arabic word *hudud* in the treaty, which Arabists say may be translated as either frontier or area, because nomadic Arabs regard the two concepts as virtually interchangeable.[1] Thus the Yemenis assumed that the British had undertaken to preserve the existing position throughout the Aden Protectorate and were furious when they discovered that British military units and civilian advisers began afterwards to pacify and administer the shaikhdoms; while the British believed that the Yemenis had agreed not to interfere with the frontier line and were dismayed when the Imam's officials, and sometimes his forces, continued to treat it with a good deal of contempt.

Whatever justification the Yemenis might have thought they had for their attitude, the British, after the Treaty of Sanaa, had no effective choice but to continue — or, rather, to begin in some earnest — their penetration of the Protectorate. By undertaking military and diplomatic action on behalf of the Protectorate rulers in the 1920's, they virtually committed themselves to further action ever after, so that a progressive modification of the *status quo* in the area became inevitable. If thirty-odd petty shaikhdoms were to be protected successfully from outside aggression, their internal disorders had to be suppressed. The defence of disorder was neither militarily nor diplomatically feasible; and the frontier could only be stabilised if the area behind it was pacified. Moreover, the growing importance of Aden as a port and bunkering station on the Suez route between the wars generated more trade with the interior, and the protection of caravans from marauding tribesmen became, therefore, a legitimate extension of commercial enterprise which even the Yemeni Imam encouraged. Gradually and irrevocably,

[1] See: Harold Ingrams, *The Yemen*, John Murray, London, 1963, p. 69.

34

therefore, the British Government was compelled to adopt a 'forward policy' in Aden and the Protectorate designed to bring to the whole area the well-known benefits of enlightened colonial rule. A first, tentative step towards this had already been taken in 1932, when Aden was removed at last from the lackadaisical control of the Government of Bombay and her old Political Resident was made a Chief Commissioner under the Indian Government in Delhi. By 1937 this, too, had begun to seem inadequate to the newly enlightened purposes of colonialism, and while Aden was then removed altogether from Indian control and made a Crown Colony under Whitehall's direction, the Protectorate was divided for the first time into Eastern and Western sections each with its own Political Agent responsible to the new Colonial Governor in Aden.

So, while the Yemen was fended off with one hand, the necessary framework of the *Pax Britannica* in the Protectorate was established with the other. Tribesmen who had spent their lives robbing and fighting each other were recruited into Government police forces and small, regular military units by the promise of a regular pay packet and a square, army meal. The new device of aerial bombing, already used against the Yemenis after the war, was turned upon remote and troublesome Protectorate villages which the arm of the law could not otherwise reach in less than a fortnight's march. With these developments, the ossification of traditional life implicit in the protectorate treaties began to take effect, as the chiefs who had inherited the right scraps of paper were automatically strengthened by the British intervention, while their rivals who had not were correspondingly weakened. And from this it followed that while the treaty chiefs were pleased and desired Britain to support them more and more, the others were disgruntled and turned increasingly to what became known as 'dissidence'.

It is necessary, I think, to elucidate this a little further, for the idea has got about in recent years that dissidence among certain tribes of the Protectorate is somehow a result of British callousness — as if bombing from the air, in particular, were carried out with such deadly intent and effect as to antagonise all right-thinking tribesmen. I am afraid this is as much of an over-simplification as the belief that a shaikh is necessarily some sort of feudal monster. Bombing was simply part of the general process of pacification, and was employed as soon as it became available as a cheap and convenient method of policing otherwise inaccessible territories in India and Iraq as well as in Arabia. The technique in the early days was essentially the same as it is now; only the machines were different. The offending village was warned in advance that it would be bombed and its inhabitants were asked to evacuate their homes. When they had retreated to the surrounding mountainsides the old R.A.F. biplanes would go droning down the valley to drop a handful of small bombs upon the empty village, while the tribesmen practised their markmanship on the aircraft as they passed. The method sounds crude, and as carried out nowadays by jet fighters with rockets or bombers with several tons of explosives aboard it can appear barbaric. Cairo Radio has certainly made it seem so, with gruesome accounts in recent years of villages 'wiped out' and 'innocent women and children killed'. But in fact these raids usually result even now in no casualties and surprisingly little lasting damage. Most of the Protectorate villages are either such flimsy affairs of brushwood and bamboo that they can be rebuilt within a few days, or such solidly fortified assemblies of rock that a blockbuster would be needed to do much more than rattle their doors off their hinges. The real disadvantages of the method are that it suffers from diminishing returns on the ground, as the tribesmen realise that a bit of bombing will probably do them little harm, combined with sharply rising criticism nowadays from abroad. On the other hand, in earlier days the bombs and the aeroplanes together presented an image of irresistible and almost magical force, giving tribesmen a decent excuse to surrender to authority without loss of face, which they could not do in battle with mere earthly forces. Indeed, as Mr. Harold Ingrams once related, when he was a Political Officer in the Protectorate, in the 1930's, the tribesmen sometimes were positively grateful to have their villages bombed as a means of concluding gracefully some tiresome squabble — and they were generous enough to congratulate the airmen afterwards upon their aim.[1]

Dissidence, then, was not, and is not now, provoked simply by firmness, or even violence, for these are qualities to which the tribes are accustomed in their rulers. It springs from the purpose to which the firmness, or violence, is directed — the attempt to impose alien standards of thought and action upon traditional Arab life; and in the late 1930's this began to go beyond mere military pacification of the Eastern and Western Protectorates to embrace the whole range of social and economic life. If proper protection from external aggression demanded the establishment of internal peace, that peace in its turn required diplomacy and economic development to give it any chance of lasting. Administration had to follow the bombs, and British political agents began to penetrate the interior more widely and more often than before, assuming the role of advisers as well as ambassadors to the

[1] Harold Ingrams, *Arabia and the Isles*, John Murray, London, 1942, pp. 97–9.

tribes. Harold Ingrams was one of the most notable of these spearheads of the *Pax Britannica* for he virtually pacified the Eastern Protectorate single-handed. Until his time the eastern territories had been in a state of chronic internecine warfare. The British had rarely bothered about them because they were 300 miles or more from Aden, neither the Turks nor the Yemenis had ever been a significant menace there, and their northern frontier hardly seemed to matter, as it vanished uncharted among the sands of Arabia's Empty Quarter. Except for one or two occasions in the nineteenth century when local rulers tried to blackmail Britain into supporting them against their neighbours by threatening to make deals with other foreign powers, the British had let the eastern states fester in mutual ill-will under nominal guarantees of protection. But by the 1930's the new state of Saudi Arabia was flexing its young muscles in the north, and seeking to extend its frontiers in every direction across the Arabian peninsula. At the same time the caravan trade with the coast was reviving, chiefly through the little port of Mukalla, and along the old incense road, up the Hadhramaut valley; while the aeroplane offered a new way of communicating rapidly, in peace or war, with communities that could not be reached previously without days or weeks of travel.

Ingrams arrived, therefore, at the right time, when there was both a new need and a new possibility of peace; and in three years of travel and tribal negotiation between 1936 and 1939 he obtained the signatures of over 1,300 local chieftains to a general truce in the Eastern Protectorate that became known, deservedly, as 'Ingrams' Peace'. Equally significantly, he also signed a series of new treaties with the five major rulers of the region, obliging them, in return for British protection, to accept the advice of the Governor of Aden in all matters concerning the welfare and development of their territory, except as it affected Islam and its customs. These were the first of the advisory treaties in the Protectorate, and were modelled on those of the Federation of Malay States, where they had already been in operation for many years. Signed as they were on the eve of the Second World War, they scarcely became effective for another six or eight years; and it was not until 1944, when Sharif Husain of Baihan signed his advisory treaty with Britain, that the principle of them was extended for the first time to the Western Protectorate. Before advisory treaties were accepted as normal working instruments throughout East and West the 1950's had begun, the Indian Empire had been dissolved, and the major Arab states of the Middle East had nearly all achieved full independence. Yet only then did Britain establish for herself the legal right and practical power to exercise even indirect rule, as well as protection, in these straggling, tribal territories between Aden and Dhofar. Before then, indeed, barely more than a handful of British officials and soldiers even knew what most of the Protectorate looked like.

The extraordinary lateness of this development can be interpreted as a particularly reprehensible example of British colonial neglect — and with the advantage of hindsight that is certainly a tenable view. Yet the neglect is understandable in its context. In the Government offices of Bombay and Delhi these Arabian territories must have appeared only as an exceedingly remote extension of India's North West Frontier, and they were treated accordingly. In Whitehall, also, they must have seemed valueless in themselves and troublesome even as strategic appendages. And to the pitifully few men on the spot, deprived as they were of the means to exercise more than a rudimentary suzerainty over the area, the shaikhdoms — perhaps inevitably — became a sort of romantic nature reserve in which their chief task was to maintain independence and the traditional Arab life rather than to import a lot of irrelevant western ways.

Thus it came about that until only thirty years ago much of the Aden hinterland could still be described in all seriousness as 'unknown'. The classic example, I suppose, is the valley of the Hadhramaut, in the Eastern Protectorate — once one of the richest provinces, and still one of the most remarkable sights, in all Arabia. The heart of it is not more than 100 miles from the sea, yet until the 1930's hardly a dozen western travellers had ever been there; and the first of them — the German, Adolph von Wrede, who penetrated the valley in disguise in 1843 — is said to have been so disillusioned by the disbelief that greeted his account of his journey that he committed suicide. That indefatigable English traveller in the Orient, Miss Freya Stark, attempting to follow the old incense road through the Hadhramaut to the Yemen in 1935, wrote afterwards that Shabwa, the capital of the ancient Hadhramaut Empire, 'was still unvisited'. She failed to reach it herself because she was taken ill, and she recorded that the direct route to it through the country of the Wahidi tribes was still 'largely unknown, dangerous and unhealthy' — in part, at least, because the tribesmen had only 'recently and possibly not conclusively decided that commerce is more profitable than murder'.[1]

It was the combination of Ingrams' Peace and the aeroplane that opened up the country; and twenty years later, when I first flew up to

[1] Freya Stark, *The Southern Gates of Arabia*, John Murray, London, 1936, p. 19.

the Hadhramaut from Mukalla, a regular air service had been operating for years. It was an odd experience to see this fabulous valley with such ridiculous ease when others had experienced such dangers and discomfort there so recently. With a touch of the old colonial romanticism in myself, I felt more than usually unheroic and diminished, as if I had joined in some rather mean jape on a very old and distinguished man. Yet visually the trip was still immensely exciting. The hills inland from Mukalla were a uniform dun colour, humping themselves gradually higher towards the Arabian plateau in what seemed an infinite series of table-lands and wadis. In their dull, oppressive wilderness there was not a flicker of life for nearly an hour after the glitter of the Indian Ocean had fallen behind us. Then, suddenly, the last of the humps was cleft away beneath us and the aeroplane dipped into a gorge perhaps two miles across and a thousand feet deep, with a flat floor and perpendicular yellow sides that looked as if they might have been cut out with a T-square. Looking down upon this closed and unfamiliar world was like seeing a coral reef for the first time through the glass bottom of an observation boat — breathtaking (for once the word is just) in its strangeness and beauty. Rippling sand dunes advanced across the floor to surround what seemed to be, at first glance, a fortress embedded in palm trees; but as the pilot obligingly dropped lower to circle this romantic place the fortress dissolved into a pattern of individual towers and became a desert Manhattan clustered upon a knoll on the bank of a shallow wadi, much as the towers of New York huddle upon the snout of their little island. This was, in fact, Shibam, perhaps the most remarkable of the Hadhramaut towns; and just as I once saw Manhattan's skyscrapers dance slowly round each other as I sailed up the Hudson river for the first time one bright autumn morning, so now I watched in fascination as we swung back and forth between the great yellow cliffs on either side and caused the towers of Shibam to float into new forms with every second, like the pinnacles of a dream city.

The facts about Shibam, I must record, are more prosaic than its appearance. Glancing at its towers from the aircraft window, it is easy to suppose that they must be at least fifteen stories high. Luckily for their inhabitants, this is an optical illusion. The prevalent manner of house decoration throughout the Hadhramaut and parts of the Yemen includes inserting above the windows on every floor a row of niches, like dummy windows, so that every building is apt to look as if it had twice as many floors as it really has. Those of Shibam are not usually above seven or eight floors high — which must be tall enough, in all conscience, for a construction that has none of the strength of steel or concrete and none of the convenience of a lift or of running water. Equally anti-climactic, I discovered later, was the manner in which these buildings were paid for. Not through fierce imposts on the incense trade did the Hadhramaut maintain these crowded towers, for all that disappeared long ago, but through handsome remittances from slum landlords in Malaya and Indonesia — Hadhramis all, whose ancestors left the valley in search of fortunes abroad when the incense trade declined. Nowadays, that source of revenue has all but vanished, too, and the Hadhramaut towns are maintained, in slightly lower state than they once knew, perhaps, on the proceeds of commerce from Saudi Arabia and the oil states of the Persian Gulf.

Thirty miles beyond Shibam my aircraft landed at the gravel airstrip outside Tarim, another of the valley's old towns. The cliffs were dancing in the afternoon heat, the mud walls of Tarim shimmered in the distance behind a shroud of palms. In the shade of a shack at the side of the strip two Arabs played draughts in the sand with pebbles. Waiting for arriving passengers was a third, in Kashmir turban and cotton kilt, at the wheel of the local taxi. It was a crinkled Austin Seven that must have existed for a good many years before Ingrams signed his Peace. With two live chickens, a trussed goat and a tin suitcase, we deposited one of our passengers in this rickety conveyance and waved him off in the direction of Tarim. With another tin suitcase, a massive stick of golden dates, and several disjointed pieces of a bicycle, we took aboard the draughts players. An hour or so later I was back in Mukalla sharing tea with a gentleman from an oil company. Plainly, the mysterious Hadhramaut was mysterious no more.

That was in 1957, and by then most of the Eastern Protectorate had settled into quiet domestication. The only significant exception was the easternmost territory of Mahra, where the ambiguous Sultan of Qishn and Socotra failed to exercise his sway. There, as late as 1964, the British Government still found it necessary to land an armed force from a gunboat for the protection of a party of prospectors from the Pan-American Oil Company. Elsewhere, Ingrams' Peace, British advice and the natural or imported wealth of the Hadhramaut had encouraged a steady development of local administration and education, and the rulers looked askance at the turbulence of the smaller territories of the Western Protectorate and the growing political agitation in Aden. Most important, however, was the absence of any power ready and able to take advantage of the disaffection of petty chieftains in the East who had been either snubbed or suppressed by Britain as a result of her treaty engagements or her pacification programme. The sands of the Empty

The late Imam Ahmad of the Yemen, at his press conference in 1957

Yemeni scribe chewing *qat*

Taiz, the southern capital of the Yemen

A mosque in Taiz

Quarter still shielded the eastern territories from any serious troubles along their uncharted border, except for an occasional foray from Saudi Arabia, and the strident call of urban nationalism was deadened by their distance from Aden. In the Western Protectorate, on the other hand, the Yemen was intervening with increasing vigour. The more the *Pax Britannica* was extended over the factious and fragmented territories of the West, the more enemies Britain made, both in the Yemen and inside the Protectorate, and the more these enemies turned to each other for support. Even the acknowledged treaty chiefs began to find the loyalty of their tribesmen wavering, as the process of pacification and administration involved greater interference with traditional life and customs. Then, as rifles and money supplied from the Yemen to 'dissident' tribes threatened to upset the old balance of power between such tribes and their neighbours, formerly 'loyal' chiefs were tempted to appeal to the Yemen — or to Britain — for similar supplies, in self-protection.[1] As with any arms race, the effects were cumulative — jealousy breeding jealousy, greed feeding upon greed, and fear upon fear in a spiral of bribery and blackmail that could only end in shooting and could only be checked by force. Although the resulting tribal skirmishes with the British remained for many years militarily insignificant, they began, in the 1950's, to become part of the folklore of the new Arab nationalism. In truth, they had almost nothing to do with nationalism as that word was commonly used in Cairo, Damascus, or even Aden Colony, but they were easily assimilated to its anti-colonial purpose; and the more vigorously the British attempted to deal with the tribesmen the more heinous was British colonialism made to seem, so that not only Cairo, but Moscow and the United Nations began to take an active and inevitably malign interest in these tiny affrays.

The crucial moment of escalation from tribal disorder to international incident arrived in 1956. In the early summer of that year, while the United States and Britain were trying, unsuccessfully, to dictate their terms for the construction of Egypt's High Dam on the Nile, the Crown Prince of the Yemen, Muhammad al-Badr, was allowed by his father, the Imam Ahmad, to tour the communist countries, establishing diplomatic relations with Russia and China and signing an agreement with Moscow for the import of Russian arms. In October 1956, even as the British and French forces were massing in Cyprus for their ill-fated 'intervention' at Port Said, the first Soviet freighter arrived at the port

---

[1] One informed guess has put the number of rifles *legally* imported, and often directly supplied to the tribes by British officials, at 100,000 over the last fifteen years. This takes no account of the number illegally supplied from the Yemen.

of Salif in the Yemen with a cargo of arms and ammunition. One month later the Anglo-French action failed, President Nasser became the acknowledged leader of a triumphant Arab movement, and the mutters of political unrest grew louder in Aden. By January 1957, the first Russian rifles had reached the tribesmen on the frontier of the Western Protectorate, and I was listening to the Sharif of Baihan's lecture on the duty of the Queen and Her Government to protect him. By then, in spite of the understandable attachment of the Sharif and his fellow-rulers to their British treaties, it was clear that in the Protectorate's *cordon sanitaire* as well as in the Colony of Aden a rearguard action had begun.

deprive Aden of its biggest single source of revenue. 'Existing in administrative separation,' wrote Sir Charles Johnston, the Governor of Aden who eventually secured the merger of the two, 'they were like a head and body cut off from each other. In this situation it was only possible to conclude that the best solution for all concerned would be a merger of the Colony and the Federation into a single unit, having a special relationship with Britain which would ensure us the retention of our strategic facilities for as long as we needed them.'[1] So British colonial idealism joined with economic interest and military hard-headedness in envisaging a full federation for the Protectorate and the Colony as the only proper way ahead.

The paradox of Britain's colonial position, however, was that while only the swift advance of revolutionary nationalism in the Arab world as a whole had created the necessary local climate of opinion in favour of such a federation, the idea of the federation in turn gave added impetus to that nationalism. Tension between the two was self-generating and created a characteristic process of political polarisation. This began in earnest in 1958, when President Nasser threatened at first to sweep all before him throughout the Arab world. Never before or after did Nasser enjoy such an *annus mirabilis* as that one, when all the glory he had acquired in his Suez triumph, all the power he had won through bargaining with the East against the West, and all the suspicions created by western policies and influence in the Middle East over the previous forty years seemed to combine in a great assertion of the Arab desire for independence and unity under his leadership. The year began with the hurried union of Egypt and Syria in the United Arab Republic, swiftly joined by the Imam of Yemen who chose to ride like a bizarre genie in Nasser's caravan as the third member of a nebulous entity called the United Arab States. It continued with an apparently sympathetic palace upheaval in Saudi Arabia that nearly cost King Saud his throne and brought his brother, the Amir Faisal, into power as Prime Minister with a mandate for reform and, it seemed, friendlier relations with President Nasser. In Lebanon, civil war began in May over a dispute that combined Muslim-Christian rivalries with pro- and anti-Nasser sympathies and resulted, after five months of desultory rebellion, in the downfall of the anti-Nasser, pro-western President Chamoun. In July, the Government of Nuri es-Said was overthrown in Iraq, the young King Faisal and his family were killed, and a republican, nationalist and apparently Nasserist regime was created by General Abdul Karim

[1] Sir Charles Johnston, *The View from Steamer Point*, Collins, London, 1964, p. 36.

Kassim. King Faisal's cousin, King Husain of Jordain, only retained his throne by hastily summoning British troops to his aid. The whole Arab world that summer seemed to be blazing with a desire for revolution and unity.

The significance of these events was not lost upon the Protectorate rulers. While most of them promptly drew closer together in self-protection under the British wing, one of them decided more boldly to swop horses — or, rather, protectors — and go over to the new United Arab Republic. He was Sultan Ali Abdul Karim of Lahej, one of the younger and better-educated Protectorate rulers, and incontestably the most powerful and wealthy, who had come to believe that his proper role was no longer to accept the rest of the Protectorate chiefs as his peers with whom he should co-operate in a milk-and-water federation, but to assume the leadership of a united South Arabian state inspired by the nationalist purposes of Muhammad Ali Jifri's South Arabian League. For this purpose he was willing to accept Egyptian help, and rumour had it that he was about to apply for formal membership of the United Arab Republic. To forestall any such disaster, the British arrested one of the Jifri family in Lahej, alleging that they were spreading subversion throughout the Protectorate. Two more escaped arrest and fled to Cairo where they were joined by Sultan Ali — himself, in effect, deposed by the British Government for condoning attempts to subvert his fellow rulers and for attempting to break the terms of his ancestral agreement not to open relations with any foreign power except Britain.

The incident alarmed Sultan Ali's erstwhile colleagues still further, and they devoted the second half of 1958, in an atmosphere of haste if not quite panic, to the swift consummation of the federation of Shaikhdoms that Britain had hoped to create four years earlier.

Now, suddenly, the cards seemed to be dealt in their favour. In one of those agonising reversals so characteristic of Arab politics, the summer's blaze of Arab unity was reduced to a sputter. Within six months, even before the South Arabian Federation papers were signed, the United Arab Republic itself was showing clear signs of internal disorder. The Yemen's membership of the United Arab States had been revealed as a political gimmick. Prince Faisal had secured a new stability in Saudi Arabia but seemed little better disposed either to revolution or to Nasser than was his brother, Saud. Husain had survived the departure of the British troops from Jordan; and although the anti-Nasser elements in Lebanon had suffered defeat, the pro-Nasser elements could scarcely claim a victory, for Lebanon had found a compromise, as usual, to obtain a peaceful future, restoring the traditional balance between Muslim and Christian communities. Most damaging of all to the Arab unity movement was the renewed quarrel between Baghdad and Cairo — now, between two republican and avowedly 'revolutionary' regimes, more bitter than it had ever been.

In spite of the usual Arab allegations of 'imperialist' intervention in their affairs, neither Britain nor any other foreign power was responsible for this renewed Arab disarray. More than anything it was a function of Arab character, a reflection of the everlasting conflict in the Arab mind between visionary and cynic, idealist and materialist, unitarian and individualist. The Arabs, wrote Charles Doughty, are 'like to a man sitting in a cloaca to the eyes, and whose brows touch heaven'. United in their dreams, they are usually divided in reality — except when confronted by a recognised and common enemy. After Suez, the common enemy was easily identified as western 'imperialism', and it generated a great emotional surge of Arab unity. But by 1959 imperialism's grosser forms had been vanquished over much of the Middle East and the Arabs were retreating again into their usual state of mutual recrimination. This seesaw between unity and division, success and failure, is a painfully familiar process in Arab politics, as T. E. Lawrence once noted: 'They have been a government twenty times since the dawn of of history,' he wrote, 'and so often after achievement they have grown tired, and let it fall; but there is no record of any force except success capable of breaking them.' Well and truly broken by success did they seem in the spring of 1959 when the South Arabian Federation emerged at last from its chrysalis to take hopeful wing. It was, to be sure, only a federation of the western shaikhdoms — and by no means all of them. Aden Colony and the states of the Eastern Protectorate had still to be inveigled into the new fold. But at least a start had been made; and as the Arabs seemed so divided elsewhere in the Middle East, British officials in Aden hoped they might enjoy a breathing space to press on with the extension of the Federation unhampered by external attacks or internal subversion. They did not get it. This bright new butterfly of enlightened colonialism was, in fact, just the sort of creature to provoke fresh unity among the Arabs — a common enemy against which the tribal Arabs of the Protectorates could make common cause with the Imam of Yemen and the urban revolutionaries of Aden and Cairo. And make common cause they did, to denigrate and undermine Britain's federal plans with renewed vigour.

To describe the Federation as an enemy of the Arabs may seem to western minds illogical, for its inauguration was accompanied by an immediate increase in British investment in its impoverished member-states. By creating an organised regional government for the first time, in place of the individual sway of petty rulers, the Federation enabled Britain to support bigger development schemes than before and to begin training local cadres for administration and security. British financial contributions to the Protectorate states ran to less than £100,000 a year for nearly a generation after the Second World War, partly because there was no administration to make effective use of larger sums. To the Federation Britain's aid soon amounted to £5,000,000 a year — a 50-fold increase. New roads, schools and clinics were opened. The Aden Protectorate Levies and the Government Guards, which had been created a quarter of a century earlier as native forces under British command, became the Federal Regular Army and the Federal Guard, and before long some dozens of new Arab officers had been promoted from the ranks to train some hundreds of new tribal recruits.

To many of the rulers, anxious to save themselves from the twin threat of nationalism in Aden and subversion from the Yemen, these changes — although alarming — seemed the lesser evil, and by 1962 membership in the Federation had grown to include 12 of the 16 major states in the Western Protectorate and one of the four states in the East. The other eastern states, so distant from both Aden and the Yemen, had yet to feel the worst of the pressures exerted in the West; and besides, they were bemused by hopes of oil discoveries in their territories that would enable them to bask in affluent independence, buying off their enemies as they pleased. In the Western Protectorate, however, the search for oil had been abandoned and similar hopes had been crushed. Federation there — on British money — seemed the only possible course. Yet the encroachments of the new administration unavoidably created fresh resentments. To the Imam of Yemen they meant that the British were tightening their grip upon an area that belonged to him. To the nationalists of Aden and Cairo they meant that Britain was strengthening Aden's old *cordon sanitaire* with a view to retaining her military base in the Colony in spite of their protests. And to many of the tribesmen and some of the disgruntled chiefs of the Protectorates they meant still more alien interference in their traditional way of life.

Thus, in the post-Suez years, the British found themselves increasingly compelled to fight on three fronts at once — against the Protectorate tribesmen, the Imam of Yemen and the Aden nationalists supported by Cairo. In theory these three should have been incompatible. The notorious medieval brutality of the Imam's regime in the

Yemen inspired no affection in either the Aden nationalists or the Protectorate tribesmen. Indeed, as long as the Imam's rule persisted it was rightly regarded by the British as one of the chief guarantees of their own position; although his shrewd acceptance of Nasser's leadership in the United Arab States enabled a few of the Aden nationalists to pretend that even the Imam was really better than the British. The Imam, for his part, rightly feared the nationalists and their friends in Cairo as the long-term threat to his own safety; while the Protectorate tribesmen despised the de-tribalised townsmen of the Colony as a Scottish Highlander might despise a Londoner — and the townsmen correspondingly feared the barbarism of the tribes. What united these three was their opposition to British policy; and the more determinedly interventionist that became, the more their unity flowered and the faster did tribal dissidence increase in scale. In 1956, in the frontier states of Dhala and Baihan, most skirmishes between dissident tribesmen and the Protectorate forces were over in a matter of hours, with perhaps one sizeable bombing raid on the rebel village to drive home the point that law and order must be maintained. 'Military tiddlywinks' was how the Commander-in-Chief in Aden described these affrays to me at the time. Two years later, five companies of British and native infantry, assisted by repeated air strikes, took ten days to rescue a Political Adviser and his police guard ambushed by a force of 300 tribesmen on a mountain in the Dhala Amirate. And at the beginning of 1964, in the Radfan district, farther from the Yemen border, 1,000 rebels with rifles and grenades kept at bay for several weeks two battalions of infantry with a full muster of artillery, armoured cars, helicopters and aircraft in support. Altogether the Radfan engagement, called by the British 'Operation Nutcracker', continued sporadically for six months and was never satisfactorily completed. The tiddlywinks by then were beginning to look not so tiddly after all.

Effectively, however, Britain had no choice in these years but to continue her effort to unite the Colony to the new Federation. To retreat into Aden alone, as if into a Rock of Gibraltar, would have been far worse. Besides being contrary to Britain's obligations under the Protectorate treaties, it would have left the shaikhdoms at the Yemen's mercy, and the military base which British policy was intended to secure would have been deprived of its old *cordon sanitaire* at just the moment when it was beginning to be seriously challenged by political agitation and subversion from within. The early loss of the base would have been virtually certain and Southern Arabia would have been left in chaos. On the other hand, to pursue a course of 'separate but equal' development in the Colony and the shaikhdoms would have deepened the existing barriers between them and postponed the day when either might achieve a viable independence.

Had the first attempt to create a federation of the shaikhdoms been successful, before Suez, there might just have developed by 1959 sufficient federal expertise in administration and politics to have permitted a merger with the Colony on more equal terms. Had the British Government — or the Government of India — adopted a forward policy in the Protectorates twenty or thirty years sooner, before the First World War instead of after it, the problems of the '50's and '60's would certainly have been mitigated. Had Arab nationalism developed a little less dramatically elsewhere, and without such needless exacerbations as the Suez affair, Britain might have had a better chance of securing local, as well as international, agreement for her Aden policy. But these are might-have-beens: and the long and short of the reality is that, by 1959, when the South Arabian Federation of shaikh-doms was born, the development of British policy there was already out of phase with the post-war surge of nationalism and anti-colonialism and there was probably not a great deal to be done about it, save to accept the burdens of the past and soldier on.

Undoubtedly, by then, the greatest of these burdens was the enor-mous disparity between the shaikhdoms and the Colony in every field of economic, social and political development. To unite the two, wrote Charles Johnston, 'was like bringing modern Glasgow into a union with the eighteenth-century Highlands of Scotland'.[1] While the shaikhdoms had only just begun their passage towards a twentieth-century life, the Colony was already in the grip of an accelerating cycle of economic boom and political unrest. With the Suez Canal re-opened and made deeper than before, the confident predictions of Aden's merchants in 1956 had been more than fulfilled. New trade was arriving from every quarter of the compass; and although the approach of independence to the East African territories and the development of a new port for the Yemen by the Russians at Hodaida might syphon off a little of the local commerce, more ships than ever were calling at Steamer Point and the new oil refinery at Little Aden worked at full blast to supply the bunkering trade. Most of all, the British decision to make Aden a major military base involved capital investment and recurrent ex-penditure within the Colony on an unprecedented scale. By 1960 the direct contribution of the British military establishment to Aden's

---

[1] Johnston, op. cit., p. 152.

economy was estimated at £11,000,000 a year, and in the following few years it rose still further.

Aden became more prosperous than it had ever been. Its sandy coves on the Indian Ocean were crowded with the families of British servicemen. Its duty-free shops at Steamer Point were jammed with the latest luxuries of the world, and the latest shiploads of tourists to buy them. New flats and houses were going up in hundreds all the way from Steamer Point to Khormaksar airfield — five miles of concrete and air-conditioning. There were new schools and hospitals, a new radio station to spread the word of Britain against the *Voice of the Arabs* from Cairo, and even the walls of the old volcano itself were torn down to widen the narrow pass from Steamer Point to Crater, to accommodate the choking influx of new cars and buses.

But it is a perpetual irony of developing prosperity that it is apt to arouse more expectations than it satisfies. Aden's boom was no exception. It created more, not less, trouble as the Colony's population was swollen with people new to the experience of contemporary wealth. Most of the immigrants came from the Yemen and the Federation to work in the port, the oil refinery and the military base. By 1962 there were between 80,000 and 100,000 Yemenis in the Colony and at least 20,000 Federation tribesmen, out of a total of a quarter of a million people.

Uprooted from their homes, removed from tribal supports and traditions, and tasting the temptations of a modern wage economy for the first time, yet without a voice in the Colony's affairs, they were easy game for political agitators. Moreover, as a relatively homogeneous group — unlike the rest of Aden's immigrant, mercantile population — they were easily organised through the Aden Trades Union Congress, which continued with its political strikes after the Suez crisis as though Lord Lloyd and his pro-consular strictures had never been heard of. In 1959 alone there were 84 strikes in the Colony, one of which virtually paralysed the port for five weeks; and by 1960 the A.T.U.C.'s political wing, known as the People's Socialist Party, had replaced the old South Arabian League as the recognised leader of the Nationalist opposition in Aden. The League's commitment to the limited objective of an independent, self-contained state of South Arabia was less fashionable, and less appealing to the Yemeni workers, than the P.S.P.'s cloudier vision of an independent, united and republican entity which would include the Yemen as well. Moreover, the P.S.P.'s leader, Abdullah al-Asnag, could hardly have been more appropriate, for he was a young, able, argumentative product of British colonial schooling and Nasserist sympathies employed as a clerk by that most characteristic institution of the twentieth century in South Arabia — Aden Airways.

For the P.S.P. the tactical first step to its enlarged South Arabian union, at least for as long as the despised Imamate remained in command of the Yemen, was to win a majority in the Aden Legislative Council through elections, and thereupon to demand independence for the Colony. The only evident way to accomplish that was to win the franchise for the Yemeni workers, whose sympathies the P.S.P. controlled. This in itself was enough to persuade the British authorities not to enfranchise the Yemenis, for they feared that with the P.S.P. in power in Aden the future of the military base would at once be jeopardised. Equally, the Aden moderates opposed the Yemeni vote because they saw in it the chief menace to their own political and commercial future, which rested, in their eyes, on the continued presence of the British. Besides this naked struggle for power, however, there was a genuine conflict of principle involved in this question of the Aden franchise. The Government's constitutional case for not enfranchising the Yemenis was simply, and reasonably, that they were not 'Adenis'. They had no stake in the Colony except their jobs. As migrant workers they were no more entitled to the privilege of local citizenship implied by a vote than, say, a Belfast shipyard worker employed in Sweden, or a London advertising executive seconded to Madison Avenue. Anywhere else in the world this might have seemed fair and conclusive. But to the nationalists in Aden it appeared as an evasion. They thought, not in British, but in Arab terms. The Yemenis, they argued, were the largest single group in the Colony and the backbone of its prosperity. Without their labour there could be no expansion. More important, they were Arabs — citizens of that putative south Arabian union of Aden, the Shaikhdoms and the Yemen to which the nationalists were dedicated, and participants in the greater unity of the Arab world which had always existed on a spiritual, if not on the political, plane. The people who did have the vote in Aden, on the other hand, were often not Arabs at all, but Pakistani and Indian merchants, Persians, Greeks and Jews, even British who had been born in the Colony or had established themselves through residence there. These, the nationalists implied, were the real immigrants, the carpet-baggers without true local status; and, significantly, they were usually sympathetic to British policy, and anxious to continue their lucrative businesses under British protection. Thus the clash of nationalists against the British over the Yemeni vote tended to coincide with those of workers against merchants and of Arab against non-Arab; and it was easy to argue from this coincidence that the exclusion of the Yemenis from the franchise was a deliberate attempt to suppress the Arab nationalist majority in the interests of colonialist exploitation. Beset by these conflicting arguments, Aden's elections — although democratic enough if the British premises were accepted — became increasingly irrelevant to the Colony's political development, resulting in a series of hollow victories for a minority of moderate, true-blue 'Adenis' over an 'Arab' opposition majority that simply boycotted the electoral process as a fraud and concentrated instead upon direct action through strikes and occasional violence.

So the polarisation process went a stage farther. While British support for an enlarged Federation of Aden and the shaikhdoms united the Yemen, the tribesmen and the Aden nationalists in opposition, the growing strength of the nationalists forced the Aden moderates into the arms of the shaikhly rulers in support of Britain. It was a familiar colonial process of pressure producing counter-pressure at every turn; and as the date approached for the merger between the Colony and the Federation the gulf deepened between the two sides and the prospects of the merger's peaceful consummation seemed to diminish. Nor were they strengthened by the terms proposed for the merger, which deliberately favoured the Federal rulers, enabling them to be sure of a majority over the Aden ministers in the Federal council and to control the internal security of Aden itself — conservative precautions which caused second thoughts even among the Aden moderates.

Yet what were the alternatives? Britain's overriding strategic aim was security for the military base. Her secondary aims in support of this were to marry the Colony to the Shaikhdoms and prepare both together for orderly progress towards independence. If the primary aim was accepted, the others followed for, as we have seen, the possible alternatives were far less plausible. In pursuing this overall strategy, the British Government adopted the tactical policy of ignoring, suppressing, or circumventing the Aden nationalists rather than negotiating with them. It was therefore logical both to weight the terms of the merger in favour of the shaikhdoms and to maintain a narrowly-based vote inside Aden Colony.

To the objection that the nationalists could neither be suppressed nor ignored, and that this tactic was based, consequently, on a false premise, there were some reasonable counter-arguments. If, for example, the Aden franchise had been widened to include the Yemenis, as the nationalists wished, the prospect of any agreed merger would have been reduced, almost certainly, to zero. The nationalists would then have controlled the Aden legislature and would have named terms for the merger — if, indeed, they had accepted the idea at all — which the shaikhs would have been most reluctant to accept. Britain would have been obliged then either to accept the continued separation of Aden from the Protectorate, or to force through the merger on Aden's terms and risk still greater disaffection in the shaikhdoms. Either way, the end might well have been the creation of an Aden redoubt in which Britain's military security rested upon the goodwill and economic self-interest of the nationalists — a prospect too nebulous to be entertained with conviction. The other possibility — that Britain might have forced a different compromise upon the nationalists and the Federal rulers — was also risky, for it could still have resulted in offending both sides and satisfying neither, and it would certainly have required no less bullying and cajoling than the merger that was, in fact, proposed.

In the circumstances of the time, therefore, the basis of British policy was less unreasonable than some critics made it appear. Its tactical aim was to find some consensus between the wildly disparate communities of Aden and the shaikhdoms on which to found the marriage of the two; and it sought to discover this in the common interest of the shaikhly rulers and the mercantile class of Aden in Britain's continued presence. The real criticism to be made was of its methods, not its purposes. In particular, the terms of the merger seemed unnecessarily favourable to the shaikhdoms, and needlessly weakened the consensus by reducing support for Britain's policy among the Aden moderates. Behind this lay, I think, three factors. First, it is likely that the Aden politicians were out-smarted by the rulers at the conference table. With all their supposed political sophistication, the Adenis may have been too self-confident, forgetting that although the rulers might be uneducated in the formal sense they had learned all the tricks of bargaining in their tribal disputes. Not for the first time, the city slickers probably allowed themselves to be taken for a ride by the country bumpkins. Secondly, there was the determination of the British military planners, warmly supported by the Colonial Office, to ensure the security of the base at all costs. To this end they were prepared to risk offence in Aden as a lesser evil than collapse or disaffection in the shaikhdoms, and to err, therefore, on the side of caution in the security arrangements. Thirdly, and perhaps just as important, some of the chief British officials in Aden were afflicted with a familiar form of colonial myopia known as 'localitis'. Most of them, except for the Governor, were old hands in Aden and the Protectorate, and they reflected in milder forms many of the old imperial preconceptions that had been voiced so vigorously by the drinkers in the Crescent bar when I arrived there in 1956. They tended to assume that Aden's problems could be dealt with in isolation from the movement of Arab nationalism elsewhere; and they spoke as if the appeal of Nasser in particular was somehow created by propaganda, bribery and intimidation alone. All these certainly were employed by or on behalf of the nationalists, but Nasser's command of Arab affections was based on two deeper factors — pride and success. As the first Arab for many a decade to kick the foreigner in the teeth and get away with it, he was a genuine and understandable source of inspiration to them; and by the same token he was a genuine and understandable cause of irritation to old British residents and officials in Aden, and elsewhere in the Arab world.

To these officials, if not always to the other residents, this was not because they looked upon all Arabs as 'wogs' who ought to be kept in their place. No British Political Agent or Adviser that I ever met in Aden and the Protectorate exhibited such a primitive outlook. It was rather because they felt obscurely that Nasser's success — and that of his nationalist admirers — elevated the wrong sort of chap in the wrong way. They had devoted their lives, often in a spirit of real, if sometimes romantic, idealism, to the protection and advice of tribesmen and their traditional rulers, but they now saw these old friends and charges being abruptly subverted or superseded by the new urban clerks and workers whom they themselves had helped to create, yet with whose outlook they had little in common. For example, I have no doubt that most of them understood and could work with the father of Abdullah al-Asnag, the nationalist and trades union leader. He was an Inspector in the Aden Government's Health Service for many years — a first-generation recruit to western ways. But they found it far more difficult to understand or work with Abdullah, who had absorbed the western influences into his very soul, so to speak, and emerged as a new kind of Arab altogether. The officials would have been more than human if they had not deep within them resented and distrusted these new, and apparently mongrel, men who were taking over their old responsibilities. They had helped, willy-nilly, to make a new world — and now they felt they could not live in it. This is a common and, perhaps, inevitable feeling in anyone who has ever served a cause or a people seriously and with some success, and it need not be counted unworthy just because the expression of it may be politically unwise. But with such a feeling ingrained in some of the senior men in the British administration in southern Arabia there was a natural tendency for local recommendations and decisions to favour the old unduly against the new. The nationalists tended to be brushed off without much consultation or consideration as irresponsible — or, as Sir Charles Johnston described them, 'utterly negative' — while the traditional rulers and the Aden merchants were said to display 'common sense' and were drawn carefully into all negotiations. Few among the British officials seemed emotionally equipped to swim for long against these pervasive habits of thought and action.

The marriage of the South Arabian Federation and the Colony of Aden was pressed forward, in consequence, upon manifestly unequal terms. Even so, there was a reasonable chance that it might have been accomplished peacefully had it not, by a surely symbolic stroke of fate, coincided with revolution in the Yemen. On September 24th, 1962, the merger scheme was presented to the Aden Legislative council to the accompaniment of nationalist opposition demonstrations throughout the Colony. On September 26th the plan was passed by the Government's narrow majority in the Council: but that same night, 200 miles away in Sanaa, the tanks of the Yemen Army rumbled into the streets of the town to shell the Imam's palace while soldiers seized the radio station and proclaimed the creation of the 'Yemen Arab Republic' and the death of the Imam. Suddenly and dramatically the nationalist horizons were widened. The cherished union of all southern Arabia with the Yemen seemed at last a practical possibility. 'If the Yemeni revolution had come one day earlier,' wrote Sir Charles Johnston afterwards, 'or the Legislative Council vote one day later, I feel pretty certain that the London Agreement [on the terms of the merger] would never have obtained the support of a majority of local members. In the new atmosphere at least one more Government supporter would have defected to the opposition.'[1] And one more would have made all the difference to the passage of the plan. That the result was so close revealed how flimsy was the basis for the merger in the first place. It had never been a love match, to be sure; but up to now it had at least been justified as a marriage of convenience. Now the news from across the border threw doubt even upon that. From September 27th onwards, the merger had to be — if it was going to be anything at all — an old-fashioned shotgun wedding.

[1] Johnston, op. cit. pp. 124–5.

4

The Shotgun Wedding

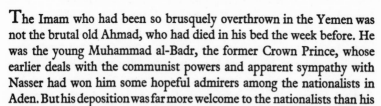

The Imam who had been so brusquely overthrown in the Yemen was not the brutal old Ahmad, who had died in his bed the week before. He was the young Muhammad al-Badr, the former Crown Prince, whose earlier deals with the communist powers and apparent sympathy with Nasser had won him some hopeful admirers among the nationalists in Aden. But his deposition was far more welcome to the nationalists than his accession, for it meant — so they assumed — the end of the Imamate itself: the downfall of the symbol of tradition, privilege, dictatorship, poverty and isolation, and the arrival of hope in the Yemen.

Their hopes and assumptions were premature, but their impact at the time in Aden was immense. When I arrived there, soon after the revolution, there was hardly a shop in the Crater bazaar that was not flying the new Republic's flag — a green star on a ground of black, white and red stripes, as close as could be to the Egyptian pattern. To the 'New York Stores', 'United Nations Stores', and 'Bandung Stores' which proclaimed the faith of Aden's humbler shopkeepers in twentieth-century progress, were now added several 'Yemen Arab Republic Stores' as the latest symbol of the new world. Within three weeks some thousands of Yemenis had left for home in the hope of finding their land reformed and prosperous under its new rulers, and within six months 500 new shops were said to have been opened by Aden merchants in the bazaars of Taiz and Sanaa in the Yemen.

This new confidence in the Yemen's future threatened to frustrate altogether the British plan for marrying the Federation and the Colony. Until the 27th of September, 1962, the nationalists in Aden had united with the Yemeni Imamate against the British for tactical purposes only, to try to win their own freedom of action. Their long-range plan for political unification with the Yemen seemed the merest pipe-dream, for the reactionary truth about the Imamate was enough to stifle the enthusiasm of most Arabs for any immediate effort to make the dream a reality. Now, however, the whole balance of power and probabilities appeared to have been changed overnight. The revolution in the Yemen, assisted by the speedy arrival of Egyptian troops, suggested, firstly, that the nationalist vision of uniting with the Yemen had become immediate practical politics, thus cutting the ground from under the Aden moderates who had been able to argue convincingly until then that it was nothing of the sort. Secondly, it threatened the Protectorate shaikhdoms with still greater physical pressure from the Yemen than the Imam had ever exerted, for it was hardly conceivable that a Yemen Republic supported by Egypt would fail to harass the British in Aden before long. As a result, the political conflict throughout the area seemed far less ambiguous than before. Gone from the alignment of 'modern Arabism' was the incubus of the medieval Imamate; and going from the ranks of 'reactionary colonialism' were the Aden moderates. The lines were to be drawn henceforth as Aden nationalists, Yemeni revolutionaries, and President Nasser, against the British and the Federal rulers — a straightforward clash, as far as Cairo's powerful propaganda was concerned, between 'progress' and 'reaction'. This impression was immediately confirmed when the Federal rulers, who had spent most of their lives fighting the new Imam's father, now became warm supporters of his son's cause. 'The friend of my enemy is my enemy,' says an Arab proverb, 'and the enemy of my enemy is my friend.' When it transpired within a few weeks that the Imam Badr was alive and raising tribal forces to challenge the Yemeni revolutionaries, the Federal rulers were eager for Britain to support him, for they recognised clearly enough that a successful republican regime in the Yemen would be a far greater threat to their existence than a reformed Imamate; and they who had been the old Imam's enemies promptly became his son's friends.

At this point the British had a short, sharp and significant debate on policy in which the Colonial Office and the Defence Ministry on one side disagreed with some of the members of the Foreign Office on the other almost as sharply as the Federal rulers differed from the Aden nationalists. Ostensibly the debate was about whether to recognise the new republican government in the Yemen, and this was said to turn upon the purely technical question of who controlled the Yemen, and how. Colonial Office and Defence Ministry officials in Aden — including Sir Charles Johnston who was, in fact, a Foreign Office Ambassador on loan to the Colonial Office — maintained that the republicans in the Yemen did not meet the minimum criterion for diplomatic recognition of any Government: namely that it should be able to exercise effective and unaided control over most of the country. Royalist forces, they said, were active over much of the Yemen, especially in the north and east, and might well have returned the Imam to power in Sanaa but for the presence of large numbers of Egyptian troops upon whose strength the republicans depended. Many Foreign Office officials, on the other hand — in the Yemen, in Cairo, and in London, too — argued that the republicans did effectively control the southern and western portions of the Yemen, as well as all the main towns and roads. The royalists were active only as guerrillas, and although they might win successes from time to time they were unlikely to overthrow the new regime. Moreover, to withhold recognition from the republicans only encouraged royalist resistance and so ensured that the Egyptian troops would remain longer in the Yemen, to the ultimate disadvantage of the British in Aden.

Within these arguments of fact and protocol, however, a far wider debate was implied about whether the security of the Aden base — and, at a further remove, the Gulf oilfields — could best be maintained through continued reliance on the conservative buffer of the South Arabian shaikhs, or through attempting some sort of deal with President Nasser and the Aden nationalists. On the whole, in my experience, Foreign Office officials seemed to favour the second course. To some of them, perhaps, there seemed a chance at this moment to repair the damage done to Britain's position in the Arab world by the Suez policy six years earlier, to which most of them had been opposed. Certainly they were conscious of the fact that a British failure to recognise the Yemeni republicans would make their task more difficult in most of the Arab capitals by antagonising President Nasser and branding Britain once again as imperialist and reactionary. And they canvassed the possibility of securing from Nasser, in exchange for recognition of his republican protégés, a private agreement to permit the South Arabian Federation to go forward without further molestation from Cairo and to accept the continued existence of the Aden base. There would have to be concessions, of course. The date of Aden's merger with the Federation might have to be postponed, and the terms would certainly have to be re-negotiated to give the Aden politicians, and especially the nationalists, more authority. But if that were done, orderly progress towards independence for southern Arabia could be resumed with the tacit agreement of President Nasser and probably, therefore, of the new regime in Sanaa. Moreover, as the Aden nationalists were both individually and collectively dependent on the economic benefits of the base, it was possible that they would willingly agree to its continuance even after independence. Beyond that, there was even the possibility of an eventual détente in the Persian Gulf, to be secured by demonstrating to President Nasser that the British Government was not automatically a friend of Arab 'reaction', that it did not wish to use the Aden base for any aggressive purposes, and that it was ready to consider any reasonable long-term plans for alternative peace-keeping arrangements in the Gulf.

This was a tempting picture, indeed, to hang upon what seemed so small a practical issue; but equally convincing visions, or nightmares, were presented by the other side. The arguments of the Colonial Office and the Defence Ministry boiled down to the assertion that the stakes were too high to permit any new gamble. The security of the base was paramount and could not be committed to any deal with so unreliable a person as President Nasser. Recognition of the republicans would, in any case, tip the scales against the Federal shaikhs in South Arabia and necessitate, as a result, a re-negotiation of the merger in favour of the Aden politicians. This would result in great disaffection in the shaikh-doms, with increased tribal dissidence and possibly collapse of the Federation and the end of Aden's traditional *cordon sanitaire*. Demands for immediate independence might follow, both in the Colony and the shaikhdoms, and Britain would be left within a year or two with no more security for her base than the whims of the Aden nationalists. Their sense of economic self-interest was not to be relied upon, as experience elsewhere in the Arab world had proved — witness Nasser's action in blocking the Suez Canal — and dreams of détente in the Persian Gulf were too visionary to be a basis for immediate policy. Besides, the best hope of long-term solutions in the Persian Gulf lay in improving Britain's relations with Saudi Arabia, and that country had emerged at once as the chief sponsor of the Yemeni royalists. If Britain recognised the republicans she would probably cast away the best chance in six years of resuming diplomatic relations with the Saudis — who had severed them after Suez — and perhaps of working out a settlement of such vexing matters as the frontier dispute in Buraimi and the smoulder-ing dissatisfaction of Saudi Arabia's tribal protégés in Oman.

Here was a nice balance of argument; and two or three months of hard thought and discourse were required at the end of 1962 to reach a decision. Had the republicans and their Egyptian allies won a quick and complete victory in the Yemen there would have been no room and no need for argument. Recognition by Britain of the new regime would have had to follow, the nationalists in Aden would have become overwhelmingly powerful and the shaikhs of the Federation would probably have trimmed their own sails to the gale. The whole basis of British policy would have been destroyed, and no course would have been left to the Government but to seek an accommodation with the nationalists and Nasser. But quick and complete victory in the Yemen was not forthcoming. Within three months it was plain that tribal resistance to the republicans was spreading and more Egyptian troops were arriving every week.

The presence of an Egyptian army on the Arabian mainland suggested to the British Government that the *cordon sanitaire* of the shaikhdoms was more necessary than ever to the security of the Aden base; and the capacity of the Yemeni tribesmen for armed resistance seemed to confirm that the hostility of tribal rulers in the Federation might be more dangerous for Britain in the short run than continued opposition from the Aden nationalists. Events therefore compelled the Government to come down again on the side of caution. Recognition of the Yemen Republic was withheld, any thought of conciliating Nasser and the nationalists was rejected, and the marriage of Aden and the Federation was made a shotgun wedding. Elections that were to have been held in the Colony were postponed to prevent the opposition making any headway, the date of the merger was advanced to give the nationalists less time to prepare any direct action against it, and in January 1963 Aden Colony became officially Aden State, its Governor became a High Commissioner, and it was formally incorporated into the South Arabian Federation. One hundred and twenty-four years after Captain Haines of the Indian Navy had severed Aden's seventy-five square miles of impoverished sand and rock from their hinterland, the two were made one again. It should have been a happy event. Instead, it looked a sorry and ill-fated union, for whatever geographic and economic advantages there were in re-uniting the port of Aden with its interior, the British had done it in such a way as to identify themselves in the eyes of much of the world with reactionary feudal chieftains against sophisticated nationalist politicians and all the forces of reform they claimed to represent.

This, at least, was the central theme of nationalist propaganda, and some of the incidental aspects of British policy seemed to confirm it. The latent anti-Nasserism and colonial 'localitis' of British officials in Aden became more prominent after the Yemen revolution. There were moments in the autumn of 1962 when all the old Suez ghosts seemed to have been raised again and dark talk was offered by one official after another of 'cutting Nasser down to size'. In some of them I sensed a feeling of personal affront that the upstart Egyptians should interfere with the land and people they had served so long; and a wish to make the Yemeni affair a direct test of Nasser's strength was rarely far below the surface of conversation. Royalist claims of 'victory' in the Yemen were persistently inflated, and republican claims of 'control' were as often denigrated. Visiting journalists like myself were offered trips across the border from the Sharif of Baihan's territory into royalist hands. 'It'll cost you nothing,' was the word. 'The R.A.F.'ll fly you up, and the Sharif's boys will see you over the line. After that, it's up to you and the royalists.' Many a reporter enjoyed this ride behind the lines and many were the dispatches published as a result telling of the Imam's forces only 35 miles from Sanaa. There was everything to be said for the reporters going if they could; but there seemed little to be said for the British Government so openly assisting them to do so, while at the same time maintaining — as it did — that it was utterly impartial in the matter. Blind eyes were turned, also, to more active forms of intervention. It was common knowledge, for instance, that guns were being smuggled across the border as well as reporters, but nothing was done to stop it. On the contrary, the ebullient Sharif of Baihan, then Minister of Interior for the South Arabian Federation, seemed rather to enjoy the role popularly credited to him of gun-runner-in-chief. No doubt he felt he had been on the receiving end of a similar trade often enough before and was delighted to get a bit of his own back. British forces were not directly involved in this trade. As far as I was aware, the R.A.F. did not fly arms to Baihan that were openly destined for the Yemeni royalists. But retired British military men, often full of romantic visions of themselves as latter-day Lawrences, were soon involved; and the extent to which British officials must have sympathised with the traffic was revealed later when Sir Alec Douglas Home, as Prime Minister, virtually admitted in the House of Commons that the *aide de camp* to the High Commissioner had been personally involved with a clandestine group giving military support to the Imam's forces. His actions were said to have been beyond the knowledge of his superiors, but it strains credulity to suppose that they did not have a very good idea of what he was doing and took some care not to find out any more.[1] It is unlikely that this gun-running from the Federation made a crucial difference to the development of the Yemen civil war over the next two years. The real support for the royalists came from the Saudis, who had quite enough resources of their own to keep the Yemeni tribesmen well supplied with arms and money to harass the new regime in Sanaa. I doubt, too, whether the British could ever have

[1] See: *Sunday Times*, July 5th, 1964, and Hansard, July 21st, 1964.

stopped the traffic completely, any more than they could stop arms coming into the shaikhdoms from the Yemen; and it seems to me possible that a really determined attempt to do so might have caused more tribal unrest than it was worth. I am convinced also, that as far as the internal situation in the Yemen was concerned, the issue of British diplomatic recognition was irrelevant. I do not think any significant number of tribesmen would have laid down their guns just because Britain recognised the republican regime; nor do I think the Saudis would have been influenced in the slightest. They were under persistent American pressure to cut off aid to the Imam, and if they resisted that — as they did on more than one occasion — they were hardly likely to have taken much notice of what Britain said or did.

Nevertheless the obvious British partisanship deepened the hostility of Nasser, the Yemenis and the Aden nationalists and probably both hastened and inflamed the clashes which followed in Aden and the shaikhdoms. It is unlikely that these clashes could have been avoided altogether. As long as Britain was determined to preserve the Aden base she was probably doomed to conflict with President Nasser and therefore with his protégés in Aden and the Yemen. And with or without civil war in the Yemen, a revival of the traditional Yemeni claim to 'south Yemen' probably was a foregone conclusion because a republican regime could not have remained true to its revolutionary principles without raising this issue before long, while an unsuccessful regime was equally bound to raise it as one way of pinning the blame for its failure upon someone else. But in the short run, at least, the conflict might have been muffled by a more genuinely impartial British attitude in Aden, and it might then have easier to win the confidence of the Aden nationalists in later negotiations on the terms of southern Arabia's approach to independence.

As it was, the forced wedlock of Aden and the shaikhdoms soon involved violence akin to rape. The political strikes in Aden continued, the Assistant High Commissioner was killed by a bomb thrown at Aden airport, Aden Ministers were attacked by gunmen, scores of P.S.P. supporters were imprisoned on a variety of charges, tribal dissidence increased in the interior, and 'incidents' along the Yemen frontier — where British and Egyptian forces now confronted each other — grew in scale and frequency and attracted the formal and disapproving notice of the United Nations. In the summer of 1963 the formation of a 'National Front for the Liberation of Occupied South Yemen' was announced in Sanaa; and in the Aden market the price of a decent second-hand rifle fell from £100 to £25 inside nine months, directly reflecting the enormous increase in gun-running from all sides. By the end of 1964, when the National Liberation Front began an intensive terrorist campaign inside Aden, with open Egyptian support, the policy of preserving the Aden base at all costs was threatening to become self-defeating, as the existence of the base increasingly provoked the unrest it was supposed to prevent or suppress. A growing number of troops from the base were required to serve as a garrison force for its protection; and the more active they became in this role, the more antagonism they created, not only in Aden and the shaikhdoms, but throughout the Arab world. Aden had become the major obstacle to better relations between Britain and Egypt, and was exploited by the *Voice of the Arabs* as proof of Britain's fundamental enmity towards all Arabs. There was pressure on both Sudan and Libya to reduce British military over-flying rights on the direct route from Britain to Aden; and there was restive talk among the young nationalists in the Persian Gulf states of Britain's 'aggressive' intentions. As Lady Bracknell observed to Mr. John Worthing, in the course of their famous interview in *The Importance of Being Earnest*, the disadvantage of owning a large estate is that 'it gives one position, and prevents one from keeping it up'. So, more or less, with the Aden base. By the end of 1964 it was dangerously close to being more bother than it was worth; and there were signs that the British Government was beginning to accept the fact. In the course of the year, it became known that the United States and Britain were co-operating in a search for suitable island bases in the Indian Ocean, with the obvious implication that Aden's days as a British sovereign base might be numbered. And after the Labour Party had formed a new Government in the autumn, talks among all factions in Aden ended with an announcement that independence would be granted to a united South Arabian state by 1968, or sooner if possible. So much for the British residents in the Crescent bar, who had assured me in 1956 that Britain would hang on to Aden for another 30 years. So much for Lord Lloyd, that same year, and the wish of Her Majesty's Government to 'make it clear that the importance of Aden, both strategically and economically, within the Commonwealth is such that they cannot foresee the possibility of any fundamental relaxation of their responsibilities for the Colony'. Just over eight years later, Her Majesty's Government had been driven to announce that Britain was on the way out.

The questions that remained to be settled before 1968 concerned only the means of Britain's withdrawal, but they were not the less difficult for that. Three of the four states of the Eastern Protectorate were still outside the Federation, and with them and their potential oil resources rested the chief hope of ultimate economic independence for a new state in this corner of Arabia. Of more immediate importance to Britain, however, were the future of the base and the constitutional structure of the state that she should leave behind. These two questions were associated, for if it had been possible to envisage an independent South Arabian state, in which the shaikhdoms would continue to dominate Aden, it would have been possible also to foresee Britain continuing her occupation of the military base. But the whole trend of events was against this outcome. The struggle for independence in Aden, the creation of the Federation in the shaikhdoms, and the civil war in the Yemen, had all hastened the emergence of a modern political structure in the traditional society of the shaikhdoms. A Federal administration was several years old, 400 Arab officers had tasted authority in the Federal forces, new roads and schools were introducing new mobility and new ideas. With every extra penny the British Government spent in southern Arabia, every extra battle it was compelled to fight and every extra soldier it put into the field, the vitality of the old tribal life was weakened and the appeal of the new way of life increased. As the Arab subalterns and sergeants learned to dispense with their British colonels and captains, as the tribesmen found more work and the camel and bandit economy of their lives was replaced by the wage incentives of a modern society, a new nursery of nationalism was being prepared.

This did not, and will not, mean that the tribes were, or can be, easily subdued, whether by Britain or the urban nationalists of Aden. I do not see the men of Upper Yafai, or Radfan, or many another tribal territory, becoming law-abiding, democratic citizens of a united South Arabian state anywhere this side of the twenty-first century — which is now, after all, only a couple of generations away. It does mean, however, that the transfer of power from the tribes to the towns, from the traditional rulers to the modern — or supposedly modern — politicians and administrators, has been and will be accelerated. Moreover, whatever the outcome of the Yemen civil war, there cannot be a return to the old Imamate; nor is there likely to be any significant revival of the moderate political forces in Aden that, not long ago, were allied to the up-country shaikhs. The traditional rulers are far less secure locally, therefore, than they were a few years ago, and ever since Britain announced a target date for independence some of them have seemed half-persuaded that their best course is to re-insure their future without her by becoming as nationalist as anyone. Sultan Ali of Lahej chose this course, we may recall, as long ago as 1958 when he sought to join President Nasser's new United Arab Republic. Sultan Ahmad of Fadhli, another powerful Federal ruler, did the same thing in 1964, when he defected to Cairo at the end of a constitutional conference in London at which he had been one of the chief delegates for the South Arabian Federation. Others, quite possibly, will be ready to follow them when they think the time is ripe; and that time now seems no longer far away, for increasing terrorism in Aden and continuing dissidence in the shaikhdoms have revealed that the British protection on which the rulers have based themselves is now on its last legs. Before independence is finally achieved, therefore, it is reasonable to expect that more of the rulers will abandon their policy of the last decade and jump on the nationalist bandwaggon. Aden then will finally dominate the shaikhdoms, not the other way about.

In the long run it is possible, also, that the whole idea of a South Arabian state composed only of Aden and the old Protectorate will prove untenable. The commercial, and even political, links between Aden and the Yemen have never been completely severed, except during the years of Yemeni stagnation under the Turks; and when South Arabia is free of the British and the Yemen is free of the Egyptians, as one day they will be, the tendency to form new political alignments embracing both territories may assert itself irresistibly.

In all these circumstances it is unrealistic to suppose that Britain has much chance of retaining the Aden base after 1968. Conceivably, she might bargain for a lease of it on the grounds that the economy of Aden would collapse without it, but the precedents elsewhere do not suggest that this argument would be effective on its own. Nationalist movements, perhaps especially among the Arabs, have more often than not been ready to sacrifice immediate economic benefits to the long-term goals of independence; and so many Arabs both inside and outside Aden are committed to the abolition of the British base along with independence that it is difficult to see how any of them could go back upon their word. There will always be others who will be ready to prevent them by invoking the magic slogans of Arabism and anti-imperialism.

Indeed, to a great extent both the nature of South Arabia's ultimate constitution and the destiny of the base have been predetermined already by a United Nations resolution of December 1963, which has become, in effect, the nationalist manifesto for independence. Pressed upon the General Assembly by the anti-colonialist nations, it called for elections throughout South Arabia on the basis of universal adult suffrage, together with the return of all political exiles, the release of all political detainees, and the withdrawal of the British base. Armed with this resolution, and spurred on by the local terrorism sponsored by the Egyptians in the Yemen, the Aden nationalists have become increasingly determined and aggressive. By the beginning of 1965 it was already clear that even if they wanted to retreat from the U.N. resolution in any negotiations with the British Government, their supporters might not let them. The scene seemed to be set, therefore, for a fairly violent last act in South Arabia that could only end in Britain's concession of defeat.

It would be easy to conclude from all this that British policy in Aden has been a total failure. I would not agree. Its tactics may have been misjudged at times, its methods often myopic; but in the tangled context of politics in southern Arabia over the years since Suez its achievements have been by no means worthless. It has kept the Aden base in being in defiance of nationalist wishes and reasonable expectation; and if the cost has seemed high sometimes in violence, estrangement and provocation throughout the Arab world, it is not easy to see that there was a real alternative except to risk a premature departure, which might have exposed the whole of southern Arabia to the sort of conflict that beset the Yemen. Compared to that, the violence in Aden and the Federation has been minimal, so far.

Britain's shotgun wedding of Aden and the shaikhdoms has not been a happy union. Given the differences of history between the two that would have been too much to expect. But at least it has forged the beginnings of a modern political structure in the region — and that, ten years ago, seemed infinitely remote. It can be argued that the whole process should have begun much sooner; and no doubt it should. But that would have required a different Arabia as well as a different Britain — in short, a different world. In the world as it is British policy has been less disastrous than has sometimes been suggested. It is true that it has steadily lost local support, ever since the day in 1956 when Lord Lloyd disappointed the loyalists in the Aden Association. But paradoxically this is a measure of success as well as of failure, for at the very least it means that some rudimentary unity has been created where there was none before. Without the irritant of Britain's presence and the benefit of her example, nationalism in southern Arabia would be far weaker than it is and factionalism and tribalism far stronger. Nowhere else in Arabia, after all, does the victory of modern nationalism seem as imminent now as in Aden and the Federation, because nowhere else has a colonial power been at work with anything like true colonial authority to act as the catalyst of nationhood.

For a year or two longer, possibly, Britain will continue in this role, playing the necessary imperialist Aunt Sally to the south Arabian nationalists, pitting her nerve and patience against their growing violence and provocation. It is not a pretty prospect, but the end is now in sight; and perhaps, in any case, some discomfort in these final years is the inescapable price that Britain has to pay for the long century when she treated Aden and the shaikhdoms as mere outposts of another, greater Empire.

5

The Kingdom of Silence

'*Ingleesi?*' The frontier guard frowned in disbelief. Yes, *Ingleesi*, the little Yemeni driver told him, and pulled from his shirt pocket the grubby paper I had obtained the day before in a dark cubby-hole in the Aden suk. By the holy order of His Majesty the Commander of the Faithful, it said, Seeker of God's Triumph, the Imam Ahmad bin Yahia bin Muhammad Hamid ud-din, this Englishman was invited to enter the Kingdom of Yemen. The guard scanned the paper and my accompanying passport. It was so, indeed. He hitched at his great curved dagger, straightened his bandolier, smiled, shook hands and bowed: '*Sala'am alaikum,*' he said with great formality, 'Peace be upon you. Welcome to our kingdom.'

The rough-hewn pole in front of the Land Rover was lifted and we bounced onwards up the stony bed of the wadi. A few miles farther on the track curled up the side of a rocky knoll to a tiny village clustered round a stone fort. The driver announced our approach with a prolonged and jubilant chorus on a multi-toned horn and by the time we reached the fort the gates were open and we drove straight through into the courtyard for Customs inspection. Around us a crowd had already assembled to view the stranger. Hands were thrust forward to be shaken, the glint of gold teeth matched the flash of dagger hilts in the sun, and small boys grinned shyly from beneath embroidered skull caps. Bolder than the rest, one man came forward to talk to me on what he sensed would be common ground. 'Suez, Suez!' he repeated, his face full of innocent glee. '*Ingleesi*, Suez!' His drift was all too plain, the ground between us all too common. 'Suez, *tamam*,' he declared next. 'Suez good. Gamal good. Gamal Abdul Nasser, *tamam*!' And, I inquired politely, knowing the answer without asking but anxious to please in this exchange of Anglo-Arab courtesies, what about the *Voice of the Arabs*? '*Aaiieeeee-wa!*' he replied, drawing out his vowels in the affirmative, as much as Eliza Doolittle elongated hers in the negative, *'Saut al Arab, tamam!'* He cupped his ear in his hand and tilted his head to the sky. *'Tamam, tamam, tamam!'* At which point, coffee arrived from the guardhouse pot and I was led ceremoniously away to eat Dutch tinned pears with a bottle of the ubiquitous Pepsi-Cola in the cool light of a white-washed room in the fortress walls, while my passport went from hand to hand among the wondering throng.

It is not often given to ordinary mortals that they should recognise themselves, at a specific point in space and time, as agents of history. That sensation is usually reserved for statesmen and diplomatists, generals and big businessmen — the captains and the kings of the world. But at that moment, in the fort in the frontier village of Rahida, I realised that I had become, in a little way, a maker as well as a recorder of history. Admittedly, it is never easy to distinguish between these two. If you record history, whether as a scholar or a journalist, you change it also by the very act of recording. But more than this unavoidable ambiguity was involved in my first visit to the Yemen. It was not so much what I was going to write about it that mattered this time as the fact that I was there to write at all. Many countries around the world, especially in the last twenty-five years, have exercised pretty arbitrarily their sovereign right to exclude 'undesirable aliens' on ground of ideology, spite, suspicion, or what-not; and journalists have often been among the first to suffer as a result. But very few countries in modern times have so determinedly discouraged visitors of any kind as did the Yemen until a few years ago.

Two centuries ago and more, its little Red Sea port of Mocha was famous among Arab and European sailors for the coffee that its merchants gathered from the Yemen mountains, but except for the expedition of the Danish naturalist, Carsten Niebuhr, in the eighteenth century, few Europeans penetrated beyond the Yemen's coast until the Italians began to show an interest in the country after their conquest of Abyssinia in the 1930's. A Treaty of Commerce was signed with Russia in 1928 — a strangely prophetic gesture towards the great new power that helped to lever the Yemen out of its isolation 30 years later — but it never amounted in practice to much more than a scrap of paper. Contact with the modern world was maintained and slowly extended through trade with Aden, and through the Yemeni emigrant colonies abroad in cities as far removed from the secrecy of Arabia as Cardiff and South Shields, where tribesmen from the Yemen mountains found work as dockers and seamen. From time to time, British Government officials from Aden visited the country on business: the Governor, for instance, was in

Sanaa in 1934 to negotiate the frontier agreement for the Western Protectorate. But in essence the heart of the Yemen remained untouched by western thought or action. Secluded behind its mountain barriers, protected by its sheer lack of physical communications and the fitful hostility of its Imams, the Yemen maintained a reputation of unusual mystery, even for Arabia, well beyond the end of the Second World War. By then, in all the rest of the peninsula, only the interior of Oman was so little known; and as the oil prospectors began to penetrate even there under the umbrella of British power, the Yemen in the 1950's seemed to be left alone in romantic isolation — a medieval survival, a kingdom of silence.

What forced the country out of this isolation was, in the broadest sense, just the twentieth century; but specifically it was the same combination of British policy and Arab revolutionary success that was at work in Aden and the Protectorate shaikhdoms. Britain's 'forward policy' in the Protectorate, and especially the efforts to create a federation there in 1954 and later, persuaded the Imam Ahmad that if he was ever to win what he considered to be his rightful inheritance in southern Arabia he must at once frustrate any further British plans and provoke the Protectorate tribes against their British overlords. Rumours of oil discoveries in the Protectorate, although they proved false, also tempted him to extend his power there. Nasser's successful assertion of Egyptian self-determination at the same time provided the Imam with new ideas of how to squeeze the British both by exploiting the discontented townsmen of Aden Colony and through international pressure. In the spring of 1956 he signed a pact of friendship with Nasser and King Saud at Jeddah, in Saudi Arabia, and learned a little more from both of them, no doubt, about contemporary diplomatic techniques. One immediate result was the dispatch of the Imam's son, the Crown Prince, Muhammad al-Badr, on a tour of the Communist capitals from which he returned with a Russian agreement for the supply of arms and promises of later economic aid. By the beginning of 1957, when the first shipment of Russian arms already had arrived at Salif, and Britain seemed to be on the run in the aftermath of her Suez miscalculations, the Imam was ready to join the fashionable new chorus and shout for self-determination in southern Arabia against the wicked imperialists.

This was where I came in, as skirmishes on the Yemeni frontier with the Protectorate flared up on a bigger scale than before and diplomatic notes began to pass between the Yemen and the British in Aden. One morning in January 1957, I presented myself at the airless little office of the Imam's commercial agent in Aden, to ask for a Yemeni visa. My request was noted, and a promise was given that the Imam's permission would be sought for me. For ten days I heard no more, nor did I expect ever to do so, for to most people even in Aden the land beyond the mountains to the north was still about as remote as the moon. Then the Imam's agent telephoned to say that my request had been granted, and by the Imam's holy order I was invited to visit the Yemen. I was off before dawn the next morning, sneaking out of the Crescent Hotel in the darkness to a hired Land Rover in one of those schoolboy-ish moments beloved of newspapermen who think they are stealing a march on their colleagues. I was not quite the first professional journalist to enter the Yemen. At least two other western correspondents had beaten me to it by a couple of years, and possibly there were others even earlier that I have never heard of. But I believe I was the first to be admitted as a deliberate act of diplomatic policy, as a potential tool in a modern public relations campaign. In fact, as I soon discovered, I was to be both agent and symbol of an entirely new kind of relationship between the Yemen and the rest of the world.

My visions of a splendid and continuing scoop did not last long. Soon enough my colleagues in Aden discovered what had happened and hastened in their turn to the Imam's agent. There it transpired that the Imam had replied to my request with a blanket invitation to any reputable journalists in Aden to come along forthwith. Had the Yemenis known anything of public relations technique at the time they would surely have sent their man to the Crescent Hotel and rounded up the lot of us at once. Luckily for me, or at any rate for my vanity, they did not, and it was four days before nine of my friends from Aden caught up with me. In that time I secured the only published scoop of the trip, with a message to *The Times* printed on January 28th, 1957. It had little merit as news or information but in about 1,000 words it described my journey to Taiz, and it was — so I was told — the first message ever cabled from the Yemen under the usual international 'press collect' arrangements. True, it had taken three-and-a-half days to reach London and was promptly followed by a deluge of messages from my colleagues as well as myself, passed by what proved to be the quicker method of a private postal service by jeep to Aden, and cable from there. True, too, the press collect arrangement, which required the fee to be calculated at a special rate for press telegrams and collected later from London, eventually proved too esoteric for the Taiz cable office to master and the Yemeni Foreign Ministry was obliged, I learned afterwards, to bear the cost itself. But that such a message was ever accepted, and still more that it ever arrived, was an undeniable triumph of the new world over the old.

My reception in Taiz, however, spoke more of the old world than the new. I was welcomed at the Government guest house by the Secretary-General of the Foreign Ministry, then acting Foreign Minister for the Yemen — a certain Sayyid Husain Ali al-Wasi, who took me by the hand, very gently and softly, and led me upstairs to a bare, white-washed room where the only furniture was a plain deal table and a suite of Egyptian Louis Quinze, cracking at the seams and shedding its gilt paint in slivers upon the linoleum-covered floor. For an hour over coffee we exchanged halting courtesies and inquiries of each other's health and happiness. Then we were joined by a young official interpreter — scarcely more than a boy — recruited for the purpose from his clerk's desk at the cable office, and our conversation began to follow with more confidence the familiar channels of Arab politics. Night came on, a meal was served, the electric light failed three times, and then, just as I was beginning to feel that the limit of my endurance had been reached — for I had been up since four in the morning and bucketed for nine hours from Aden over one of the roughest tracks I had ever experienced — the *chargé d'affaires* of the British diplomatic mission in Taiz arrived to look for me. He had heard from the buzz that was already around town that a new *Ingleesi* had arrived.

The immediate consequence of his coming was the adjournment of our party to the extra privacy of Sayyid Husain's bedroom in the guest house, where he slept with two small sons because his wife was ill and his household was disrupted. On an iron truckle bed under a red hospital blanket the children slept soundly together. On another red blanket on a second truckle bed the Yemen's acting Foreign Minister sat cross-legged among a litter of papers and lit a hubble-bubble. Under the bed were a few old shoes and a sack of dried tobacco leaves spilling on the floor. Around it in a semi-circle, passing the pipe peaceably from hand to hand, were the British *chargé*, myself, the young Yemeni interpreter, an Adeni clerk from the British mission acting as the *chargé's* official interpreter, and an American whose role was then obscure to me but who had materialised from the recesses of the guest house dressed in shoes, socks and a printed cotton kilt and was blessed, so he informed me, with the unlikely name of Bruce Alfonso de Bourbon Condé.

A less likely setting for diplomatic exchanges could scarcely have been imagined, yet those were just what followed. Sayyid Husain was splendidly oblivious of any incongruity in the situation. He was, as I came to recognise afterwards, a typical representative of the Yemeni aristocracy of sayyids. His eyes were large, dark and liquid, his cheeks hollow almost to the point of emaciation, his complexion sallow and his features aquiline. He wore a wisp of black beard and an expression of suffering disdain that drew all the lines of his face mournfully downwards until he looked like a black-robed saint from an El Greco painting. Bill Monteith, the British *chargé*, was scarcely so striking, yet he was no inconspicuous figure. Tall, lean and rather rakishly handsome, he had, as I remember, the sort of eyes that are possessed only by a certain type of Englishman, usually of a romantic temperament — startlingly blue, but deep set, and expressing behind a superficially quizzical look an infinite reserve and self-containment. Between these two now the diplomatic ball was batted back and forth. The latest Yemeni note to the British Government was analysed point by point; the possible form of the British reply, not yet in Monteith's hands, was discussed. Suez raised its head briefly and was skilfully pushed down again by Monteith. Israel popped up periodically like a figure in a fairground cock-shy, for Sayyid Husain to pelt with a few routine verbal missiles. From time to time Sayyid Husain sought to draw me, too, into expressions of opinion about Yemeni rights or wrongs; and I sought rather priggishly to protect my observer's status by declining to take sides. The interpreters and Condé were invited — and were more ready — to have their say. For two hours we enjoyed a diplomatic *tour d'horizon* while the children slept in the corner and I swayed on my chair, dizzy with fatigue and slightly sick from the sweet stench of the pipe, until Monteith at last took pity on me (and perhaps on himself) and brought this first strange session to a close. There were many more equally odd to come; for the incongruity of the Yemen's medieval ways with my twentieth-century standards and demands was forever being made apparent.

The Imam Ahmad, priest-king of the Zaidi Muslims, had inherited and perfected a complete autocracy. Possessed of the authority of a descendant of the Prophet and of a royal line that began in the ninth century, he ruled with minute command and brusque brutality. In the vast spaces of Arabia his kingdom seemed surprisingly small: 75,000 square miles — less than the area of England — between the coastal desert of the Tihama on the shores of the Red Sea and the disputed sandy wastes of Najran where Yemeni claims conflicted with the Saudi empire. Its heart was in the jagged, granitic mountains and high plateaux between Taiz and Sanaa, where the bulk of the people lived — perhaps three, perhaps five million; no-one could be sure. Here was the centre of what the Romans knew as *Arabia Felix*, and what others had called the Green Gardens of the High Plateaux, where the last autumnal whisper of the monsoon against the peaks brought a steady, refreshing rain and made the Yemen the most verdant and populous corner in all Arabia.

It remains a land of astonishing drama, wildness and beauty, where the plunging, rocky slopes have been terraced with such infinite complexity that the mountains seem to have been whorled with the fingerprints of gods. But it has never been ruled by anything much save force and fear. More often than not its mountains have frustrated any effective central control whatever, and its tribes under their local rulers have led a Balkan life of feud, intrigue and battle. Only strong men and strong powers have ever succeeded in subduing the tribes or obscuring their divisions. The Egyptians under Ibrahim Pasha attempted to conquer the Yemen in the early nineteenth century but were never more than sporadically successful and were compelled to give up within twenty years. The Turks who followed them, to take up again where they had left off after their first occupation of the Yemen, 200 years earlier, held on through the rest of the nineteenth century as much by default as by force. Like the modern Egyptian army in the Yemen today, they controlled most of the towns and left the rest of the country in chaos. When the Imam Yahia raised a new revolt against the Turks in 1905 he opened eight years of war in which he was as much concerned to protect himself against other Yemeni claimants to his title as he was to drive the Turks out of the country. That he succeeded in both, eventually, was testimony to his personal skill and strength of character — and owed something, besides, to the final collapse of the Ottoman Empire in the First World War.

Yahia was in the great tradition of the Zaidi Imams, one of the few who did contrive to unite his mettlesome people. For thirty years he ruled with a just severity until, like so many of his predecessors, he was murdered, in 1948. His son Ahmad had to fight for the succession like his father, but mercifully won his struggle in weeks instead of years. When he was established on his throne, as securely as any Imam could be, he proved himself another in the line of strong rulers. Both less just and more severe than Yahia, he terrorised his kingdom. Under his theocratic monarchy nearly every position of authority was in the hands of the Zaidi Muslims, although they did not number more than 40 per cent of the whole population. The Imam was their leader, and with the aid of the Zaidi tribes from the north he was able to suppress, when he could not win over, most of the Shafii Muslims of the south and west who would not otherwise accept the Imam's spiritual and temporal supremacy. Especially important, because they held all the senior administrative offices and all positions of tribal authority among the

Zaidis, were the sayyids — aristocrats, chiefs and hereditary holy men, of whom there were said to be some 50,000 all descended from previous Imams and therefore in direct line from the Prophet.

But upon them as much as upon the peasantry, the Imam laid his ubiquitous power. Not an aircraft, a lorry, or a camel could move nor any man journey far without his consent. No-one might enter or depart the country without his fiat. Every legal appeal came to his office, every Government purchase, from a roll of bandages to a shipload of Russian tanks, required his authority. In the structure of Government, the checks and balances were scrupulously arranged to prevent the emergence of any independent responsibility. There was, for example, no single capital city. The Foreign Ministry, one of the Imam's main palaces, the chief merchants and the British diplomatic mission were all in Taiz, handily placed for their necessary contacts with Aden. The Crown Prince and the other Ministries, with the Egyptian and Italian Legations, were in Sanaa; while the Imam spent much of his time taking medicinal waters in a little palace at Sukhne, near the Red Sea coast, and his household and principal advisers were forced to swelter in the port of Hodaida, not far away. Faced by such barriers to independent action, the first necessity of every traveller became the cultivation of patience; while that of every inhabitant was the adoption of acquiescence.

The system had the virtues of its defects. At least a man knew the limits of his freedom; and if the law was harsh, it was certainly effective. Under both Yahia and Ahmad the Yemen was outwardly more peaceful than the Aden Protectorate under the British, and once a foreigner was accepted by the Imam he could travel safely wherever the Imam chose to let him go. Through Sayyid Husain Ali al-Wasi, the Imam chose to let me go at once from Taiz to the disputed Protectorate frontier at Qataba, where his territory marched with the Aden Amirate of Dhala and the skirmishing was then increasing. It was a strange journey over tracks rougher, if anything, than the boulder-strewn road from Aden to Taiz, and it was interrupted by two nights and a day in the town of Ibb. Here, among tall, whitewashed houses that seemed to be tossed upon the dark and tumbled sea of the mountains like stiff, white foam, I glimpsed a world still buried in the Middle Ages. In the whole day's drive to Ibb the only wheeled vehicle we saw besides our own jeep was one broken-down lorry; and as far as I could discover when we arrived no other European had set foot in the town since the British botanist, Hugh Scott, had been there, twenty years before.[1] A few miles away from Ibb, a little off the main track from Taiz, in the town of Jibla,

[1] See: Hugh Scott, *In the High Yemen*, John Murray, London, 1942.

there was — so my hosts assured me — no record of any previous European visit whatever; and when I went there with Sayyid Husain I thought I experienced a little of the authentic thrill that must have come to all Arabian explorers until the very recent past, whenever they found themselves breaking quite new ground. Our jeep could not be got over the ancient pack horse bridge into the town, so that our coming, on foot, seemed somehow more appropriate — or less starkly desecratory — than it might have been. We arrived on Jibla's terms, as it were, not mine; and for an hour or two I could fancy that this was a place still genuinely inviolate, in spite of my own incongruous presence — a virgin community amid the twentieth century's world-wide rape.

But even in Jibla, medievalism was not quite intact. The mosque was already equipped with electric light, for certain Ismaili groups elsewhere in the Muslim world had raised money for a small generator and some simple wiring, in praise of Allah, on account of some particular historical connection between the town and their sect. As it happened, Sayyid Husain was an amateur archaeologist and had brought me to Jibla chiefly so that he could examine the mosque, which he said dated from the ninth century; and, as he paced out its courtyards and arcades with melancholy deliberation, the townsfolk — held at bay in the doorway by two fierce, armed guards — peered in, wondering to see even so distinguished a holy man at such strange devotions.

My own reception both in Jibla and Ibb was roughly that of a man from Mars. Whenever I appeared in the streets I was besieged by staring, laughing, but friendly crowds. If I was alone they walked beside, behind and in front of me leaving only a small respectful circle in which I could move freely. But once when I walked with the sons of the Mayor of Ibb, three young sayyids, the circle was widened and the way ahead was cleared by an embarrassing show of force. The eldest of the Mayor's sons was my guide — a lad of eighteen or so. The two others were my guards — children of nine or ten, carrying bamboo canes with which they attacked the legs of anyone who came too close. Just so, perhaps, might two young seigneurs have treated their peasants in France or England in the Middle Ages.

This spectacle of some hundreds of heavily armed tribesmen, every one of them equipped with dagger, rifle and assorted ammunition, sheepishly accepting a public whipping from two small boys on account of an *Ingleesi* revealed a good deal about the methods and effectiveness of the Imam's law throughout the Yemen. Obedience and respect for traditional Muslim law were exacted all over the country by strict application of the prescribed Koranic punishments. Not only did thieves have their hands severed and murderers lose their heads in public, but women caught in adultery were still liable to be stoned in the market place. My arrogant young guides in Ibb pointed out a mummified hand nailed to a post inside the town's main gate — a grisly reminder of the fate of one who was said to have robbed a Jew a few years earlier. Challenges to the Imam's authority were dealt with particularly ruthlessly. There were many dark reports of tribal hostages and prisoners incarcerated in remote mountain dungeons; and in Taiz I found a flourishing trade in photographs of the public beheadings of a group of revolutionaries who had tried to unseat Ahmad two years earlier.

What I was immediately concerned with, however, was the Imam's own challenge to the authority of the British across the border, and to that end the Naib, or Governor, of the frontier province of Ibb evidently had received instructions to provide some demonstrations for me, to constitute the second step in the Yemen's new public relations campaign. Our stay in Ibb, as it turned out, was not so much determined by a wish to let me see the local sights as by the Naib's need of an extra day or two to get his tribesmen organised. By the time I reached Qataba in his company, after another day's drive, he had assembled a group of dissident Protectorate shaikhs and their retainers to impress me with their complaints about the brutal British, together with an exhibition of the remains of British mortar bombs and bullets which had allegedly been fired upon Qataba and other innocent Yemeni habitations, and a peaceful demonstration of Yemeni tribesmen demanding United Nations protection from British aggression. This last met us as we drove into Qataba in the afternoon. Five hundred armed men were gathered beneath the town's mud wall, and as we passed through the gates into an irregular, dusty space within, they surrounded the Naib's scarlet jeep, hammering on the roof in welcome, waving rifles in the air and maintaining a high-pitched babble of comment and ejaculation like a girls' school at a hockey match. The Naib stopped his vehicle and we climbed together upon its roof to survey the throng, I in crumpled trousers and a dirty bush shirt — the picture, no doubt, of a decadent imperialist — he in his white robe and black cloak, tall and commanding, an imperious eagle beside me. 'You see,' he murmured, 'they ask you, the *Ingleesi*, for peace.'

The scene was like some exotic wedding celebration, for in every man's hand a piece of ruled schoolbook paper had appeared, and these were now fluttering like confetti all over the square. As they were crudely gathered in by a few eager cheer-leaders and thrust up to me in sheaves on the roof of the jeep, I saw that each was covered with Arabic writing. The local scribes must have burned the midnight oil, for later examination showed that all these scores of messages were written by only two or three hands, with the same number of variations upon a standard theme. The Yemen, they said, wished only to live in peace with her neighbours, yet she had been unjustly and barbarously attacked by Britain, and would welcome, therefore, the interest and protection of the United Nations in her plight. This brief message was stretched, in the Arab way, to unimaginable length, with frequent calls upon the mercy and compassion of God and many and tedious references to the benign wisdom of the recipient; but I took leave to doubt, in my bottomless western cynicism, whether one in a hundred of that cheerful, shoving, shouting crowd of tribesmen knew any more about the cause they were all supposed to be advancing than a mob of extras on a film set. Still, it must be said that they performed their task with theatrical devotion, and for the rest of the afternoon I could not venture about the town without some laggard running up to me with yet another petition.

Late that day, my solitary state as the only foreigner in the vicinity — with the exception of the American, Condé, who had accompanied us and was doing his not-very-convincing best to dress and talk like a Yemeni — came to an end when my colleagues arrived hot-foot from Aden, having done the whole journey by a shorter route in two days. The afternoon's peaceful demonstration, I then realised, must have been intended for all of us, but by arriving early I had scooped the pool. The others were still in time, however, for the *pièce de résistance* of the trip, which proved to be a battle with the British forces across the frontier, thoughtfully arranged that very night before the windows of the Qataba guest house. By the scale of the frontier skirmishes in those days, it was an unusually protracted affair, lasting a full seven hours from just before dawn, when we were all awakened by the rattle of machine-gun fire, until two o'clock in the afternoon. As we put the story together afterwards, it was begun by a group of Yemeni tribesmen who had crossed the Protectorate frontier on the previous night and, after lying up for a day, had moved on the night we arrived towards the town and army encampment at Dhala, about eight miles from Qataba inside Protectorate territory. There they engaged the British forces briefly — a few of the party in Qataba heard this first exchange of fire at about midnight — and then withdrew towards Qataba with the British in pursuit. By first light the frontier, barely half a mile from the Qataba guest house, was apparently aflame — just as the Naib of Ibb must have intended. British mortar bombs were thumping down upon the stony ridges just in front of us, where the Yemenis lay secure in rocky sangars and fox-holes. British jet fighters swooped low over the town repeatedly, never firing, but causing the inhabitants to duck their heads involuntarily behind the mud wall, where they stood in a ragged line watching the battle just outside. Machine-gun fire from the British side was almost incessant, yet at a range of not much more than a mile not a single bullet seemed to reach the town, nor did many of them find a mark elsewhere. At the end of the day there were just four Yemenis wounded out of several hundred in action.

On both sides it was a battle of more noise than achievement. From the Yemeni side, fire was disorderly and perforce confined mainly to rifles, but it was as incessant as the British. A few of the tribesmen had brand-new Russian army weapons, first fruits of the Crown Prince's agreement in Moscow, but most had ancient, long-nosed pieces of uncertain range and penetration. They possessed only one machine-gun — a water-cooled relic of the First World War that jammed repeatedly until an American photographer, impatient for pictures of its crew in action, executed a few running repairs and gave a quick and successful lesson in its operation. From a hill behind Qataba a solitary cannon cracked from time to time with erratic fire apparently directed at a point well to the left of the British line where its shells disturbed nothing but the sand. In the guest house there was pandemonium. Buglers stood upon its roof sounding messages to and fro while the governor of the town was besieged on the ground floor among the ammunition boxes, doling out bullets in handfuls to the tribesmen who scurried in from the 'front line' screaming cheerfully for more. Small boys were under everyone's feet, running among the mortar explosions on the frontier to dig for metal fragments in the still hot and smoking earth and scuttling back to lay their discoveries before the governor and his assistants who broke off from distributing bullets to buy these offerings for a few small coins. The fragments were later displayed to the visiting journalists as part of the evidence of British aggression.

When all this was over, and the siesta hour settled upon an unharmed, and remarkably unfrightened, Qataba, we drove back to Taiz by another and quicker route to await the last stages of the Imam's publicity operation — a press conference with the Commander of the Faithful himself. Now we learned at first hand the virtue of patience in the traveller in the Yemen, as a week went by with no word from the Imam's palace at Sukhne. Like some of his subjects we began to feel imprisoned and sought release in the coffee shops, the mountain gardens and the doleful *qat* parties of Taiz. This was still in many ways a medieval town, yet a flickering, hesitant shadow of things to come was already clearly visible. The gates were still locked every night at 10.30, and the women still hoisted their veils and scattered, in a rippling alarm of black gowns and wine-red scarves, at the sight of a stranger; but the most insistent noise in the *suk* was the radio playing 'I Love Paris in the Springtime', and the most persistent nuisance was the man who wanted to sell us pictures of Gamal Abdul Nasser.

In the hills above the town the terraces climbed like giant staircases past fortified villages and stone watch-towers that spoke of violence never very far away. Yet here, plainly, was the *Arabia Felix* of history and legend. The fertility, after the barrenness of many other parts of Arabia, was astonishing. Sometimes the bright green of young maize traced semi-circles around a valley like the seats of a great amphitheatre. Sometimes the green strips slashed from top to bottom of a steep gorge, like a narrow flight of steps. There were peach trees in tiny pink bloom, papaya, bananas, pomegranates and fig trees throwing out bare, silvery boughs from the hillsides like a Greek landscape. There were vegetables too — carrots, potatoes, onions, beans — and there were even smiling women, far less afraid to show themselves to the stranger here than in the streets of the town. They were unveiled, and worked with their long gowns hitched about their hips to reveal tightly trousered legs, with pants cut like blue jeans and embroidered at the ankles in gold and silver thread. Their jewellery hung heavily about their arms, legs and neck — ponderous squares of amber, silver anklets, golden bracelets and chains of weighty Maria Theresa silver thalers, or golden sovereigns for the lucky few. Away from their menfolk among the crops, or washing clothes in a mountain stream, they would giggle flirtatiously, rubbing yellow turmeric powder on their cheeks to emphasize what they hoped might be their beauty, and grinning slyly at us through lashes heavily lined with kohl. Let one of their own men appear and they were subdued in a flash, vanishing behind the nearest rock or bush, but on their own they presented to the stranger a totally new aspect of Arabian womanhood, replacing the arid secretiveness of the veil with the open welcome of a smile.

On the higher terraces, where the famous mocha trees once had grown, the coffee that had been the Yemen's fortune in earlier centuries had given way to *qat*. The leaf of this narcotic shrub seemed to hold in fee the entire nation. It was at once the chief release from squalor and frustration and an additional reason for their continuance. Every afternoon in Taiz, the whole male population retired into the shade and began a rhythmical, bovine chewing, its cheeks bulging with a green cud, its lips smeared with a green scum, indolently tying more firmly about its collective neck the millstones of ill-health and poverty. The servants in the guest house sprawled upon the back steps, munching; the shopkeepers squatted in their dark alcoves, glassy-eyed and ruminating; the guards at the town gate chewed and dozed and dribbled their green saliva like cretinous infants with a packet of bulls-eyes. Not a man in the place, it seemed, but was determined every day to crunch and mumble and spit his way through a bag of greenstuff big enough for a small pony.

Qat is not a strong narcotic, and I am not sure that it is even a genuinely addictive one; but consumed in large quantities throughout life as it is in the Yemen, it becomes a substitute for food and its juices subtly corrupt the blood, so that debilitation and a hazy sense of placid well-being go hand in hand. Several times we visitors tried it in Taiz but, accustomed to the stronger stimulus of alcohol, forbidden to the Yemeni Muslims, we found no more solace in an occasional bag of *qat* than we might have done in a mouthful of suburban privet — whose taste, indeed, it seemed to me to resemble. For our hosts, however, it seemed to be alcohol, tobacco and food combined — the last, self-inflicted shackle of a poor and imprisoned life.

In this week of wandering in and out of the Middle Ages we had three firm companions. One was the young interpreter from the cable office, who was pathetically eager to practise his English on any subject under the sun. A second was another Yemeni youth, bigger, more handsome, and bursting with truculent self-confidence, who attached himself to us one day in the streets of Taiz, announcing in a strong Welsh accent that his name was Raymond. He was one of the Yemeni seafaring colony born in Cardiff's Tiger Bay who had been persuaded, so he told us, to return to a homeland he had never seen on the understanding that he would thereafter be awarded a Yemeni Government scholarship at some university in Britain. Now, after nearly a year in Taiz, there was still no sign of a scholarship and he had been unable to obtain the Imam's permission to leave the country again. He was trapped, and when no other Yemenis were in earshot, he abused the Imam and his own misfortune with all the forceful command of gutter English to be expected of a boy from Tiger Bay.

Our third companion was Bruce Alfonso de Bourbon Condé, whose role now became more apparent. He was an ardent Yemenophile seeking, it seemed, to ingratiate himself with the Government by acting as their self-appointed public relations man. Whether the idea of inviting us to enter the Yemen *en masse* had originated with him, we never established beyond doubt, but he certainly approved of it whole-heartedly and set himself to convert us to the Yemen's cause. He was an inexhaustible fount of information which, whether reliable or not, was poured by the hour into our numbed and captive ears until for some — less polite, resilient or curious than the rest — the major problem of each day became how to escape Condé's relentless instruction. He was an odd and slightly pathetic figure, somewhat out of both his time and his depth. Nervous, even in full flow, he seemed to belong nowhere, and to be yearning romantically for the impossible, to be accepted as a Yemeni. In his daydreams, perhaps, he may have seen himself as a new Lawrence, or a St. John Philby, but he had neither the grace and sensitive intelligence of the first, nor the toughness and perspicacity of the second; nor had he chosen his moment, or his masters, as well as they did. He appreciated the Imam's sagacity, and accepted his case against the British, but he was no admirer of brutality or isolationism and knew that the Yemen might not much longer survive on such outmoded recipes of government. He wanted to help to change this country he had fallen in love with, and in us he may have seen his first real chance. Yet he seemed fated by nature to be the sort of man whom other people use and discard, as we did then; and that, I believe, was his eventual fate in the Yemen. In the next few years he became a Muslim, changed his name, adopted Yemeni citizenship and strove to identify himself with such national progressive movements as he could find around the Crown Prince Muhammad. But long before the revolution of 1962 he was thrown out, and figured briefly in the world's press as a stateless person, shuttling ignominiously to and fro between Cairo and Beirut, looking for a resting place. For all his faults, he deserved better, for I believe he was sincere, and in his way he probably did the state some service as one of the early conductors of the modern current into its ancient world. But perhaps we were the intimation of his end, as well as a hoped-for beginning — the harbingers of something that was soon to grow too big for him to handle.[1]

When the Imam's word came through at last to Taiz we were flown to Sukhne in one of the Yemeni Airlines' DC 3's. These were modern conveniences that the Imam had embraced of necessity, along with a group of Swedish pilots to fly them. They did treble duty, flying unscheduled passenger services to Aden and elsewhere, carrying the Imam and his officials between their various palaces and capitals, and distributing elements of the tribal army in emergencies. Ours dropped

---

[1] In 1964, Condé turned up in the news again, fighting as a 'general' with European mercenaries in the Yemeni royalist army. At least he was loyal to his old friends.

us at noon on the Tihama desert, with the mountains inland hidden in a yellow dust haze and the little white palace alone at the head of a shallow wadi seeming far too small and insignificant to contain the Imam's almost legendary power.

The Imam himself, however, was as legendary as they come. He was a short but immensely burly figure running to fat in old age, for he was 68 when he held this, the first and only press conference of his turbulent life. His dress was that of any Yemeni sayyid — a black, gold-edged cloak, white gown, and white turban bound round a brightly-embroidered, cylindrical hat. He wore a gold-handled dagger and sat hunched over a table in a white-washed room surrounded by his bodyguard, with two small sons at his feet and another small adopted son at his right hand. The Director General of the Foreign Ministry, Sayyid Hassan Ibrahim, a courteous, soft-spoken, small-boned man who had once been Ambassador to the Court of St. James and had the feline inscrutability of a born diplomatist, stood by his chair to interpret for us.

What the Imam said is no longer important, except that he reiterated his claim to Aden and the Protectorates and spoke feelingly about the chances of oil being found there. The way he spoke, however, revealed a remarkable man. His voice came in rapid, hoarse gasps, as if he was in pain — as, indeed, he might have been, for he spent his days at Sukhne only in order to treat his chronic rheumatism in the water from the local hot springs. He was popularly reputed to be suffering also from half-a-dozen other less mentionable diseases; and although blood analyses performed by American doctors some years later scotched one old canard by proving that syphilis was not among the old man's afflictions he certainly looked as if his frame and his mind alike had been taxed beyond the strength of most men. His face worked uncontrollably with every utterance, his hands tugged at his black-dyed beard, and his eyes — starting from his head with goitre and the effort of speech — rolled like white marbles only tenuously anchored to his sallow flesh.[1] At a glance one might have thought him literally staring mad. But if he was he remained uncannily alert. Nothing in the room escaped him: his eyes could be riveted in the instant upon the slightest movement, and he listened to every questioner with an intensity so fierce and so impatient that he seemed at times about to leap up, crying 'Off with his

[1] It is worth noting, perhaps, that the story that Ahmad regularly tied a cord round his neck in his youth to make his eyes pop and increase the general fearsomeness of his appearance, is almost certainly untrue — although it has been repeated in several respectable places.

head!' like the Queen of Hearts in *Alice in Wonderland*. He answered everything without a note or a consultation, pausing only to allow Hassan Ibrahim to translate his replies, with the gratuitous aid of the Imam's adopted son, who evidently fancied that his command of English was as good as any old Ambassador's, and who followed the whole bizarre scene with sharp attention. The boy was, we learned, the offspring of the Imam's former chauffeur who had died protecting the old man in the last attempt on his life; and the Imam seemed to favour him even beyond his own sons, patting him indulgently at his interventions and sharing a fearful, mocking smile with us as he did so.

These flashes of grim, ingratiating humour, when the full lips were drawn back over broken teeth and the dark brows were lowered over popping eyes, gave an extraordinary humanity to what might otherwise have seemed a mere, broken monster. One grasped not only the power, cruelty and suspicion of a total despot, not only the weaknesses of pain, sickness and age with which his will seemed to be in open, tigerish conflict, but also the sense of a man fearfully alone. Beyond the boy — or perhaps, the boys, for his own young sons were no doubt objects of his affection, too — there was probably no-one in the room whom he trusted. Like all absolute rulers, he was doomed to be absolutely solitary; and he derived such human warmth as he could only from those who were not yet in a position to betray him. Yet even this he seemed to feel was a weakness, and he sought to cover it with sardonic humour — distancing himself from his own indulgence towards the boys by sharing a joke at his own expense with us. He was, I think, an intensely self-aware man who knew that if he ceased to calculate and observe his own actions for an instant he opened the door to betrayal. By no stretch of the imagination could he ever have been described as attractive, physically or temperamentally. On the contrary, he was fearsome and ugly. But he had the same sneaking, human appeal, the same capacity to compel reluctant admiration, as Shakespeare's Richard III. And here I recall that it was not Lewis Carroll's Queen of Hearts who first cried 'Off with his head!' in such a peremptory fashion, but that same Richard.

> *Talks't thou to me of 'ifs'? Thou art a traitor:*
> *Off with his head!*

At the time, the resemblance between the two men did not occur to me; but in memory, it is compelling. They share to my mind the same ferocity, quickness and suspicion, the same grim quality of laughter. They share an obvious physical weakness — at least in the Imam's later years — and a compensating sense of immense and steely will-power. They share their inevitable solitude, and even, I believe, the same pride in their powers of sexual conquest. Years after my only meeting with the Imam I heard from sources who, although impeccable, shall remain nameless, of his preoccupation with his failing sexual powers in the last year or two of his life. He weighed by then nearly 300 lb., for he had given up walking anywhere and generally had to be lifted into his car on a specially powered seat that swivelled out to one side. But he still enjoyed the company of women and sought to impress them, with all the vanity of an old man; and great was the rejoicing in his palace one day when, after a long course of hormone drugs supplied by an American doctor, he called in his household to observe that he had achieved an erection for the first time in eighteen months.

Essentially, and above all, however, Richard III and the Imam Ahmad shared a medieval background. Often coarse, cruel and sombre, their worlds were each full of enmity and conflict, dominated by dynastic rivalries and family treachery. Nine of Ahmad's brothers died violent deaths, often at his instigation; and when Ahmad's father, Yahia, was machine-gunned to death in 1948, and a rival briefly seized the throne, Ahmad, preparing for his own successful *coup*, might well have echoed Richard's speech:

> *Why, I can smile, and murder while I smile . . .*
> *Can I do this, and cannot get a crown?*
> *Tut! Were it further off, I'll pluck it down.*

For two weeks in 1955 Ahmad was overthrown by a half-brother and imprisoned in his palace at Taiz. Then again, more than ever, we might have heard another echo of Richard in the field at Bosworth as the Imam one day snatched a Bren gun from a careless guard and mowed down his captors single-handed.

> *Slave! I have set my life upon a cast,*
> *And I will stand the hazard of the die!*

For Ahmad the dice rolled well. Where Richard died, he lived for a few more years to end his life, against all the odds, in bed. But in preserving his life and kingdom with all his force and all his skill he had, willy-nilly, opened windows upon a new world that nobody could close again. When we left him in his little room in Sukhne, his eyes rolling, his lips drawn back in a farewell grin, we were taken to a long cool chamber elsewhere in the palace where a meal had been laid on trestle tables. The first course was Russian salad from a Heinz tin. With facetious thoughts of the Crown Prince in Moscow and Soviet rifles on the Aden frontier, I turned to one of the Yemeni officials and asked what significance we should attach to this strange coincidence. 'None,' said he, 'except that it is the Imam's favourite dish. He just likes mayonnaise.' Within three days this curious intelligence from an unknown dateline in the Yemen was published in several of the chief newspapers of Britain and America. The kingdom of silence had been breached at last.

6

The Path of Good Intentions

In the years that were left to the Imam Ahmad between his first essay in modern public relations and his death six years later, he spent most of his considerable, but failing, energies trying to hold the door closed upon the crowd of contemporary demands and pressures whose first elements he had himself helped to admit. Like the Dutch boy with his finger in the hole in the dyke, he could not, dare not, relax for a moment.

Only once did he do so, in 1959, when the Italian doctors who then attended him persuaded him to visit Rome for medical treatment. His absence for four months almost brought his regime to a premature end. He entrusted his kingdom to the Crown Prince, Muhammad al-Badr, whose admiration for President Nasser had led him to believe that he could and should reform the Imamate. 'Yemen,' said a broadcast on Sanaa radio at the time, 'today enters on a new era. Yemen today abounds with hope, particularly since the people realise the genius of the Crown Prince, who traces the outlines of the enlightened future with far-sighted wisdom. . . . May God preserve His Royal Highness as a treasure and the hope of the nation and country.' Every Friday for several weeks, in that spring of 1959, the Crown Prince traced the outlines of the enlightened future from the pulpit of the main mosque in Taiz. There would be reforms in the Civil Service and the law, there would be an end to nepotism and corruption, there would be bigger and faster development programmes, and more Arab nationalism and positive neutrality in the manner of Gamal Abdul Nasser. Egyptian teachers and advisers were swiftly imported to assist in these changes, and in case all this did not inspire the people of the Yemen to support him, the Crown Prince also told the Army that they would have 25 per cent more pay and free medical attention.

The result, in theory, should have been a spontaneous upsurge of support for al-Badr, establishing him as the Yemen's favourite son.

Instead, there were riots in several of the main towns, the Army mutinied because its promised extra money was never paid, and al-Badr found himself forced before many weeks were out to call upon the Zaidi tribes of the north for armed support and to put several individuals to the sword in passable imitation of his father's severity. This was not the first time al-Badr had contrived some forceful corrective action in the Yemen. He had won the title of Crown Prince from his grateful father by successfully raising the tribes in his support when Ahmad was temporarily overthrown in 1955. But he was no chip off the old block. He inspired no terror in anyone, and not much confidence either except among his personal friends and the tribes who followed him because he was the son of the Imam and Ahmad's designated successor. Reports that he was an alcoholic and a drug addict may have been as unreliable as the story that Ahmad was syphilitic, but he was certainly moody and erratic in his behaviour, and naive in his judgements of both persons and policies. He never seemed to grasp that he might become Nasser's dupe until after his overthrow in 1962, when he complained bitterly to reporters in his mountain headquarters in north Yemen that he had been deceived in thinking Nasser was his friend. Al-Badr was, in fact, what is usually described as a woolly-minded liberal, sincerely anxious to reform his country without much idea of how to set about it or what passions reform might release. He was full of good intentions which ultimately, and appropriately, paved the way to his downfall.

But not yet. The Imam himself, defying speculation that he was at death's door, returned refreshed from Rome, fulminating against the Egyptians under the thin disguise of 'the tools of alien countries' and determined, so he said, to rule his kingdom according to the laws of religion. Within a week or two the dungeons of Hajja in the northern mountains were filled with hostages, executions without trial cowed rioters and mutineers alike, most of the Egyptians were expelled in a body, and a number of frightened administrators — including my old and once imperious acquaintance, the Naib of Ibb — fled across the frontier of the Aden Protectorate to seek asylum with the British. Once more silence fell upon the Yemen. Once more the Imam had put his shoulder to his country's creaking doors and — apparently — jammed them shut.

But this was the last time he managed to impose himself with his old success. As he was growing older and weaker the forces that opposed him were gathering strength. They had roots both inside and outside the country, in both old and new discontents. The traditional opposition was tribal, religious and dynastic, and although Ahmad's unusually stern rule had effectively suppressed all the outward signs of this, it had also correspondingly increased the inward resentments. Most of Ahmad's direct dynastic rivals had been disposed of by 1955 but the Crown Prince had a strong rival for the succession in the Imam's brother, Prince Hassan, who had been posted as the Yemen's representative to the United Nations to get him out of the way. Hassan's friends were not disposed to let Ahmad and the Crown Prince conspire to usurp his place without a struggle. Tribally, the Imam's support was strong, for he had the loyalty of the two great tribal federations of the north, called the Hashid and the Bakil, who were reputed to be able to raise 100,000 men and were known by tradition as 'The Wings of the Imam'. But without the aid of these Zaidi warriors, he could hardly have hoped to contain the discontent of the Shafii majority of the south and west, which had never accepted the Zaidi Imamate except on sufferance and now, after a dozen years of Ahmad, would probably have been delighted to see the Imamate and all it stood for overthrown.

The modern opposition was utterly different — less coherent, and numerically weaker, but in the long run more dangerous. There were a few army officers and fewer intellectuals who nursed genuine revolutionary principles, and there were a few business-men and a large number of assorted and more or less de-tribalised townsfolk, especially in Sanaa, Taiz and Hodaida, who were ready to work off old scores and win power for themselves. They were supported from outside by Egypt, and by an organisation in Aden known as the 'Free Yemenis' which had been spreading propaganda against the Imam ever since he forcibly established his succession to the throne in 1948. The 'Free Yemenis' drew their strength from among the tens of thousands of Yemeni workers and business-men in the Colony; and with consistent Egyptian support in the 1950's they advocated the overthrow of the Imamate in favour of a republican regime.

Around the Crown Prince, on the other hand, there was a group of younger chiefs and noblemen calling themselves the 'Young Sayyids' who had been influenced, like al-Badr, by the success of Nasser in Egypt and who sought to use the throne as an instrument of reform. It was with their support, and Ahmad's necessary blessing, that al-Badr had eased open a window to the world by his first approach to the communist powers shortly before Suez, to seek aid in the cause of positive neutralism and the fight against the British. His success in Moscow and Peking was not confined to arms. Not long after the first shipments of Russian weapons arrived, the first communist civil aid and technicians reached the Yemen, too. The Russians had agreed to extend and modernise the old port of Hodaida. The Chinese came to build a new motor road from there to Sanaa, in the central highlands. These agreements, small as their contents seemed at the time, were to prove decisive instruments in promoting the ultimate revolution.

As all these pressures accumulated Ahmad's ageing shoulder was not strong enough to hold the doors of the Yemen tight against change forever. He tried, therefore, not merely to suppress changes but to contain, deflect, or even exploit them. He was quick to learn the techniques of this, from enemies as well as friends. His flirtation with the communist powers through his son was obviously inspired by Nasser's example in exploiting the new possibilities of neutralism. His later dalliance with Nasser himself, however, as a member of the United Arab States, was a piece of home-grown political shrewdness — and not unenlivened, I suspect, by the Imam's peculiar, grim humour. When Nasser reached his most triumphant moment with the creation of the United Arab Republic, the Imam had the wit to see — as his neighbour, King Saud, for instance, did not — that this sudden achievement of Arab unity was bound to dazzle Arabs everywhere and that the best thing to do was to jump aboard the band-waggon, not to try to stop it. Accordingly, he elected to be the first Arab ruler to accept Nasser's invitation to form a larger federation with the U.A.R. As it turned out, he was not only the first, but the only one to do so. He sent the Crown Prince to Damascus in March, 1958, to sign an agreement establishing the 'United Arab States' with the Yemen and the U.A.R. as founder-members. As the founder-members were also the only members, it was deemed courteous that the larger partner should defer to the smaller and agree that the capital of the new federation should be the fly-blown, crumbling old port of Hodaida. The Egyptians and the Syrians were patently embarrassed by this unexpected response to President Nasser's appeal for recruits to the Arab union. The rest of the Arab world looked on in astonishment — and some ribaldry — at so incongruous a partnership. But the Imam was reported to be gleeful, for he had made a gesture by which he could pose as a champion of Arab nationalism without surrendering any significant portion of his sovereignty. Only the Crown Prince appeared to be taking the new federation seriously. As sincerely liberal and well-intentioned as ever, he sat through a round of meaningless festivities in Cairo and Damascus with all the solemnity of a bridegroom at a High Church wedding service.

For the U.A.R., federation with the Yemen was at best a formal genuflexion to the ideal of Arab unity; at worst it was a humiliating farce. Not only did the United Arab States never come to life, while the shining image of President Nasser was sullied by his apparent association with a medieval despot, but even the venomous propaganda of the *Voice of the Arabs* was muffled for the time being by the obligation to be reticent about this alleged new friend and ally of President Nasser. The old genie of the Yemen had proved himself once again, in fact, to be a master of political tactics. Yet the Imam's strategy remained, perforce, that of a holding operation which, in the long run, could not hold. His country, which had been sarcastically described as plunging madly forward into the thirteenth century was actually being sucked irresistibly into the twentieth. Little by little, for all his efforts, his medieval theocracy was beginning to crack.

After the mass visit of journalists at the start of 1957, the Imam thought again about the value of cultivating representatives of the world's press — for they had not, after all, given his case or his country a very sympathetic airing — and he never again permitted more than one or two isolated reporters to enter the Yemen. Equally, he refused to relax his vigilance about the Egyptians who tried to come; and except for those who were invited by the Crown Prince in 1959, during his absence, not more than a handful managed to establish themselves officially in the Yemen before the Imam's death in 1962. But even Ahmad could no longer keep out the whole world. By ostensibly joining Nasser's camp he might have closed one door, for the moment, against direct Egyptian attack. But by accepting communist help to challenge Britain's position in the Protectorate, he had exposed another opening. By the end of 1958 there were 500 Russian technicians and instructors in the Yemen, and another 1,000 Chinese working on the Hodaida-Sanaa road. The Swedish pilots of the Yemeni Airlines had been replaced by Yugo-Slavs, and a score or more of Yemeni students had accepted scholarships in communist countries. As a specifically communist influence it is unlikely that any of this was of much significance; and there is no doubt that the Imam calculated that Russians and Chinese in the Yemen were less likely to subvert his regime than the Egyptians, who spoke the language of Arabism, both literally and emotionally. Moreover the Imam was careful to restrict the activities of these foreigners within his frontiers, so that the communist technicians never managed to establish themselves outside the three main towns. Most of the heavier Russian arms, which included tanks and aircraft, rusted in storehouses and on the airfields, and the Yemen Army remained a puny and ill-ordered instrument — apparently no great threat to a strong regime. As a modernising, or just disruptive influence, however, this sudden massive influx of foreigners, and the accompanying sense of wider international contacts being established at last, were bound to take effect, adding to the other forces already working in the same direction.

Of these, the appeal of Nasserism grew steadily in importance. Even though the Imam kept the Egyptians out of the country physically, he could not exclude the potent spirit of their politics. The *Voice of the Arabs* was never silent about Egyptian achievements even when it was restrained about the Imam's shortcomings; and the mere presence of President Nasser in the wings, waiting to take advantage of whatever might happen in the Yemen, was enough to encourage both royalist reformers and republican revolutionaries to press on with whatever plans they had in the belief that they would win Egyptian support whenever they needed it. Both the Crown Prince and the 'Free Yemenis' maintained close contacts with Cairo and there was at least tacit encouragement from Egypt for the Crown Prince's first efforts at reform in 1959. In retrospect it looks as if those efforts and their aftermath only made the eventual revolution more certain. It was then, in all probability, that the Egyptians were able to make their first direct contacts with the potential revolutionaries inside the Yemen, including the future President, Abdullah Sallal, who was at that time in charge of the port at Hodaida.[1] A few Yemeni soldiers had been trained in Egypt in previous years, and at the Crown Prince's invitation an Egyptian military training mission was sent to the Yemen during his brief regency and succeeded in maintaining a small staff there for the next two years, in spite of Ahmad's hostility. At this time, too, the Egyptians must have realised the uncertainty of the Crown Prince's grip upon the country as they watched his efforts to control the troubles that his hasty reforms unleashed. Certainly, from then onwards al-Badr's relations with Cairo grew more ambiguous. The 'Free Yemenis', with their republican aspirations, were nearer to Egyptian sentiment than any monarch, however ostensibly liberal, and after 1959 they became Nasser's favoured agents, while the Crown Prince struggled to preserve his undisputed right of succession through the Imam's declining years.

Even the Imam's swift and successful campaign of repression when he returned from Rome to correct the blunders of his son probably played into the hands of the republicans and their Egyptian friends. To raise the northern tribes in his support during his troubles, the Crown Prince had paid them substantial sums from the Imam's treasury. Concerned at the heavy loss of funds, Ahmad tried to get the money

---

[1] This is plausibly argued by Harold Ingrams in *The Yemen*, John Murray, London, 1963.

back. The result was a simmering discontent among the tribes, which was suppressed — but made secretly more bitter — only when the Imam beheaded one of the tribal chiefs in a characteristic piece of ruthless trickery. Three years later the tribes concerned remained aloof from al-Badr's campaign to recapture his lost throne. Had they been with him, he might have succeeded before Egyptian military strength in the Yemen had become as overwhelming as it did. Had they not been alienated in the first place it is just conceivable that the revolutionaries might not have found the courage to strike.

Before these chickens came home to roost, however, the Imam had one more shot in his locker which he fired off with typical, if somewhat Pyrrhic, gusto after Syria seceded from the U.A.R. in September 1961. Encouraged by this evidence that Nasser's domination of the Arab world seemed to be weakening, the Imam published a long poem of his own composition, addressed to 'the Arabs' and condemning Egyptian socialism as an irreligious scandal. It revealed how keenly the *Voice of the Arabs* had pricked him with its past propaganda: 'Why do you pollute the atmosphere with abuse?' he asked, 'Why do you shout over the microphone with every discordant voice?' President Nasser, having lost Syria from the U.A.R. already, saw no harm after this in shedding the Yemen from the U.A.S., and promptly replied by announcing the dissolution of that moribund federation. For the remaining months of his life the Imam paid for his last, poetic gesture with constant abuse from the *Voice of the Arabs* and repeated calls for revolution in his kingdom. As this Egyptian pressure grew, and the Imam's powers ebbed away, turbulence in the Yemen increased. Reports of demonstrations in Taiz filtered through to Aden, and attempts upon Ahmad's life were rumoured frequently. Later analysis revealed that in the last twelve months of his reign there were at least seven attempts to assassinate him. In one of them, in March 1962, he fell to the floor with four bullets in his body. But the man who had murdered so many people in his lifetime was not to be murdered in his turn. He died in his bed, in September 1962 — one of the last, and in many ways most remarkable, of the archetypal rulers of a vanishing Arabia.

The date of his death, according to the new Imam Badr, broadcasting on Sanaa radio the following day, was September 18th. In a speech from the throne after Ahmad's burial two days later, al-Badr returned to the theme of reform that he had been forced to abandon so abruptly three years earlier. Once more he traced the enlightened future, promising 'equal rights' and 'rising standards' for all, and full co-operation in establishing a 'unified Arab nation'. A general amnesty for all political prisoners and exiles was announced, elected national and municipal councils were to be established, and development plans prepared. Abdullah Sallal, whom al-Badr had known for some years, and believed to be essentially a reformer like himself, was appointed Army Chief of Staff. But once more al-Badr's good intentions betrayed him; and with ironic aptness he reaped the bitter harvest of those agreements he had signed with Russia and China six years before. On the night of September 26th, several of the Russian tanks he had brought into the country, and which the small Egyptian military mission had helped to keep secretly in good repair, rumbled into the dusty square inside the main gate of Sanaa and began to shell his palace. Other troops, armed with Russian weapons, seized the radio station, and in a series of revolutionary broadcasts proclaimed the birth of the Yemen Arab Republic, announced the names of several 'Free Yemenis' from Aden who would shortly join the new government, and revealed al-Badr's friend, Sallal, as leader of the *coup*.

Unknown to his attackers, al-Badr escaped from the palace and fled northwards to raise support for the third time among the Zaidi tribesmen to whom he could now appeal as their Imam; but while the tribes laboriously gathered their traditional forces — and some, as we have seen, refused to contribute — the revolutionaries turned at once to the Egyptians in the wings and were not disappointed. Within a few days the first Egyptian troops began to arrive by air to support the latest, glorious Arab revolution. Within a fortnight they were pouring into Hodaida by sea. Once more the luckless al-Badr's past caught up with him. The new port built by the Russians and the new road to Sanaa built by the Chinese had been completed only the year before. They now provided the Egyptians with the facilities for a swift concentration of modern forces in the Yemen without which they might never have contained the traditional counter-attack that al-Badr and the tribes were preparing. This time, nobody could hold the door closed. Between them, the dead Ahmad and the refugee al-Badr had contrived, after all, to wedge it open. Thus, although the twentieth century never quite defeated the fierce old man, it promptly overwhelmed his well-meaning son. The only question that remained was whether the thirteenth century had strength enough to fight back without old Ahmad's inspiration.

7

Hurrah for Revolution!

Hurrah for revolution and more cannon-shot!
A beggar upon horseback lashes a beggar on foot.
Hurrah for revolution and cannon come again!
The beggars have changed places, but the lash goes on.

W. B. YEATS

Outside the tall, arched gateway of the Republican Palace in Sanaa at the end of 1962, a crowd of shouting, kilted tribesmen assembled every day. Daggers glittering, rifles waving, fists raised aloft with scraps of paper on which some local scribe had scrawled a few words, they waited in vain for access to their new President. Petitions of loyalty fluttered in the brisk, highland air; complaints about taxes, crops, camels and trade, appeals for more land and demands for better houses, announcements of births and laments for deaths, all rattled upon the indifferent ears of the guards.

There was no-one to accept those crumpled messages, no-one to interpret those incoherent cries. From dawn until dusk, day after day, disorder swarmed at the palace gates. Only the Egyptian soldiers of the President's bodyguard and assorted visitors in western suits were able to shoulder their way in and out, to and from the new seat of power. They, and they alone, it seemed, were the V.I.P.'s of the Yemen's revolution. Upon them, the ragged Yemeni guards smiled a bewildered welcome, then turned again immediately to beat back any of their clamouring compatriots who sought to sneak through the gate themselves. The Egyptians had arrogance, authority and the President's ear. The men in western suits might be business-men with a million dollars or journalists with a million readers. The tribesmen at the gates had nothing but their expectations. The revolution had been proclaimed for the sake of the Yemen, but it had been taken over by the world; and while the Yemenis waited for the millennium to arrive, their new masters from elsewhere proposed or disposed of their country's future strictly in their own interests.

Ever since the night of Sallal's *coup*, the contenders in the Yemen's revolution had seen their causes adopted by powers embarrassingly greater than themselves. Their struggle had acquired in the Arab world an ineffable symbolic purity. All Yemen was divided, for the sake of the argument, into republicans and royalists. On one side were President Sallal and his heroic republican revolutionaries, supported by President Nasser and his many followers. They represented the glories of Arab nationalism and social progress — or, if you preferred, the evils of subversion, and Egyptian imperialism. On the other side stood the Imam Badr, enlightened and all-wise — and mercifully saved from the murderous republicans, after all — leading his loyal, royalist tribesmen into battle with the support of King Saud and King Husain of Jordan. They were the champions of legitimate government and peaceful evolution — or the arch-demons of black reaction. Behind these lines, at a discreet distance, stood still greater powers. The Soviet Union and the communist nations were on the republican side, Britain — with some show of reluctance — was backing the royalists, and the United States was attempting to straddle the two in the interests of Middle Eastern stability. In this joust of the black and white knights of Arabia, the Yemen and its problems seemed to have become simply pawns.

Yet pawns have a way of asserting themselves, especially when they are overlooked, and the story of the following years was to be largely that of the gradual re-assertion of Yemeni realities over foreign pre-conceptions. A hint of this future development was vouchsafed to me within a couple of hours of my arrival in the Yemen soon after the revolution. It was a marvellously clear November morning, with the mountains knife-edged and blue to the north as we lumbered aloft from Khormaksar airfield at Aden in one of the old DC. 3's of the Yemeni Airlines, bound for Sanaa. The pilots this time were neither Swedish nor Yugo-Slav, but Egyptian. The passengers were eager young Yemenis returning home as if to the promised land. There were smart young men in Italian suits with tartan canvas luggage, who had been studying in European technical colleges; and there were grubbier young men from Aden, in cotton kilts and sandals, with tin suitcases painted with flowers, who had been working in the port. Their spirits were high, their hearts were full. The hated Imamate had been overthrown, the Yemen was now their oyster. Sanaa, they said — metaphorically, anyway — here we come.

But we did not. Unexpectedly we put down at Taiz, thumping rudely upon the gravel airstrip from a great height and rolling to a stop in front of a small crowd of cheering tribesmen. There we were turned out, our luggage was unloaded and the aircraft was towed away to a far corner of the field. 'We stay,' said the Egyptian pilots, and without further explanation departed in a jeep for the town of Taiz. Grumbling, we stayed. Inquiry of the Yemenis on the spot established that we would probably have to wait before resuming our journey for a demonstration which the Egyptian authorities had arranged in Taiz that morning to welcome a large number of pilots from the Saudi and Jordanian Air Forces who had lately defected to Cairo in protest at the reactionary policies adopted towards the glorious Yemen revolution by the respective governments.

Ninety minutes later an Ilyushin of the Egyptian Air Force arrived and discharged an Egyptian Air Marshal, accompanied by the former Commander of the Jordan Air Force and one Saudi Arabian pilot, both of whom had, indeed, defected. In another jeep they, too, left for the town amid a few thin cheers from the tribesmen at the airfield. The passengers who had arrived from Aden waited. Another two hours dragged by until the airmen returned from their triumphal tour of the town, boarded their Ilyushin and took off again for Sanaa. In their wake, sharing the final cheers, came our Egyptian pilots, who crossed the airfield, boarded our aircraft for a few minutes, climbed out again and locked the doors, got back into their jeep and set off again for Taiz. We managed, with a flying wedge of frustrated passengers, to stop them at the airfield gate, and demanded information about our flight. Cancelled, they said brusquely; the weather is too bad. And they pointed at the sharp peaks to the north, towards which the Ilyushin had disappeared a few moments earlier, and where now, to be sure, a wisp or two of cloud had just formed to deter any further foolhardy flying. '*Too* bad,' the Egyptians repeated and drove off. As the passengers began to look for other transport into Taiz to find a bed for the night one of the smart young Yemenis with the tartan luggage turned to me in a forgivable flash of temper. 'Look,' he hissed, serpent-like and red-eyed with momentary fury, 'These Egyptians! We must fight them for our freedom next!'

Over the next week or two this angry remark from a republican supporter assumed a greater significance as the extent of Egyptian hegemony in the Yemen revealed itself. Already the Egyptian Army was installed as an army of occupation. There were then about 12,000 Egyptian soldiers in the country and more were arriving at Hodaida every week. Egyptians swarmed through the Sanaa *suk*, forcing up the prices of local goods and buying up the imported luxuries from Aden. They showed propaganda films to the populace of Hodaida, marched brass bands through the streets of Taiz and drove their vehicles everywhere with scant regard for other people's convenience. President Sallal never appeared in public without a bevy of armed Egyptians fore and aft of him; and there was hardly a government office in Sanaa that did not have either an Egyptian guard or an Egyptian adviser attached to it, and usually both. Sanaa radio was run by Egyptians, and Egyptians controlled the port of Hodaida and the airfields everywhere.

No doubt much of this was inevitable. Once President Nasser had adopted the new republic he could not afford to be half-hearted. Nor could he have afforded to stay aloof in the first place. Whether or not he personally directed the revolt from Cairo — and it is inconceivable in the light of what happened that he did not know something of it in advance — it was a foregone conclusion that the revolutionaries would turn to him for support. Equally it was foregone that he would agree to help them, not only because his agents and his propaganda had openly encouraged them beforehand, thereby morally committing Nasser to their cause, but also because he simply dare not leave them at the mercy of King Saud. To have done so would have betrayed the vague hopes of social justice that Nasser had aroused among the Arabs, and would have seriously diminished his stature as an Arab leader.

Besides, the revolution offered the best opportunity so far of upsetting the Saudi regime, which had repeatedly led the Arab opposition to Nasser. With his troops in the Yemen Nasser had a foothold in Arabia for the first time, from which to menace the Saudi kingdom whenever he chose. Even more significant, the successful establishment of a republican regime dedicated to the Nasserist ideals of socialism and Arab unity would provide the first radical alternative in Arabia to Saud's extravagant and antiquated form of government. Subversion by example might then reinforce subversion by propaganda and conspiracy. Similarly, a successful revolution in the Yemen would undermine the British position in Aden. For positive as well as negative reasons, therefore, President Nasser could hardly stay out of the Yemen imbroglio; and in the beginning, at least, there was every sign that he actively wished to be in it.

All the same, the arrival of his troops in the Yemen was a daring departure from the Arab norm. Never before in modern times had one Arab country sent its army into another's territory in quite this way. There had been Egyptian troops in Syria before 1961 but only under the terms of the union between the two countries. There had been a joint Arab force in Kuwait after 1961 when General Kassem claimed the shaikhdom of Iraq, but only by invitation of the Kuwaiti Government and under the auspices of the Arab League. The Egyptian intervention in the Yemen was far closer to unilateral action. It was invited by the republicans, who had duly proclaimed themselves the Government of the Yemen, but it was sanctioned by no other Arab government, was opposed by several, and was clearly intended to protect the new regime from the natural consequences of its actions — specifically, the threat of counter-revolution which it seemed too weak to contain.

In other contexts such a manœuvre would have been condemned as imperialism. Neither the Soviet Union in Hungary, for instance, nor the United States in South Vietnam or the Congo, was immune from widespread criticism that they were deliberately propping up unpopular governments for the sake of imperialism, Eastern or Western style. But initially President Nasser was free from similar objections in the Yemen, partly because the first contingents of his soldiers were sent in secret and their numbers were never officially disclosed, but chiefly because few people and fewer governments cared to appear by implication as supporters of the Imamate. The Imam Ahmad's reputation as a blood-thirsty tyrant quite over-shadowed his son's promises of reform, and enabled President Nasser to declare with his customary conviction — and possibly even with sincerity — that he was only doing his duty by helping his Arab brothers to secure freedom and social justice. Egyptian soldiers in the Yemen, pressed by people like me to explain what they thought their purpose was, turned on these Presidential phrases with unctuous alacrity. 'We must help our brothers,' they would say, 'That is our duty.' But behind the unction the sense of brotherhood remained strictly rhetorical. The stocky, peasant soldiery of Egypt had little in common with the lean, Yemeni highlanders. They regarded the people as barbarians and their country as a wilderness, to be treated with fear, astonishment or disdain. Fear was often stark upon the faces of many Egyptian army drivers, for example, as they negotiated the endless twists and hairpins of the Chinese road to Sanaa. They had joined the army for a square meal and a regular wage, no doubt, and relief from the crowded, stifling poverty of the Nile valley. Now, hunched over their steering wheels, tense and tired, they ground upwards in bottom gear hour after hour, towards the cold air of the highland plateau, shivering in their thin summer uniforms and bewildered by the towering crags and tumbling precipices around them. Not one in a thousand, probably, had ever seen a real mountain before, and none could ever have driven on a road like this.

At intervals of a few miles all the way up from Hodaida to Sanaa lorries had overturned in ditches or upon sharp corners, and disconsolate crews sat by the roadside waiting to be rescued. At every village, posses of wild tribesmen waited, flashing their daggers and firing volleys from their rifles in warning or welcome. They were a motley lot, the men upon that road, clad in more various uniforms than the cast of a Ruritanian musical, from padded old Russian winter great-coats and antique Italian tin helmets to the jacket of a Green Line bus conductor and several pairs of cast-off knee socks from what I judged to have been the Arsenal Football Club. When darkness fell, and the army convoys ground on — more afraid to stop even than to continue — the appearance of such strangely assorted brigands in the headlights was enough to impress the hardiest soldier. The Egyptians, fresh from their billets in Assiut or Alexandria, were not just impressed — they looked often, and with reason, terrified.

Once they were established in authority, however, the Egyptians assumed — as foreign governors of any nationality are apt to do — a perceptible arrogance towards the Yemenis. It was one of the more piquant experiences of my post-revolutionary stay in Sanaa to be hailed by most of them with a chummy affability that implied as clearly as any words that they and I were somehow in this thing together as embattled representatives of civilisation in the midst of savagery. 'What can you do with these people?' they would often laugh, in tones of vastly superior deprecation, 'They are not like us, you see. . . .' Having come directly from British colonial Aden I recognised the symptoms all the more easily. Creeping imperialism is a catching disease, and those Egyptians were only a step away from clapping their hands together and shouting, 'Boy!' when they wanted service.

This Egyptian compound of fear and superiority was further confused by an apparently bottomless ignorance about the country. Both soldiers and civilians were surprised by the very appearance of the Yemen. Like many people in Europe and America at that time they seemed to have absorbed only the legend of a 'desert kingdom' and they were dismayed to find rugged mountains where they had expected a land of rolling sand-dunes and palm-fringed oases. Of its tribalism, its history, and the Imamate's methods of administration they knew little, if anything. I doubt if more than one in a hundred knew that Egypt had sent soldiers there more than a century before.

Once, driving down from Sanaa to Hodaida, I stopped to exchange words with an Egyptian colonel who was leading a convoy of armoured cars and personnel carriers in the opposite direction. Hopefully, the colonel asked me if he was near the top. I told him he was only half-way. He was disbelieving: surely the road could not go on climbing like this forever? Not quite, I said, but as it climbed to nearly 9,000 feet, and he was only at about 4,000 feet at the moment, he might well think he had to climb to heaven. He was dejected. 'I never expected anything like this,' he remarked, 'You see, I have no map.'

Such a degree of unpreparedness requires some explanation. At first glance it may suggest that the Egyptians were not expecting to dispatch their forces to the Yemen in the wake of a revolution — and it is, of course, possible that this is so. In my view, however, it is an inadequate, even unlikely, explanation. Efficient staff-work in any army requires contingency planning, and when Cairo was publicly urging the Yemenis to revolt and privately plotting to help them to do so, the possibility of an Egyptian expeditionary force being required to help them must have been foreseen by President Nasser and his senior generals. The speed with which the force was assembled and dispatched suggests that this was so; and the failure to brief and plan the force properly with basic information about the nature of the country and its people seems more likely to be an indication of the weakness of Egyptian army staff work at lower levels than of the total inability of Nasser and his generals to look farther ahead than tomorrow morning.

It is also symptomatic, however, of a wider weakness in the Egyptian approach to the Yemen, which appears fairly clearly in retrospect to have been one of over-confidence based on ignorance. True, Egyptian ignorance about the Yemen was shared by many people. Not for nothing had this been the kingdom of silence for so long. But in the few years immediately preceding the revolution Egypt had shown more interest in the Yemen than most other nations and, in spite of the Imam Ahmad's efforts, her agents had probably enjoyed better access to information about the country than most other foreigners. That, apparently, they were either misled or misleading was due, probably, to three factors. First, the reluctance of most Egyptians, especially in foreign countries, to do any consistent leg-work. It seems to me entirely likely that the Egyptians in the Yemen before the revolt made little serious effort to discover what sentiments might prevail about revolution and its possible aftermath outside the main towns where they had established themselves; or that if they did, they discounted what they did not wish to hear. Secondly, the nature of Nasser's relationships with his subordinates. Perhaps without realising it, Nasser — like most dictators — has often been shielded from unpleasant facts by the unwillingness of subordinates to reveal them to him. In particular, this weakness often seems to vitiate the work of his foreign intelligence services which tend to feed Cairo with selective accounts based on what agents in the field think their superiors would like to hear. These in turn may be winnowed before reaching Nasser, with the result that his picture of the world appears sometimes to be sharply at variance with reality.[1] Perhaps this was even more likely to happen in the Yemen than in other parts of the Arab world, for there are few areas that, by nature, the Egyptians seem so ill-equipped to understand.

Thirdly, there is the general Arab tendency to take the word for the deed, the wish for the accomplishment, and to believe that obstacles can be overcome most easily by being overlooked. It follows from this that to call attention to obstacles is to be more of a traitor than a critic, because it automatically diminishes, in Arab eyes, the chances of wish-fulfilment. As an example, it is part of the Nasserist and Arab nationalist faith that tribalism or any other traditional source of Arab disunity is in some way an invention of imperialist reaction that will be swept away as soon as the truth of revolutionary Arab unity is revealed. Let someone point out that the Kurds in Iraq, for instance, have no reason to welcome Arab unity, or that the Christians of Lebanon might have reason to be afraid of total domination by Muslims in a united Arab world, or — greatly daring — that one of the reasons why the Arabs lost their war against Israel was that they could not trust each other enough to fight together, and he will be dismissed as an 'imperialist' who wishes to divide the Arabs. The fact that he does no more in reality than ask for rational consideration of divisions that already exist is overlooked in the emotional conviction that divisions are undesirable and therefore do *not* exist. To admit that the undesirable does exist, and may well go on existing, is a very un-Arab trait. President Nasser himself appears no longer to cherish such characteristic Arab illusions, for he has had enough setbacks in his pursuit of Arab unity to induce more realism. But he still sometimes talks publicly in the old, visionary terms, and his followers still appear to believe them; and I think it likely that they contributed significantly to Egyptian ignorance and arrogance in the Yemen by causing the provision of accurate but possibly unwelcome information about the country to be regarded as more of a vice than a

---

[1] e.g. Egyptian miscalculations about the chances of a revolt in Saudi Arabia after the Yemen revolution — see below, p. 132. Similar Egyptian ignorance has been revealed in Tunisia, Lebanon, Iraq and Oman among other places. In another field, several western diplomatists in Cairo have been convinced that Nasser has never been fully informed about the economic cost to Egypt of some of his policies.

virtue. It was easier to suppose that revolution was inevitable, and must therefore succeed, than to ask what natural or political barriers it might have to overcome and what attributes it would need to do so. It was simpler and more truly Arab to assume that by doing your revolutionary 'duty' you must be on the winning side, and that your enemies would crumble before you, than to attempt a realistic assessment of potential enemy strength. It seems likely that such preconceptions took Egypt into the Yemen without much idea of how much she would have to do there, or for how long, or at what cost. Perhaps Nasser believed, like some Englishmen in 1914, that he could have the boys home again for Christmas. If so, it was a sad miscalculation for by the end of 1964 — three Christmases later — he still had between a quarter and a third of the Egyptian Army in the Yemen, and there was no end to their stay in sight.

What President Nasser had committed himself to, in fact, was the simultaneous success of political revolution and economic development in a country that was starting its modern life from scratch. Divided by its mountains, its tribes and its religious schisms there was no natural sense of unity in the Yemen, and few ready means of promoting it. Besides the Chinese road from Sanaa to Hodaida there was only one other road in the whole country, built by American engineers from Taiz to Mocha, which could be tackled safely without a four-wheel drive. There was no single undisputed capital city, and no administrative system save that of a despot, now destroyed. Outside the ranks of the sayyids — most of whom were on the Imam's side — there was only a handful of educated men, and little education was available except that of the traditional Islamic schools. Except for a few foreign doctors in Taiz and Sanaa who had mostly served the Imam and the royal family, there was no modern medical service whatever; and except for the local agents of the Aden merchants there was little that could be called modern commerce. Not one of the revolutionary leaders had any experience of government, and several of them, coming from long years in Aden or Cairo, had little experience of the Yemen. None of them knew for certain what wealth they had acquired in the Imam's treasury, or what Imamic bank accounts existed abroad, or whether, if there were any, the revolutionary Government would have access to them. They had neither the skill nor the system to administer foreign aid effectively, even if it were forthcoming. They had not even a reliable armed force to protect them, for in spite of the Russian arms agreements and Russian and Egyptian attempts to train a professional army before the revolt, the Yemen Army was too weak to control the tribes single-handed. In short

The tall houses of Ibb

Hawks and shaikhs in Bahrain

Former slaves, now divers on a Persian Gulf pearling dhow

Yemeni children

the revolution had inherited nothing. Its leaders were urging their country into the twentieth century with less equipment and fewer resources than the ill-fated rulers of the Congo. It was hardly surprising that they became, at once, the captives of the people to whom they turned for help.

It is easier to see this in retrospect, of course, than it was at the time. A powerful euphoria surrounded the overthrow of so notorious an institution as the Imamate, inducing wishful thinking in many people, Yemenis and foreigners alike. To begin with, moreover, the republicans seemed to be both popular and successful. Early visitors to the Yemen after the revolt found the country apparently both docile and elated. Two months afterwards, when the Imam's resistance had become established in the north and east, I was still able to travel by road all the way from Sanaa to Aden without hearing a single shot fired in anger or seeing any other sign of royalist activity. In the towns there was genuine relief — or every appearance of it — at the disappearance of the Imamate. Young men in the *suk* in Sanaa seized me by the arm and urged me to tell the world how poor the Imam had left them, and how the revolution would change their lot. An ancient tea-seller in Taiz offered me a free glass of his brew and cried, in stumbling but understandable English, before an approving crowd, 'Sallal, very good! Imam fuggoff!'

Repeated royalist claims of a 'triumphant march on Sanaa', issued through broadcasts from Mecca and Amman, were obvious nonsense which reduced the credibility of the Imam's resistance with every repetition. Equally, the Imam's allies reduced his appeal to the world outside the Yemen. King Saud was nobody's favourite ruler, and King Husain had been on the defensive against Nasser and many of his own people for several years. To support the Imam Badr, they had formed — not for the first time — an alliance of monarchs which brought them into swift and vociferous disfavour throughout the Arab world and was followed promptly by rumours of impending *coups d'état* in their apparently shaky kingdoms. King Saud, indeed, was soon forced to surrender control of his Government to his more enlightened brother, Faisal, who promised to initiate widespread social and political reforms in the feudal structure of the Saudi state; and whatever plans may have existed for Saudi-Jordanian armed intervention on behalf of the Imam in the Yemen were stillborn when, at the mere supposition of such action, the armed forces of both countries suffered some highly-publicised defections.[1] Several times, Egyptian aircraft from the Yemen

[1] See above, p. 98.

even bombed or dropped arms on Saudi territory, without effective retaliation. For a few months it seemed as though the forces of 'monarchist reaction' were in full flight before the new Arabian challenge, and the revolution would march on to inevitable, and generally welcome, success.

For the great powers standing behind the principal combatants this prospect had widely varying implications. The possibility of liquidating Britain's Aden base and spreading unrest throughout the Arabian Peninsula was sufficient inducement for the Soviet Union immediately to take the side of Nasser and Sallal in their struggle against 'reaction'. But, perhaps because they had already experienced some of the uncertainties of working in the Yemen, the Russians did not press their luck too hard. Within a couple of months four or five hundred Russian technicians and military advisers had returned to the Yemen but there was no overt attempt to acquire any stranglehold on the country and no disposition to pour unlimited aid and effort into a container that might prove to have no bottom. With nothing much to lose, the Russians could afford to let the Arabs fight each other with no more than a few prods to help them on and a modest stake on the likely winner.

The British, on the other hand, had an overriding interest in protecting the Aden base, and chose to do so by withholding recognition from the republicans and giving tacit support to the Imam, thus placing themselves on the side of 'monarchist reaction'. Not so the United States, however. Unlike Britain and Russia, her interests were at stake on all sides. In Egypt since 1959 she had wagered £200 million worth of aid on President Nasser as a genuine nationalist and the best antidote to communism in the Middle East. In Saudi Arabia she had a huge financial and strategic interest in the oil production of ARAMCO. In Jordan she was financially committed to helping King Husain and wished to see him remain in power lest his downfall should precipitate another round in the Arab-Israeli conflict. In Aden and the Persian Gulf her interests marched with those of Britain. None of these could America readily surrender, none of them could she safely elevate at the expense of the rest. For the United States, therefore, stability in Arabia was the first essential: if there had to be change, it must be orderly. Out of the Yemen crisis President Kennedy tried to secure both, by judiciously banging together the heads of most of the combatants. He stationed American aircraft in Saudi Arabia and ordered naval demonstrations in the Red Sea to deter Egypt from any further attacks upon Saudi Arabia. He publicly welcomed the Amir Faisal's proposals for Saudi reforms as a means of procuring orderly change. And to both Cairo and Riyadh he sent some plainly worded private messages urging the withdrawal of support from both sides in the Yemen so that the Yemenis might settle their own affairs under guarantees of non-intervention from any foreign quarter. In exchange he promised American recognition of the republican regime.

Securing the necessary agreement from Egypt and Saudi Arabia took longer than he expected. His representative in the Yemen, Mr. Robert Stookey, was in Sanaa when I was there, waiting to extend official recognition to the republicans, and although at first he had spoken of leaving again within a few days, he ended by having to stay over a month, in the squalid haven of the Government guest house. Surrounded as he was by his fellow-guests — Egyptian advisers and Russian technicians, western journalists and brand-new Yemeni ministers — exposed to the frailties of the Yemen telegraph service and the unwhole-some necessity for burning top-secret telegrams in lavatories already overflowing with other waste matter, it was no wonder that the nature of Stookey's mission was an open secret in Sanaa at the time. Even Radio Djibouti, on the other side of the Red Sea, knew what he was up to, and was apt to announce his latest move almost before he knew what it was going to be himself. Luckily, the guest-house, although sordid, was friendly. On one occasion when Stookey was sitting at breakfast at the long table shared by all the guests, the man who was known to everyone present as the chief Russian security officer in the Yemen rose from his place, picked up Stookey's heavy brief-case as he passed his chair and without pausing made as if to leave the room with it, un-noticed by Stookey. At the door he turned with a booming laugh, held up the brief-case and cried for us all to hear, 'Ah, Meester American, what carry you here?' There was a pause for maximum effect, while Stookey looked up from his breakfast in consternation, and then the Russian added, with a marvellously swooping intonation, 'Gold so-overrreigns?' With which he returned the case to Stookey's chair, gave the American an avuncular pat on the back and walked off beaming with pleasure, having let it be known to his appreciative audience that he knew — as, for that matter, did nearly everyone else in the room — that it was something more valuable than sovereigns that caused Stookey to carry the brief-case with him everywhere: it contained the American cipher books.

In such surroundings it was probably too much to expect that the Kennedy settlement would ever succeed. Non-intervention in a state so totally undeveloped was doomed to be only a pious hope. In the end, it is true, the agreements were forthcoming from both Cairo and Riyadh, and with non-intervention thus formally assured American diplomatic recognition of the Yemen Arab Republic was announced on December

19th, 1962. But the *Pax Americana* proved largely illusory. Egypt continued to send in troops, the Saudis still supplied arms and money to the Imam's forces, and an increasing number of adventurers, mercenaries and propagandists of various nationalities became involved on one side or the other. Fundamentally the weakness of the American position was that their interests in the dispute were too evenly balanced. Where nothing can be surrendered, no risks can be taken; and the United States could no more abandon the Saudis to unqualified Nasserist pressure than cut off aid to Egypt and hand Nasser to the Russians on a plate. She was unable, therefore, to employ any sanctions to enforce the settlement she thought she had procured. Instead, the Americans had to be content with a certain insulation of the affair from the more inflammatory influences of the cold war and the confinement of the physical conflict to the Yemen, for the time being. Neither full stability nor orderly change was guaranteed; but total instability and utter disorder were avoided in the acceptance of an Arabian stalemate.

Over the next two years this stalemate remained unbroken in the Yemen, and not all the embroidery of Arab rhetoric nor the blood of Arab fighting men could impose any substantial change. The vicissitudes of the struggle were hopefully charted by propagandists on both sides, and bemusedly followed by the world at large in the fading hope that some rational settlement might emerge. But none did. For over a year, the United Nations was involved, in the belief that an international observer force might supervise the 'disengagement' of Egypt and Saudi Arabia; but although the U.N. officials reported that the Saudis appeared to have stopped supplying the royalists for a few months, they found no sign of the departure of Egyptian troops. By the time the U.N. observers were withdrawn, in September 1964, the Saudis had resumed their supplies to the Imam. Two months later, a cease-fire was signed by republicans and royalists, with the encouragement of Egypt and Saudi Arabia, but it was dishonoured almost before the ink was dry. A peace conference was called but never met. Several times President Sallal was reported to be ill, and out of favour, and regarded by the Egyptians as expendable — but he remained, doggedly, the republican President. Just as often, the Imam Badr was said to be unpopular with the Saudis, and as expendable as Sallal — but he remained, tenaciously, the royalist leader.

The depressing tale of claims advanced and denied, of hopes raised and dashed, and of bloodshed unceasing, was told succinctly in the newspaper headlines of the period. The affair had begun with confident claims from the republicans of 'Imam of Yemen Killed in Palace

Shelling' (*The Times*, 28/9/62) and 'New Regime in Control of Almost All Yemen' (*The Times*, 9/10/62). Three weeks after the revolt the story was still, 'Yemen Rebels Confident of Success — No Appeal for Egyptian Help' (*The Guardian*, 17/10/62) although Egyptian troops were already pouring into the country by that time. Then came the announcement of the Imam's survival — ' "Dead" Imam Appeals for World Support' (*The Times*, 12/11/62) — and a gradual abandonment of early hopes began. 'Mediation in the Yemen' was welcomed by *The Guardian* on November 29th, but by December 19th its headline read more realistically, 'Haggling in Yemen'. With the arrival of the new year, after the United States had reached her agreement with the combatants, fresh doubts were visible. 'U.S. Warning on Middle East Rivalries,' *The Times* reported (7/1/63), and 'Arab Doubts on Effectiveness of U.S. Move — "Miscalculation over Egypt"?' it added, somewhat clumsily, the next day. Thereafter the headlines may speak their dismal story for themselves.

Yemen Army Move Against Royalists — Both republican and royalist forces say that the Yemen civil war is now entering its final, critical phase. . . .	(*The Guardian*, 1/3/63)
Crisis at U.N. Over Yemen	(*The Guardian*, 10/6/63)
General Von Horn Begins his Yemen Assignment	(*The Times*, 14/6/63)
Royalist Successes in the Yemen	(*Sunday Times*, 16/6/63)
Internal Rivalries Keep Yemen Divided	(*The Times*, 19/6/63)
Tribes' Plan to End Yemen War	(*The Observer*, 14/7/63)
Imam's Forces Are On Top	(*Sunday Times*, 21/7/63)
Sallal Wins Over the Tribesmen	(*Sunday Times*, 13/10/63)
Yemen — End to the Affair?	(*Economist*, 19/10/63)
U.N. Force Stays in Yemen	(*The Guardian*, 1/11/63)
Peace Hope in Yemen	(*The Observer*, 10/11/63)
U.N. Observation Mission to Remain in Yemen	(*The Times*, 4/1/64)
Growing Strength of Yemeni Royalists	(*The Times*, 4/1/64)
U.N. Mission Stays in Yemen	(*The Times*, 4/7/64)
Yemen Republic Finally Has a Real Government	(*Sunday Times*, 5/8/64)
Yemen Capital is Shelled	(*The Times*, 15/8/64)
A Nasser Victory in the Yemen	(*Sunday Times*, 30/8/64)
U.N. Team Leaves the Yemen	(*The Guardian*, 5/9/64)

HURRAH FOR REVOLUTION!

Cease Fire in Yemen's Civil War	(*The Guardian*, 6/11/64)
Compromise Near on the Yemen	(*Sunday Times*, 8/11/64)
Yemen Conference Doubtful	(*The Times*, 27/11/64)
Conference on Yemen Next Week	(*The Guardian*, 9/12/64)
Confusion Again in the Yemen	(*The Guardian*, 16/12/64)
U.A.R. Faces Crisis in the Yemen	(*The Observer*, 27/12/64)
Campaign to Oust President Sallal	(*The Times*, 4/1/65)
Yemen Regime in Stronger Hands	(*The Times*, 7/1/65)
Setback for Republican Regime	(*The Times*, 11/1/65)
President Nasser's Vietnam	(*The Guardian*, 12/1/65)

Up and down, the see-saw swung. Now the republicans and their Egyptian allies were on top, now the royalists and their Saudi Arabian friends seemed more successful. For domestic political reasons King Husain of Jordan switched sides, deciding to offer the Republic his belated recognition. But this diplomatic success for Cairo was more than offset by the war's continuing strain upon Egyptian resources. The casualties on both sides were heavy. In just over two years the Egyptian Army was thought to have lost at least 3,000 men killed and probably another 20,000 wounded — although the official losses were given at the beginning of 1965 as only 105 officers and 1,502 men. Under Egyptian attacks, with high explosive and napalm bombing from the air as well as armoured columns on the ground, the Yemeni casualties were probably far greater. Their dead must have been numbered in tens of thousands, especially when the victims of disease and malnutrition resulting from the war were added to those killed in battle. Yet as 1965 opened the basic stalemate upon which the tragic see-saw pivoted remained unchanged. The irresistible force of Arab revolution had met the immovable object of Arabian reaction, and a lasting compromise between the two seemed almost as far away as ever.

From the years of unremitting war, however, several truths about the Yemen had been discovered, or re-discovered, by the beginning of 1965. In the light of hindsight they might look platitudinous, but when the revolt took place in Sanaa they seemed a lot less clear.

1. *No simple military solution was possible in the Yemen.* Not since the first three months of the republic had the Egyptian Army in the Yemen numbered less than 20,000 men and for most of the time its strength had been nearer 50,000 and possibly even more; yet it had never been able to subdue the hostile tribes. The main towns and roads had been secured, parts of the south and west had remained fairly peaceful, where the Shafii tribes were traditionally hostile to the Imamate, but about

half the country had remained for over two years a no-man's land of guerrilla warfare, while large areas of the Zaidi north and east had never been under Egyptian or republican control. This was nothing new in the Yemen's history. Ibrahim Pasha and his Egyptian Army in the nineteenth century, and the Turks after him, experienced similar difficulties; and in 1911 when the Imam Yahia was fighting to regain the Yemen's independence, the Turkish Governor-General was moved to declare that if he had under his command such warriors as the Yemeni tribesmen, he could 'subdue all Europe'.

But if modern armies could not defeat tribal guerrillas in these conditions, the guerrillas were equally unable to defeat the armies. The tribesmen had never accomplished their 'triumphant march on Sanaa' and there was little reason to believe they ever would as long as the Egyptian Army remained there, and President Nasser was determined not to yield to 'royalist reaction'. Military victory for either side had to be eliminated, therefore, as a possible means of settlement.

2. *The cost to Egypt of remaining in the Yemen was greater than the cost to Saudi Arabia of helping Egypt's opponents there.* Because tribal guerrilla warfare is more easily maintained than full-scale military counter-action, the financial (and human) burden of the Yemen war fell more heavily on Egypt. How big a role it played in her balance of payments difficulties cannot be known in the absence of reliable figures, but it could not have been insignificant to a country that was compelled, in 1964, to sell a quarter of her gold reserves to meet her short-term foreign debts. Official Egyptian figures of the cost of the war must be viewed with scepticism, but for what they are worth they were given early in 1965 as £6 million in foreign exchange and about 15 million Egyptian pounds annually (between £10 and £12 million sterling) in local currency.[1] It can be taken for granted that these were the lowest conceivable figures the Egyptian Government could put forward, and even at their face value they represented a serious and unwelcome addition to Egypt's many other economic burdens.

Saudi Arabia, on the other hand, blessed with a steadily rising income from oil, was able to maintain her less costly support of the Imam without difficulty; and there were indications that Iran was also offering help to the royalists as reprisal for Egyptian attacks upon the Shah.[2] In the financial contest, therefore, Egypt was at a serious disadvantage.

3. *In the long run, the Yemenis themselves would settle their dispute on their own terms.* In fact, this was just what they were doing, and were

[1] and [2] *The Observer* 28/2/65.

likely to do increasingly, whatever Nasser or the Saudis wished to say about it. Possibly, without foreign intervention, the dispute would have been settled within a few months, but no-one can be sure. Historically, strong central government in the Yemen has usually been provided by strong individuals, like Yahia or Ahmad, and their deaths have been followed, as a rule, by periods of tribal fragmentation and warfare. It was always on the cards that the death of Ahmad would be followed by such a spell of comparative anarchy, because of the weakness of his successor. Had Sallal himself been a sufficiently ruthless man, or better-placed within the Yemen's structure of dynasties, tribes and religions, he might have succeeded in imposing his Government; but he, too, suffered from several disabilities. He was a Zaidi, but only a black-smith's son and therefore — whatever his attitude to the Imamate — unlikely to commend himself as a ruler to many of the Zaidi chieftains. At the same time, he could not entirely overcome the traditional sus-picion of the Shafiis, many of whom, although they welcomed the downfall of the Imamate, never gave him more than passive support, and were showing distinct signs of unrest after two years of his non-government. Moreover, like al-Badr, Sallal was personally unimpressive. When I met him in Sanaa he was unshaven, crumpled, doleful in his looks and lacking in authority. His officials whispered among themselves while he talked; his Egyptian bodyguard seemed to diminish his stature. He was already a man out of his depth.

With weakness in the leadership of both sides, the struggle among the Yemenis often seemed to outsiders to be incoherent, given meaning only by the intervention of the Egyptians and the Saudis with their respective commitments to 'republicans' and 'royalists', or 'revolution' and 'reaction'. But these twentieth-century labels were only part of the story. Within the Yemen the traditional facts of political and social life, unchallenged until so recently, re-asserted themselves with vigour. The lack of communications and administration, the sharp divisions of mountain, valley and desert, of tribes and religions, did as much as anything else to dictate the course of events. Alliances were made and unmade for local reasons unconnected with the world's preconceptions, and campaigns were often won or lost for reasons other than simple military supremacy. When the crops had been safely harvested and sown again in the autumn, the tribes harried the Egyptian soldiers through the winter and spring, and the newspapers talked of 'royalist victories'. When the fields demanded attention in the summer, the Egyptians often achieved some temporary command, and the com-mentators spoke of 'republican successes'.

Gradually, however, the most important truth about the Yemen was discerned in the flux:

4. *The more anyone else tried to impose a solution, the more the Yemenis would combine to resist it.* This was just another form of the familiar nationalist proposition that ranks are always closed against outsiders in the end. President Nasser had invoked this successfully in many a clash with the western powers, but in the Yemen it appeared to be working, gradually, against him. Not only had the Egyptians been unable to subdue the royalist tribes, they had also experienced increasing difficulty in retaining republican support. Saddled with the strains of war and its own incompetence, President Sallal's administration had never begun to come to grips with the civil problems it inherited. Ministerial corruption burgeoned, and the peasants who waited at the palace gates were no better off than before. In 1962 they stood there in Sanaa patiently, offering their pledges and petitions, confident on the morning of revolution of miracles on the way. Two-and-a-half years later, no miracles had been vouchsafed. Instead, freedom had bestowed its inevitable disillusionments, and the peasants were less patient.

Equally inevitably, it was the Egyptians who felt the draught. They who came as saviours had manifestly failed to save. Instead, they had remained to govern — and were not even very good at that. They had become not just the revolution's shield, but its spine, its limbs, its brains and its nervous system. They were not only President Sallal's bodyguard, they were his puppet-masters. Indisputably, they were the cuckoo in the Yemeni nest — and with increasing clarity the Yemenis showed their resentment. Disturbances in Sanaa were followed by executions, executions by more rumours of disturbance. A state of emergency was decreed, and ministers were tried in secret tribunals. But attempts to sustain a responsible Yemeni administration under President Sallal failed repeatedly, and one cabinet after another collapsed. The resentful hint of my young student in Taiz, two years earlier, that the Yemen would end by fighting the Egyptians for its freedom, seemed more than ever prophetic.

Like the Americans in Vietnam, the Egyptians had staked their prestige on an overseas war which they showed ever less likelihood of winning; where, indeed, every step they took to secure outright victory only seemed to make ultimate defeat more probable. Thus they were caught in the classic colonial paradox, where the irritation of their presence undermined the very position they were hoping to secure. Indeed, perhaps the real parallel was less with the Americans in Vietnam than with the British in Aden and the South Arabian Federation. In many ways the British and the Egyptians were the mirror image of each other. While President Nasser was supporting 'revolution' against 'reaction', pitting the townsmen against the tribes, Britain was trapped by history on the side of 'reaction' against 'revolution', supporting the tribal rulers against the towns. Each was well on the way to failure, both were seeking the means to withdraw, yet neither could easily and honourably find the way to do so.

The result was a nice, historic irony. Wittingly or unwittingly, Egypt had assumed in the Yemen in 1962 the same colonial burdens as Britain south of the border — of pacification, administration, economic development and the rest. Voluntarily or involuntarily, she also inspired the same resentments. And just as Britain was ending her role by provoking increasing nationalist discontent in her old dependent territories, so Egypt seemed likely to become the catalyst of modern nationhood in the Yemen. Both north and south of the border the tribes were putting up a valiant fight for the thirteenth century against the twentieth, if you like; and no doubt they would go on doing so for some years yet. But their successes were bound to be Pyrrhic in the end, because they were won only by adopting the twentieth century's weapons. In the old British Protectorate, the dissident tribes destroyed their old ways even as they fought for them by accepting the bribes of modern weapons and easy money: and the loyal rulers undermined their own authority even as they tried to preserve it by creating their modern federation. In the Yemen the same paradoxical processes were at work. It was not only the Egyptians and the republicans who used modern techniques of publicity and propaganda, for example; the royalists and their friends had a publicity machine, too, with broadcasts from Mecca and interviews in the world's press, public relations men in London and lobbyists in Washington. This was a far cry, indeed, from the day when the Imam Ahmad invited me to enter his silent kingdom for the first time. The republicans were not the only ones, either, who talked about reform and liberation, Arabism and social justice. The royalists had pinched all those liberal clothes. They wanted to 'liberate' the Yemen, too — and not only from 'feudal reaction' like their opponents, but from 'Egyptian imperialism' as well. Did the Egyptians sponsor a 'National Front for the Liberation of South Yemen'? Then the royalists sponsored a 'National Front for the Liberation of North Yemen'.[1] They, too, wanted economic development and Arab unity and all the right and proper joys of the modern world. Although the world still called them royalists, they had even accepted the end of royalism. In

[1] Its formation was announced in November 1964.

1964 they produced a formal proposal for a 'constitutional Imamate' in which the Imam would hold only spiritual authority, while temporal power would be vested in an elected body. In such proposals, no doubt, lay the germ of the eventual compromise that would restore unity to the Yemen one day and open the way to the withdrawal of Egyptian troops.

All this did not mean that the old Yemen was dead already, any more than the remote shaikhdoms of the Aden Protectorate were fitted already for immediate induction into twentieth-century life. When all was said and done, the Yemen was still rent by ancient as well as modern feuds, still deprived of all but the most elementary equipment for contemporary life. Unity would be difficult to achieve, reform would be hard to begin, peace would be onerous to preserve. For many years to come, the rulers of the Yemen, whoever they might be, would have to consider the tribes and sects, the mountains, deserts and seasons as vital elements in the equations of government. But the fact remained that the old framework of the Yemeni state had been shattered beyond repair. Neither the medieval theocracy nor the traditional isolation could ever be restored. The scarred and wrinkled carapace of centuries had fallen. Ahead, there were only the infinite hopes and disillusionments of the modern, universal, world.

8

Dissolution in the Desert

There is nothing like a Friday in Saudi Arabia for inducing galloping melancholia even in the stoutest extrovert. Confronted with the inspissated gloom of the Saudi Sabbath, temperate men accustomed to nothing more intoxicating than a glass of tonic wine at Christmas develop a sudden craving for strong liquors. Faithful husbands and clean young bachelors dream of illicit love; and as the muezzin booms his call to prayer from a thousand amplifiers on a hundred minarets and the religious police stalk the streets to enforce observance of his cry, even an atheist from the occident may lament the lost freedom of the Christian Church.

Saudi Arabia is the home, and spiritually the creation, of the Wahhabi Muslims — the Calvinist 'wee frees' of Islam who, by putting their opponents to the sword for the past two centuries, extended their puritan rule over most of central Arabia, and are now fighting fiercely to defend it against the modern erosions of secular liberalism. At first glance their struggle seems depressingly successful. Alcoholic drinks are absolutely prohibited, even to foreign diplomatists. Saudi women remain in strict purdah, and not even foreign wives are permitted to drive a car. Nothing but Muslim religious institutions may function, and no Christian priest is allowed into the country — unless he gets himself a second passport and describes himself as a 'teacher'. Nowhere in Saudi Arabia is there a public cinema, for representations of the human form are forbidden under the Islamic law; and when, in 1963, Mecca Radio employed its first woman announcer, the religious leaders of the nation delivered to the Prime Minister, the Crown Prince Faisal as he then was, a solemn protest at such ungodly goings-on.

But, like the 'wee frees', the Saudi puritans are fighting a rearguard action. 'My friends,' Prince Faisal is reported to have told the protesting *ulema*, 'you'd better get used to women's voices on the radio, because you'll be seeing their faces on television soon.' Just how television images of either sex can be reconciled with the strict Wahhabi interpretation of the Islamic law is a matter for the theologians to decide, if they can. Most Saudis, I suspect, will not care one way or the other as long as they get the telly. And get it they surely will, for as modern oil affluence, technology and Nasserism exert their pressure, reform and re-organisation are beginning to change the face and habits of the Saudi kingdom. To the outsider, long accustomed to envisaging Saudi Arabia as an hypocritical hell of pious sentiments, brutal autocracy and fabulous but ill-distributed wealth, any reform and any organisation may seem long overdue, and what there is of these things so far may seem pretty unimpressive. Yet if one stands back for a moment to acquire an historical perspective, he may reflect, as Dr. Johnson did of the dog walking on its hind legs, that the surprising thing is not that it is done badly, but that it is done at all.

In 1900 the fortunes of the Saudi family of Najd were as reduced as they well could be. Fifty years before, leading the Wahhabis in the conquest of Arabia, they had ruled, plundered and exacted tribute from the tribes as far south as Oman and as far north as Kuwait. A hundred years earlier they had sacked the holy city of Kerbala, in Iraq, and occupied Mecca. But at the turn of this century most of the family was in virtual exile in Kuwait and the rival house of the Rashidis of Hail occupied the old Saudi capital of Riyadh. The history of the modern Saudi state did not begin until two years later when the late Abdul Aziz ibn Saud, then just out of his 'teens, vaulted the mud walls of Riyadh one night to lead a group of Saudi warriors in recapturing the town. It was another ten years before he managed to drive out the last feeble Turkish garrisons from the province of Hasa, on the Persian Gulf, and during the First World War his position was still so insecure that the British had to maintain him with a subsidy and treated him like any other petty Arabian chieftain. Not until 1925, when he captured the western kingdom of the Hejaz and its holy cities of Mecca and Medina from the Hashemite Sharif Husain, did he emerge unquestionably as Arabia's premier Lord. Two years later Britain recognised his new status in the Treaty of Jeddah, acknowledging his absolute independence and his title as 'King of the Hejaz and of Najd and its dependencies'; but it was only in 1932 that the name of the Kingdom was changed in ibn Saud's honour to Saudi Arabia, and only in 1933 that the first and ultimately revolutionary oil concession was granted. Saudi Arabia's total annual income then was a mere £600,000, chiefly from the pilgrim traffic to Mecca and Medina. In 1945 it was still less than £5 million. One strong man like ibn Saud could still rule the country without a modern administrative system — and did, for nowhere had any administration been established save that of ibn Saud's family connexions. To be sure, these were extensive enough. With the aid of thirty-three sons and an unknown number of daughters — the progeny of a multitude of judicious tribal alliances — ibn Saud had established a personal domination within Arabia unmatched by any of his Wahhabi predecessors.

Yet the richest and most fertile parts of the peninsula still lay beyond his control, in the green valleys of the Yemen and Oman and the ports of Aden, Muscat and the Persian Gulf. His was strictly a desert kingdom, held together by traditional Wahhabi fanaticism and his personal leadership — a country nearly as big as the whole of Western Europe whose frontiers were as yet uncharted, whose wealth was negligible, and whose tribal manners were almost undisturbed by modern politics or government.

Almost — but not quite. Like the Prophet Muhammad 1,300 years before him, ibn Saud had brought to the interior of Arabia an unaccustomed sense of discipline and stability. He settled some of the nomads and checked their tribal warfare, and in doing so opened the previously inaccessible heart of the peninsula to the influences of the modern, external world. Often he argued personally with bigoted religious leaders to persuade them to accept modern inventions like the motor car, the radio and the telephone; and by granting the first oil concession to the Arabian-American Oil Company (ARAMCO) he determined the country's present path, even though in his last years he regretted the corruption of morals and customs caused by the vast new wealth that resulted from this action. In short, he laid the foundations of a modern state in place of a traditional tribal federation, and when he died, in 1953, he achieved the last great act of a great man in securing the peaceful succession to his throne for his eldest son, Saud. His many other sons did not dispute his judgement, and for once a great Arabian empire survived the death of its founder apparently unimpaired. Where there had been faction and disorder there was the rule of royal or theocratic law; where there had been strife, there was peace.

This was revolution enough in the space of 50 years, but it was only the beginning of still greater changes whose shape the old man dimly, and somewhat fearfully, foresaw, and to which, unfortunately, his eldest son proved unequal. Within five years of his accession, and in spite of soaring revenues from oil, Saud's misjudgements had emptied the royal treasury and induced needless discontent both at home and abroad. Sheer royal extravagance was part of the trouble — extravagance in the traditional, open-handed way of the desert, applied with far less discrimination to the new dollar millions than ever it had been to the old handfuls of gold sovereigns. King Saud's new Nasariyeh Palace in Riyadh, for example, had cost him at least £25 million, and included four separate palaces for his reigning wives, 32 mansions for his scores of concubines and their retinues, and 37 villas for various princes, as well as royal schools, a hospital, a museum, a zoo and what was said to be the world's largest air-conditioning plant.

A great deal of the rest had gone on other members of the royal family who had been only slightly less profligate than Saud himself. Towering new blocks of flats in Beirut and Cairo were evidence of the foreign business interests of many of the Saudi princes, and trails of Cadillacs and gold watches recorded their many pleasure trips around the world. Prestige inflation of the armed forces consumed nearly a quarter of the annual income, and millions were devoted to 'anti-imperialist' political activities in other Arab countries, especially in the years just before and after Suez when the Saudi disputes with Britain over Buraimi and Oman were particularly inflamed. At that time the King seemed to have been persuaded by his advisers, with some encouragement from the American State Department, that his money and his status as the guardian of Islam's holy places would enable him to seize the leadership of the Arab world, and he dispensed his largesse with patent delusions of grandeur. When Jordan terminated her arrangement for an annual budget subsidy from Britain, in the turbulent aftermath of Suez, King Saud stepped in with a commitment to King Husain of £5 million a year. When President Nasser was in economic difficulties after the Suez crisis, the Saudis sold oil to Egypt on such favourable terms that they lost about one dollar in every three. A little money had been devoted to genuine development, such as the railway from Riyadh to Dammam on the Persian Gulf, opened just before the death of ibn Saud. There had been improvements to the roads from Jeddah to Mecca and Medina to assist the pilgrim traffic; a few new hospitals and schools had been built; and a 'King Saud University' began its first classes in Riyadh in 1958, under an Egyptian director. But scarcely one productive enterprise had been developed in the whole country outside the oil-fields, and such public services as the railway, the airlines and the water supply companies never came within loud-hailing distance of sound commercial management. Attached to every transaction were corruption, incompetence, waste and lack of foresight on a truly monumental scale; and it was no surprise to anyone except the Saudis to discover that by 1958 the country was spending 25 per cent more than it was earning, and the value of the Saudi currency had fallen to only two thirds of its normal value. Under pressure from more enlightened, and perhaps more worried, members of the royal family, King Saud summoned international experts to help him to correct this imbalance; and at the beginning of 1958 an Egyptian and a Pakistani, seconded from the International Bank, produced for him the country's first genuine budget. There had been one other attempted budget, in 1953, but it was less detailed, less comprehensive, and in practice utterly unfulfilled. The 1958 budget was the first rational attempt in Saudi Arabia to introduce modern administrative methods suited to the needs of the new state. Announcing its provisions for reducing State spending, Mecca Radio declared with pride that, 'His Majesty King Saud began with himself and reduced his personal expenses;' and the estimates duly revealed that the allocation for all the royal family and their appurtenances was only about ten per cent of the total income. The old concept of the state as the ruler's personal fief had come to an abrupt, ignominious and permanent end.

Equally abrupt and ignominious, but not then as permanent, was Saud's loss of authority immediately afterwards, and the elevation of his younger brother, the Crown Prince Faisal, to effective power for the first time. The circumstances of the change were remarkably similar in 1958 to those of October 1962, when Faisal assumed power again, immediately after the Yemen revolution. A loss of confidence in Saud's leadership was associated with the appearance on the Arabian mainland of a threat of nationalist revolution and Egyptian power. The first time, as it turned out, the threat was more apparent than real, and the changes that resulted were, in consequence, largely temporary; but they provided a trial run for the more permanent changes that have taken place since 1962, and they presaged, in particular, Faisal's eventual accession to the throne in place of his elder brother.

In the atmosphere of nationalist hysteria that swept the Arab world after the creation of the United Arab Republic in February, 1958, King Saud panicked. Less shrewd than the Imam Ahmad in the Yemen, who simply jumped on to the unity bandwaggon by entering the spurious federation of the United Arab States, Saud sought to beat Nasser instead of to join him, spreading his agents and his money through the Arab capitals in an anti-Egyptian propaganda campaign. But Nasser was far better equipped for that kind of battle, and replied forcefully through broadcasts from Cairo and Damascus, and by whispering campaigns among the hundreds of Egyptian teachers and civil servants employed in Saudi Arabia. In March, Colonel Abdul Hamid Sarraj, the chief of Syrian Army intelligence, alleged in Damascus that King Saud had offered him £2 million and the Presidency of Syria if he would assassinate Nasser and frustrate the union of Syria and Egypt. Four days later the Crown Prince Muhammad al-Badr of the Yemen signed the charter of the United Arab States on behalf of his father, and for the first time in over a century it seemed possible that Egypt had won a foothold on the Arabian peninsula. The effect of these two events inside Saudi Arabia was alarming. King Saud promptly disappeared from public life, while passionate appeals for 'loyalty' had to be issued over Mecca Radio, and a substantial majority of the King's brothers insisted that Faisal should take over the Government.

He did so as Prime Minister, committed to a programme of administrative reform, and for a week or two it seemed to triumphant commentators in Cairo that Nasserism was about to conquer the Arabian heartland forthwith. But nothing so dramatic happened. Instead, the Muslim fasting month of Ramadhan intervened, damping Arabian energies and spirits. At the end of it King Saud emerged from his retirement to make his customary pilgrimage to Mecca, and the crisis was over.

If revolution had been avoided, however, the need for reform and re-organisation remained appallingly clear. By a lucky coincidence of timing, it was just at this moment that I made my first visit to Saudi Arabia, and there have been few occasions in my life when I have felt so acutely a sense of social disintegration all around me. Admittedly, my view was coloured — like that of most visitors I met there — by the difficulty of getting into Saudi Arabia in the first place and by the frustrations imposed by the demands of Ramadhan in the second. My application for a visa had been made more than four months earlier, and without much hope of success. An earlier application had never been answered, let alone granted. When my visa did arrive, therefore, I lost no time in travelling before someone in authority changed his mind about admitting me, with the unfortunate result that I reached Jeddah soon after the start of Ramadhan. This month of fasting by day and feasting by night induced in the Saudis a sleepy and indifferent euphoria. All was for the best in the best of all possible worlds: and please, they would murmur in bewilderment at my fury, when I was offered my tenth cup of coffee at three o'clock in the morning, please Mister David, do not be nervous. No doubt the sensible course would have been to do as they implied — surrender all hope, eschew all effort, and follow the local customs as far as possible. But I was brought up in a conscience-driven world, and as my hotel was costing £10 a day I felt that surrender would have been a less than proper use of my time; so I maintained instead a fruitless and exhausting battle to accomplish something — indeed, anything — before I was buried by the drifting sands of Saudi indifference. I did not succeed. For three weeks I scarcely saw a single Saudi official before ten o'clock at night, when the day's fast had been broken, nor could I secure permission from anyone at any hour to set foot outside the bounds of Jeddah. I never saw Riyadh until Ramadhan was over, and then I was not allowed to leave the airport — where, piling insult upon injury, the police confiscated a copy of *Holiday* magazine that I had brought with me to read on the aircraft on the grounds that it contained infidel representations of the human form. (I learned afterwards that this was a profitable racket. Magazines so obtained commanded a handsome price on the black market.) Only after prodigious waste of time and effort did I get permission to spend three days in the ARAMCO town at Dhahran, towards the end of my visit. But when I wished to leave the country by flying directly from there to Bahrain, a mere twenty minutes away across the Persian Gulf, I was firmly re-directed to Jeddah again, for the sole reason that as I had entered Saudi Arabia there I must leave from there, too. Having thus spent the better part of a month like Alice in Looking Glass Land, running as hard as I could just to stay in the same place, I discovered back in Jeddah that it was almost as difficult to get out as it had been to get in, and I spent nearly another week in constant attendance at the offices of 12 different officials to secure my exit visa.

The Saudi bureaucracy was dropsical beyond belief, staffed by nepotism and Parkinson's Law, and graced with as many niceties of style and rank as the civil service of Whitehall or Washington. Beneath its blubber of appearance there was little skeleton of structure or command, no capacity for decision and no will to act, and often its grandest titles were sheer make-believe. The farcical affair of the Foreign Press Department in Jeddah was a case in point. One night during Ramadhan when all other diversions had been exhausted I asked to be taken on a tour of the Ministry of Information. It was an extensive building, like all other ministries, whose corridors were always peopled by scores of servants and sweepers hawking and spitting in blank idleness, and whose offices were full, on floor after floor, of shaikhly figures in white nightshirts and gold wrist-watches listening in equal idleness to the chatter of ten different visitors at once. One of these rather pasty grandees with the rank of Under-Secretary summoned a Palestinian refugee employed in the Ministry to escort me on my tour. When we were out of the Under-Secretary's earshot the Palestinian introduced himself as a product of

British education under the Palestine mandate and desired me to know, as one rational man to another, that I was wasting my valuable time in this place. I was under few illusions about that, anyway, but I said perhaps we could just have a look at the Foreign Press Department and then we might seek some refreshment and have a talk. He looked startled. How did I know there was a Foreign Press Department? I explained that I had seen the title on a door that appeared to be locked, and I wondered why no-one had bothered to take me there. 'I will show you', he said, with a hint of mischief, and led me through the corridors past the coffee-sipping shaikhs to the very door. Putting his shoulder to it, he heaved, and with a swift susurration of disturbed paper it opened sufficiently for us to squeeze inside and switch on the light. We were in a large and quite uninhabited room knee-deep in unopened newspapers and magazines from all over the world. *The Times* of London and *The Times* of New York lay where they had been thrown, with *The Guardian* and the *Herald Tribune, Le Monde, Der Spiegel,* and the *Neue Züricher Zeitung, Time* and *Newsweek* and *Paris Match* — an elephant's graveyard of all-too-mortal words. Most of them were still in their postal wrappers and anything up to two or three years old. Scattered among them were drifts and avalanches of little brown envelopes, likewise unopened, bearing the imprint of an American news cuttings service. On a table by the door someone had left two cardboard files. One was labelled 'Joseph Alsop', the other, 'Anthony Nutting'. I felt a twinge of envy that the reputations of these two journalists should, apparently, so far exceed all others. But when I opened them I discovered, with miserable gratification, that the files were empty. 'Ah,' said the Palestinian, in high sardonic humour, 'they are for what you British call immediate attention — *insha'allah*! — by the will of God!'

Nothing ever got immediate attention in Saudi Arabia, in my experience, and few things got belated attention, either. The prevailing attitude to time, indeed, made largely irrelevant any distinction between now and later, by bundling most things into the bottomless pit of never. The wags of Jeddah called this attitude A.M.T., or Arabian *Ma'aleesh* Time, because, as every Middle Eastern traveller knows, *ma'aleesh* means 'never mind,' and never minding time in Saudi Arabia was the chief national occupation. And no wonder, for most rational measurements of time were in a state of ineluctable confusion. Besides the universal acceptance of A.M.T., four other kinds of time were recognised in varying degrees. Two of them were new and western, one was old and Arabian, and the fourth was a compromise that did nobody any good. To begin with there was Dhahran Time — a device employed by ARAMCO and the United States Air Force base at Dhahran for getting their men to work at the crack of dawn by adding one hour of summer time to Dhahran Standard Time between April and October. Such was the importance of Dhahran's oil industry in the life of the nation that Dhahran Time had to be taken into account sometimes in Riyadh and Jeddah too. Then there was ordinary Standard Time, or G.M.T. plus three or four hours, according to longitude. This was accepted in Dhahran and Jeddah — but not in the reactionary fastnesses of Riyadh — as the basis for international airline schedules and the programmes of Mecca Radio. At the other extreme was Muslim Sun Time, which was determined locally by establishing midnight as the time of sunset each day. This regulated Riyadh and all the offices of the Saudi Government, as well as the wrist-watches of most shopkeepers in the *suk*. Between these two lay the compromise of European Local Time on which most foreigners relied, setting their clocks six hours behind whatever Muslim Sun Time happened to be. Thus a traveller arriving in Dhahran at eight o'clock on Sunday evening by the airport clock (D.S.T.) would discover that for his taxi driver it was already about 1.25 on Monday morning (M.S.T.) while his hotel was run on the assumption that he had arrived at about twenty five minutes past seven (E.L.T.) and at the ARAMCO office just down the road they were under the firm impression that he had landed at nine p.m. (D.T.). A swift decline into the timeless resignation of A.M.T. seemed, for most people, the only rational answer.

At every level such idiotic incongruities were repeated — the offspring of an abrupt and total war between contemporary demands and old ways. At the highest level this had resulted in national bankruptcy. At lower levels it produced constant equivocation, and the frequent appearance, if not the fact, of plain bad faith. The day before I left Jeddah at last, an American television crew arrived in my hotel to make, so they happily informed me, the first documentary film about Saudi Arabia. Unfortunately, they had been asked to leave their equipment in Customs for some technical reason they did not understand, but they had been assured that it would be released within 24 hours, and as their trip had been arranged through the good offices of the Saudi delegation to the United Nations in New York they were confident of success. As it happened, I was able to explain the 'technical reason' for the impounding of their equipment. Having already suffered a similar fate with my own small still-camera, I knew that it was because of the religious prohibition upon photography, which, by extension, prevented the import of photographic equipment as well. I knew also that the shops of Jeddah openly sold cameras and film, nevertheless, and that the Ministry of Information was happy to supply visitors with its own photographs, if only it could find them. I knew also that my own camera had been released eventually after repeated protests — but only on condition that I employed a Government photographer to use it for me. And finally I knew that, having done so, the Government photographer had immediately disappeared with all the film, never to be seen again by me. All this cast some gloom upon the Americans' day, but it was not until I met them again in Beirut some months later that I learned the still gloomier outcome of their endeavours. They had stayed in Jeddah for six weeks, trying to get their cameras released from Customs, but had eventually retired in a state of total mental exhaustion, leaving their equipment still impounded. I believe it was only returned, eventually, to New York after vigorous intervention by the American Embassy.

There was not only meddling and misunderstanding in such irksome affairs, but often graft and deception, too, for in the clash between the modern and traditional worlds corruption had bitten deep into the Saudi spirit. The absence of any modern commercial law, for example, and the Islamic prohibition of interest charges on money loans as 'usury', were comprehensible in a desert society where trade was based on barter and banks had never been heard of. But in a country with an income of £150 million a year and a flourishing international trade, such restrictions only forced every merchant and every bank into subterfuge and evasion in their most humdrum business dealings. Other religious prohibitions were brought similarly into disrepute. Music was a strictly forbidden joy, and many an unfortunate western resident, arriving in the country for the first time with his gramophone records or his tape-recorder in his luggage, had protested in vain as the Saudi Customs officers indignantly confiscated these instruments of the devil. Yet they would probably be on sale in a back room of the *suk* before long, and the officials would be a few ryals the richer. Smoking and games were prohibited in public, too, but in every coffee shop there were usually Saudis to be seen with cigarettes cupped furtively in their hands, listening to the forbidden whine of an Egyptian singer on the radio, while barefooted lads in white nightshirts played football in the dust outside.

The royal treasury financed a powerful force of conscience-keepers, splendidly entitled 'The Committees for the Encouragement of Morality and the Suppression of Vice' — but more commonly and simply known as the religious police — who were empowered to compel all Muslims to pray five times a day and arrest anyone, Saudi or foreign, who infringed the laws of Islam. They worked hard and conspicuously at their invidious task — and not, so it was said, without obtaining some financial advantage from it — but they could no more halt the decay of the old culture than the Imam Ahmad could keep the twentieth century out of the Yemen. The most notorious abuses, in which they were constantly involved, concerned the trade in alcohol. This was not always totally forbidden in Saudi Arabia, but the story of how it came to be so is still relatively little known and is perhaps the classic example of the swift degradation that overtook the puritanical desert life through the combined influence of easy money and modern living. In the 1930's, when foreigners began to enter Saudi Arabia for the first time in any numbers, mostly in the search for oil, ibn Saud gave them a special dispensation to import and consume alcoholic drinks. As their numbers grew, and local incomes rose, and increasing travel abroad altered the tastes and perspectives of the wealthier young Saudis, the foreigners were exposed inevitably to pressure from royal princes and other influential citizens who wished to evade their own laws. In the post-war years, especially, the illicit distribution of liquor from some foreign stocks became a commonplace. One night early in 1952, one of ibn Saud's younger sons, by then a well-known drunkard, is said to have called at the house of the British Vice-Consul in Jeddah for a drink. The Vice-Consul, seeing him a little the worse for wear already, and reasonably reluctant to have a drunken royal prince on his hands, refused him. The prince left, disgruntled, but returned a few hours later, having succeeded in his quest elsewhere, and threatened both the Vice-Consul and his wife if he was not promptly satisfied this time. When the Vice-Consul resisted he was shot to death. Ibn Saud, in the old manner, offered a life for a life — his son's head for the Briton's death. The offer was refused, but compensation for the widow was accepted, at a reputed figure of £70,000. The son was imprisoned, but was released in a general amnesty which accompanied the accession of his brother, King Saud, two years later, and when last heard of he had been re-instated in a splendid villa on the outskirts of Jeddah. Eight months after the incident, ibn Saud — shocked and disillusioned by his son's behaviour, and no doubt influenced in his last, ailing years by the views of the more fanatical *ulema* — withdrew the foreigners' concession for the import of alcohol. 'Our sharia[1] forbids liquor' said the royal decree which announced his decision, 'and considers it the mother of crises and the basis for all corruption, and having been informed that the use of it has spread in the country by the importation

[1] i.e. the Islamic law.

thereof by persons who had the facilities therefor because they were not Muslims, leading to a state of overflowing and greed among certain individuals who have been led into great corruption, therefore in order to fulfil the rules of the Islamic sharia and as a protection, we have given the explicit order to forbid the importation of liquors into our country, of all sorts and names and brands by Muslims and non-Muslims, citizens and non-citizens, and whoever violates our order shall be subject to severe consequences. If the party is a citizen and there is proof that he imported liquor, he will be lashed one hundred times and put in prison for a year, and if he is a non-Saudi, he will be deported from the country immediately by virtue of such proof.'

Poor man, he was playing Canute. The result of his decree was more, not less, corruption. Among the American community in Dhahran the home manufacture of liquor became a vital by-product of the oil industry, and the purchase of rubber tubing and enamel baths for the purpose was a necessary part of every trip to the Christian freedoms of Beirut. The experts created charcoal-flavoured 'whiskies', and juniper-flavoured 'gins', and a simple colourless distillation of date sugar known appropriately as *siddiki* (friend) was drunk by Arabs and foreigners alike. In Jeddah I found respectable bank managers with bottles of whisky buried in their window boxes and business-men who kept their gin in disinfectant bottles under the kitchen sink. Scotch whisky was obtainable in the *suk* at £15 a bottle, and among the essential qualities of the art of Jeddah party-giving, and party-going, were a reliable knowledge of which Saudis drank and which did not, and how to get the offending stuff replaced quickly by lemonade when some rare incorruptible arrived. At one western embassy, where liquor was imported through the diplomatic bag, the disposal of the empties was one of the more bizarre chores in the calendar of the Ambassador's wife. Every week she filled a canvas diplomatic sack with the bottles, laid it on the stone floor of the courtyard of their house, and beat it with a hammer until the contents were reduced to splinters and powder. These remains she poured into an innocent-looking airline satchel, which was then carried aboard the embassy's private launch in Jeddah harbour as part of the paraphernalia of a week-end picnic. Once at sea, the broken bottles were dumped overboard, safely out of sight of the Morality Committees. It was, so the Ambassador's wife assured me, astonishing how many bottles you could get into one airline bag if you only beat them hard and long enough upon a solid stone floor.

By 1958 evasion of this sort had become the rule rather than the exception in both Jeddah and Dhahran, where most of the money, and the foreigners, were accumulated; and I had no doubt that even then the example of these two cities was creeping swiftly through the country. Superficially, Jeddah still looked more like the old Arabia than the new. Ten years earlier its old mud wall had been pulled down, and the rubble had filled the foundations of a new pier, but the dhows were still becalmed upon the glassy harbour, and the heavy, timeless smell of every Arabian seaport lay like a hot poultice over the waterfront — an unwashed, sour-sweet compound of dung and rotting fish, sweat and dust and the sea. Behind the harbour was the crumbling, drowsy, Turkish town that Lawrence described forty years earlier, when he led the warriors of Sharif Husain in their revolt against the Turks. Within the circle of asphalt road that had replaced the old wall it was as crumbling and drowsy as ever. The tall, grey, mud-and-coral houses leaned in weary intimacy across the unkempt alleys, their bleached walls veiled from top to bottom in the intricate lattice-work of harem balconies where the women sat in purdah, seeing but unseen. There, in the heat of day, the dogs lay panting in the dust, the soft shuffle of sandalled feet died in the still air, and the time was always yesterday. But outside this closed circle of the past, the dissolution of the present was beginning. Released from the bond of its old wall, Jeddah was spreading in a disordered fantasy of Riviera mansions and concrete palaces, lean-to workshops and abandoned motor-cars; and where lately only camel tracks had led off across the desert to the holy places of Islam, modern highways and motor buses now carried the pilgrims to Mecca and Medina.

As the Ramadhan fast ended, and the succeeding feast of Id al Fitr began, I saw the lights go on for the first time in a new café on the waterfront. Jeddah had seen nothing like it in its life — a fashionable, sparkling, vaguely Venetian sort of place, with floodlit fountains and bright umbrellas and coloured fairylights above the black lagoon. 'Al Montazah Welcomes You' said a sign in English; and a giant Coca-Cola bottle winked in neon glory above the gate. The fountains, alas, would not work, and the ornamental fish pool had sprung a disastrous leak, leaving phosphorescent corpses to decorate its sides. The owner did not know to the nearest hundred how many customers he could seat at his tables, nor the number of waiters they would require; and the times of opening and closing had been left to Allah to decide. 'Ma'aleesh!' said the owner, 'Tomorrow we will see!' 'Insha'allah!' his white-robed customers gravely replied, 'Truly we are content.' But truly also, yet scarcely knowing it, they were in the middle of a spiritual holocaust.

9

The Challenge of Dhahran

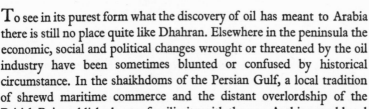

To see in its purest form what the discovery of oil has meant to Arabia there is still no place quite like Dhahran. Elsewhere in the peninsula the economic, social and political changes wrought or threatened by the oil industry have been sometimes blunted or confused by historical circumstance. In the shaikhdoms of the Persian Gulf, a local tradition of shrewd maritime commerce and the distant overlordship of the British Raj established some familiarity with the non-Arabian world and even — in places like Kuwait and Bahrain — a sense of comparative sophistication, long before oil was discovered there. In towns like Jeddah there was a history of urban settlement and a tradition of Turkish administration to obscure the direct impact of modern wealth upon the old ways of the desert. But in Dhahran before oil there was nothing except Arabia's own nomadic life. This was an Arabian *tabula rasa* where the confrontation was absolute and uninhibited between the international culture of the oil industry and the introverted ways of the desert.

In 1938, when the first oil well in Saudi Arabia was brought in at Dammam, a few miles away, there was nothing at Dhahran to speak of except sand. Dammam was a small Arab village, and on the coast nearby a few mud huts and a dhow or two comprised Al Khoba, ARAMCO'S first Gulf port. At Ras Tanura, twenty miles to the north, where a massive refinery and the main loading facilities were built later, there was only a sand spit. Now in these four places there are at least 150,000 Arabs, and virtually every one of them over the age of twenty has had his life transformed by oil. The younger ones have simply grown up with the new life — and are already seeking tentatively to transform that, in their turn.

Dhahran itself, where 4,000 Americans live in the ARAMCO Senior Staff compound, is the heart and symbol of this extraordinary process. The compound is much more than a typical American small town, as some casual observers have described it. Nor is it just the *suburbia deserta* of the local wits. It is rather the apotheosis of American small town and suburban life, far more perfect than any American reality, full of the sanitized promise of twentieth-century wealth. It exhibits all the stock features of American life except a tavern and a church. Both these are forbidden under the Wahhabi laws, but are surreptitiously replaced by home-brewed liquors and a private chapel in the house of a company chaplain who calls himself a 'teacher'. There are serve-yourself groceries and soda-fountain bars. The Rolling Hills Country Club is down the road and the baseball park is round the corner. There is the smell of charcoal-broiled T-bone steaks and french fried potatoes in the restaurant. There is milk for lunch, supper at six o'clock, and lemon-and-meringue pie on the cafeteria counters; and there is everywhere the hiss of air conditioning and the bottle of pine deodorant standing in the corner of the room. This is the American way of life under glass, as it were, as polythene-wrapped and flavourless as the frozen hamburgers at the local Rendezvous Club.

But for the people among whom this functional machine has been created it is a force of enormous vitality. Besides being immensely rich and sanitary, it is also an open society, where a Harvard Law School graduate is the next-door neighbour of a Texas driller, and rigid social hierarchies are anathema. In the compound there are no rich and no poor, none privileged and none deprived. The Americans are not altogether free from patronage towards the Arabs with whom they work, nor is race consciousness always absent — the racialism of some Texans has caused trouble more than once in Arabian oil-fields — but they seem generally freer from assumptions of superiority based on class or rank than are British expatriates in comparable situations. The British approach is institutional, founded like so much of British society upon definitions of status and authority. The American approach tends to be fluid and dynamic. If it lacks coherence it can achieve more vigour. Combined here with vast wealth and modern technology it has accomplished in the last twenty years a social and economic miracle.

Within ten years of the end of the war, when ARAMCO began serious exploitation of their pre-war oil strikes, the company had trained some 30,000 Saudi Arabs in every sort of technical skill. In twenty years illiteracy among the company's local recruits dropped from 95 per cent to somewhere near 20 per cent. Several hundred native born Saudis and naturalised Arabs from elsewhere showed their competence as supervisors and foremen, and several score reached — and some have already left for other jobs — the Senior Staff grade that was once reserved for Americans and Europeans.

Disease around Dhahran has been reduced, water supplies provided, agriculture stimulated, and new imported foods have widened local diets as much as they have maintained the accustomed standards of American homes. With Saudi pay packets averaging more than £500 a year, the mud hut villages of Dammam and Al Khoba have blossomed beside the model uniformity of the Dhahran compound into small-town America, with drug stores, shoe shops, summer suits and candies. The whole complex now seems not merely unrelated to the immediate Arabian past, but almost a flat denial that any past ever existed. Between these modern towns and the world in which Abdul Aziz ibn Saud lived most of his life, the only obvious sign of continuity is the brisk trade with American residents in the Arabian curio shops, selling 'antiques' from a past that collapsed only twenty years ago but has now disappeared physically from this district almost as completely as the eighteenth century in England or the Indian culture in America.

It needs no great insight to suggest that such radical social and economic changes cannot remain unaccompanied for long by equivalent political adjustments. The only questions are what form will these take and how will they be achieved? One way of achieving them is by agitation from below — and that, in a small way, has already begun. There have been several strikes among oil workers and others in the Dhahran district in recent years, and in the summer of 1964 the Saudi Government accompanied a sudden spate of arrests there with public denunciations of 'communists' who were seeking to spread 'a subversive creed originated by a vile Jew' in the land sacred to Islam.[1] How many of those detained were really communists is another matter. No doubt a few of them were, for communists in Aden and Bahrain joined with others from Saudi Arabia not long before these arrests to create something called the 'Union of Democratic Forces in the Arabian Peninsula'. But many were probably only critics of the regime who could find no outlet for their views except underground agitation, and all were saluted by the Egyptian press at the time as 'nationalist opponents of Faisal's feudalist regime'.

This accolade from Cairo suggests that in Saudi Arabia, as elsewhere, the internal spokesmen of political change from below cannot easily be separated from those who seek to provoke changes from outside. The chief of these is certainly Egypt. Although President Nasser's open attacks on Saudi Arabia have been sporadic, dictated by the constantly shifting patterns of the Arab alliances, the tacit challenge of his revolution and his leadership has been unrelenting, and more threatening so

---

[1] *The Guardian*, August 4th, 1964.

far than any purely indigenous Saudi movement. Except during the Suez crisis, when the Saudis stood up to be counted with Nasser like practically every other Arab in the world, Nasser's greatest moments of political triumph have often been those of deepest anxiety for the Saudis. In 1958, as we have seen, they were badly shaken when Nasser seemed about to carry all before him in the Arab world, and Faisal for the first time assumed some of the powers of his brother, King Saud. But the crisis then was short-lived, and, as the drive towards Arab unity and nationalist revolution shuddered to a disillusioned halt in the following years, Saud took heart again and removed Faisal from his new office. He was not re-instated until immediately after the Yemen revolution, when the same threats to Saudi security took, suddenly and unexpectedly, a far more potent form. Within a week or two of the Sanaa coup and the arrival of the first Egyptian troops in the Yemen, in September 1962, three Saudi Air Force pilots defected to the Egyptians, four rebellious younger brothers of the King flew from Beirut to Cairo to embrace President Nasser's leadership, and artillery had to be posted protectively outside the King's palace in Riyadh. Under pressure, from his frightened family and friends, Saud disappeared again from public life, as he had done in 1958, and recalled Faisal to the post of Prime Minister.

This time the Saudi regime seemed to be backed against a wall in a fight to the death. In the six years that had elapsed since the first serious Egyptian challenge, the dissolution of the old Arabian life had been accelerated by increasing prosperity; and if revolution could come to the backward kingdom of the Yemen, where money had never had much chance to erode the old structure, it seemed sensible to suppose that it was now more likely to spread to its wealthy neighbour. Certainly the Egyptians appeared to think so, and, as their troops landed in the Yemen to establish their first foothold in Arabia for over a century, a good many other people hoped, or feared, for the same thing. From Sanaa there came hints of a 'United Republic of Arabia' that would bring revolution and justice to the entire peninsula; from Cairo there were calls for revolt against all royal tyranny; from the United States there were deprecatory douches of cold water upon Egyptian hopes, and gestures of support for the Saudi regime. When the Saudis struck back by supporting the Yemeni royalists, the Egyptians attempted to carry the war into their territory with bombing raids beyond the Yemen frontier, and as late as four months after the Sanaa coup they dropped arms and ammunition by parachute along roads north of Jeddah, apparently in the hope of inspiring a rising there that would exploit the old dislike of the people of the Hejaz for the conquering Saudis of Najd. But no rising took place, and as the Yemen revolution degenerated into civil war, with the country pulled and pummelled between tribal conflict and Egyptian occupation, the Saudis regained their poise again, confident that impatient revolutionaries could now see in the Yemen the dangers of going too far, too fast.

King Saud, indeed, grew rather too confident, and on his return from an apparently cordial meeting with Nasser in Cairo, early in 1964, he tried once more to take back from Faisal the reins of power. It was his last attempt to re-assert the authority his father had left him. On March 13th he sent his brother a letter demanding restitution of his kingly rights, and several of his sons distributed leaflets in Riyadh calling on the Army and the National Guard to rise against Faisal in support of the 'legitimate ruler'. Faisal summoned the chief *ulema* and elders of the royal family to consider the King's challenge. They declared, as he had expected, against Saud; and, although the King at first tried to reject their verdict, they issued a decree on March 30th naming Prince Faisal as Viceroy, with sole responsibility for the conduct of the kingdom's affairs. By the same decree they halved Saud's annual allowance from the privy purse, abolished his separate *diwan*, or royal cabinet — which had been a constant source of friction with Faisal's own ministers — brought the Royal Guard under the control of the Minister of Defence instead of the King's personal command, and absorbed his personal bodyguard into the Interior Ministry. Seven of the King's sons were also discharged from official positions, including one who was Governor of Mecca. Saud was virtually deposed, and the elevation of Faisal to the throne the following November was little more than a formality.

The conflict between the two brothers was one of principle as well as personality. It was not just that Faisal was the more able and determined man: he was also — which is not necessarily the same thing — more far-sighted. While Saud stood simply but ineffectively for the retention of the chiefly prerogatives that his father had exercised in his desert kingdom, Faisal represented a rational response to the new economic and political pressures. He was no revolutionary. On the contrary, he was, and is, a conservative by temperament, and an austere and devout Muslim who still begins every speech with enough salutations to God and Muhammad to do credit to a Wahhabi hot gospeller. His policies include few overt concessions to democracy, socialism, Nasserism or the wilder dreams of Arab unity. Like Saud's, they are directed essentially to the preservation of both his family and the state; but he is shrewd enough to see that they can only succeed through intelligent adaptation, not by standing pat. He is, therefore, the embodiment of a third response to the challenge of Dhahran — not agitation from below, nor subversion from outside, but reform guided from above. The significance of the decree of March 30th, 1964, which confirmed his supreme power in Saudi Arabia, lay in the recognition of that challenge and the acceptance of that response by the elders of the biggest and most influential of all the Arabian states. Six years earlier the same challenge had been sighted, but the response had been half-hearted, and the necessary policies were soon suspended. From 1964 onwards, further suspension seemed impossible. The Saudi regime was committed henceforth to forestalling revolution by instigating its own reforms.

When Faisal became Prime Minister for the second time, after the Yemen rebellion, Saudi Arabia was not much changed, administratively or politically, from the way he had found it during his first curtailed essay in office. It was solvent again — indeed, richer than ever — for after the 1958 budget had set the pattern of financial control Saud had never been able to return unhindered to his haphazardly open-handed ways. But it was still self-enclosed, wrapped like a mummy in its ancient habits. Faisal's first acts in the urgent atmosphere of the autumn of 1962 brushed some of these bandages away. Immediately, he revealed a more extrovert attitude than any Saudi ruler had shown before by opening the country's doors to practically anyone who wished to go there. Unprecedented press conferences were held in Riyadh, and business-men, technicians, diplomatists and journalists began to penetrate corners of the country that until then even an explorer like the late St. John Philby, for all his personal friendship with Abdul Aziz ibn Saud, had scarcely visited in a lifetime of endeavour. The holy cities of Mecca and Medina remained closed to the Christian interloper; but on at least one occasion in 1963 the Anglican Archbishop in Jerusalem was seen in transit at Jeddah airport wearing his purple surplice and gold cross with never a Wahhabi eyebrow lifted in his direction.

The misuse of power by the religious police was one of Faisal's early targets. With the characteristic knack of a radical conservative for leading his people backwards into the future, he disguised his intentions with some splendid Saudi gobbledygook. 'Immediate steps' would be taken, he announced, 'to improve the conditions of Benevolence and Anti-Abomination Societies to enable them to achieve the sublime aims for which they were instituted and to uproot the causes of abomination from the hearts of the people.'[1] Which meant, when translated into

---

[1] Policy statement, November 6th, 1962, reproduced in *Prince Faisal Speaks*, published by Saudi Arabian Government.

action, that the religious police had to do rather less intimidating and rather more persuading in seeking to enforce observance of the Prophet's laws. Less bigotry was appropriately accompanied by more education. Within 12 months, the Government's spending on education had been increased by 15 per cent and expenditure on girls' schools in particular had been doubled, although it was only three years since Faisal, in the final months of his first spell in office, had been forced to call out the army to open the country's first girls' school against the violent protests of Wahhabi traditionalists.

Communications, health services and municipal development were all allotted more money than before, but, in spite of the Egyptian military presence in the Yemen, defence got less. Plans were drafted for a new telephone service, for port extensions, for new road and water surveys, and — in that Saudi gobbledygook again — 'because His Majesty's Government believes that the economic, commercial and social development which has prevailed in our society during recent years, still lacks organisation,'[1] Saudi Arabia's first commercial law was prepared to replace the obsolete prohibitions of the *sharia*.

The action which most caught the fancy of the rest of the world, however, was the abolition of slavery. In the Yemen this had been one of the first reforms announced by the revolutionaries, and Faisal was evidently determined that, in a matter emotionally so crucial to Arabia's contemporary image in the world, he was not going to be outbid by his neighbours. His father had, in fact, begun the legal process of abolition in 1936, with a decree prohibiting traffic in slaves; but slavery as an institution had not been outlawed, and the temptation to continue the traffic illegally had often proved irresistible — as the British revealed in the dispute over Buraimi, when Saudi slave traders operated there in the early 1950's. Goaded now by a greater challenge than his father ever knew, Faisal used his first policy statement of 1962 to announce total abolition.

'It is known that the Moslem Sharia urges the manumission of slaves. It is also known that slavery in modern time lacks many of the stipulations imposed by Islam for the justification of slavery. The Saudi state has, ever since its inception, faced the problem of slavery and taken gradual steps towards its abolition. . . . Now the Government finds the time opportune for the total abolition of slavery and the manumission of slaves. It will compensate those who deserve compensation.'[2]

A few months later a terse announcement from Riyadh stated that all slaves in the central region of Saudi Arabia had been bought by the

[1] and [2] Policy statement, op. cit.

Government and given their freedom. At a price of £1,785,000 for 1,682 slaves,[1] they cost the Government rather more than £1,000 a piece, which was a good deal more than any slave-owner would have paid for them in the first place. A strong boy or girl in the Buraimi market, so I am told, rarely cost more than £300. But the Saudi treasury could afford the money, and no doubt Faisal thought it better to compensate the owners handsomely and secure their willing co-operation than to be mean and court their displeasure.

It is a mistake, I think, to see this downfall of slavery simply as a moral victory of right over wrong, or as no more than a frightened Saudi response to the revolutionary promptings of the Yemen. The moral condemnation of slavery was a western import into Arabia, and had not been strongly felt there except when enforced by British power. The Yemeni prompting was important in determining the timing of the Saudi decree but it was not its exclusive *raison d'être*. In the most general sense the Saudi action revealed a realistic, if somewhat belated, recognition of the fact that the new economic and social environment made slavery as much of an anachronism as the absence of a commercial law. In the old desert world of Arabia, where individual freedom was often valued above all else by the nomadic tribesmen, the enslavement of another group was necessary for many elementary social tasks — just as it was in Athens, for that matter, where a great city of freemen was built on the backs of slaves in the Lavrion silver mines. But when the tribesmen themselves began to surrender some of their freedom for the security of a steady job and the temptation of a good wage, slavery became superfluous. Particularly since the great oil rush began in Arabia a genuine alternative to slavery has existed for the first time for both masters and slaves. For the slaves, the oilfields have offered work and good wages as well as freedom to replace the old security of bondage. For the masters there has been money enough to pay for other and often better forms of service. And for the Saudi Government, we may add, there was money enough to pay generously for the slaves' release. In this context the formal abolition of slavery in Saudi Arabia is as much another response to the challenge of Dhahran as a moral or political triumph.

In spite of such responses, however, not much change was immediately visible in the outward aspect of Saudi Arabia when I visited the country again at the end of 1963. Faisal had then enjoyed 15 months of power, and was plainly making a sustained and disciplined effort to open his country's windows to the modern world, but when I landed at Dhahran airport from Bahrain one morning, the old, introverted spirit

[1] *Daily Telegraph*, August 18th, 1963.

of Arabia hit me in the face once more, like a wet cloth. The day was Friday, and the gloom was as intense as ever. The airport was empty, save for a couple of surly officials, two or three misguided souls like myslf who had chosen that day to disturb their Wahhabist contemplations, and a villainous little man with three days' stubble who misread my health documents and insisted upon stabbing me with a cholera needle that was both painfully blunt and alarmingly tarnished. My hotel was like a tomb and besides water there was nothing to drink but the usual sticky sweet things and a non-alcoholic concoction from Denmark, got up temptingly in green bottles and gold foil to look like lager, and tasting infuriatingly like stale lemonade. The clocks showed, as I had remembered, three or four different times, and my futile attempts to make a few local telephone calls revealed that Arabian *Ma'aleesh* Time was still the only one that really mattered. The women, to judge by their absence from public view, were still in purdah; and the only person from whom I could extract more than a few disgruntled words all day was a Dutch airline official who sunnily informed me that after eighteen months in Dhahran he now knew what life imprisonment must be like.

And yet the changes were there all right. To revert to that Johnsonian image — however unfortunate it may seem in the Arabian context, where dogs are held in some contempt — the dogs were walking on their hind legs all over the place. Instead of waiting for a week to get permission to fly from Dhahran to Jeddah, I simply bought a ticket and boarded the appropriate aeroplane. Instead of twelve different officials taking a week to produce my exit visa, four officials managed the job in only two-and-a-half days. Nobody ever asked about my camera, or objected to its use; and in spite of the law prohibiting representations of the human form, children's dolls and ornamental plaster busts and statues were displayed in shop windows, American magazines and paper backs with lurid covers were available to all comers, and picture postcards of Saudi tribesmen — and even of their women — were on sale in the hotels. Whisky was now smuggled so efficiently that the price on the black market had dropped from £15 to £7 a bottle; and try as they might, the religious police no longer seemed able to enforce the closure of every shop and business for the five prescribed occasions of prayer each day. Even on Fridays, I discovered in Jeddah, a European could usually slip beneath the half-drawn shutters and find the shopkeeper ready to serve Mammon as well as Allah.

Not exactly a great leap forward, you may say. Yet in Saudi terms all these changes implied a daring departure from the norms of tribal authority and medieval religiosity. There are those who still think the departure altogether too daring — like the *ulema* who protested to Faisal about the women announcers on Mecca Radio. But the oil of Dhahran and the revolution in the Yemen have given them their answer. It is, of course, still possible that what happened in the Yemen in 1962 may yet happen in Saudi Arabia: a regime that could not rely on its Air Force officers and its royal princes then may not be able to rely on its Army colonels and its under-secretaries in, say, another five years time. But it is virtually certain that if revolution did come to Saudi Arabia in the foreseeable future, the aftermath would be even more confused than it has been in the Yemen. Saudi Arabia, like the Yemen, is ill-adapted to revolutionary coups — and for the same reasons, only more so. With a population less than half the size of London's, scattered over an area as big as Western Europe, a successful coup would be difficult to accomplish even with an efficient central administration to direct it and a large and coherent army to enforce it. Saudi Arabia, in spite of its recent changes, has neither. Its civil power is still split into thirds, between the royal seat in Riyadh, the Foreign Ministry, diplomatic missions and commercial houses in Jeddah, and the vital oilfields in Dhahran. Its bureaucracy is still overblown with shaikhly relatives and retainers in a happy conspiracy of nepotism, and is painfully far from being efficient. The Saudi regular army is only 16,000 strong, and, although the 4,000 troops of the Royal Guard were added to it after the deposition of King Saud, the two together remain separately administered from the Beduin territorial, or 'White Army,' which is a tribal force of 20,000 men recruited especially as a loyal instrument of the ruling house. Whatever revolutionary aspirations some of the budding young Nassers may nurse in either of these forces they are unlikely to have the power or the cohesion to put them into effect without clashing with each other and meeting resistance across the length and breadth of the peninsula. The likeliest outcome of any *coup*, therefore, would be the swift disintegration of the Saudi state.

In these circumstances, President Nasser ought to view any prospect of a Yemeni-style *coup* in Saudi Arabia with genuine alarm. That is not to say that he will do so. It is conceivable that he is as ill-informed about the situation there as he appears to have been about the Yemen; and in any case the Saudi regime remains undeniably the richest and most obvious target for the sort of nationalist and socialist revolution which he has so often advocated throughout the Arab world. But if the Yemeni model is anything to go by, a Saudi insurrection at this stage would involve Egyptian troops in a war they would stand little chance of winning, and that might easily end in Nasser's own destruction.

King Faisal, on the other hand, has been given *carte blanche* to avert such disasters, and with his programme of reform and development he has made a fairly promising start. But a dilemma familiar to all reformers, especially in the undeveloped world, is already visible: by speeding the reforms, he may hasten the revolution. As the Crown Prince al-Badr discovered in the Yemen, every new road that is built, every new school opened, every new arms agreement concluded with a foreign power, every government department prodded into greater efficiency, means that an attempted *coup* will have more chance of success. In short, Faisal must ask, if the lid is loosened, will it not blow off? Perhaps it will, one day; but probably not yet. And anyway, if the lid is always screwed down tight, an eventual explosion only becomes more certain. So, inevitably (because there is no real alternative) yet hesitantly (for fear of the unknown future) the transformation of Saudi life begins.

The dissolution of the old culture is already far advanced, and nothing can restore it. I noticed on my last visit that the old town of Jeddah had almost disappeared. The mud walls and latticed balconies of the Turkish houses that were still intact six years earlier had decayed into dust and matchwood, and the streets were deserted by all except the panting dogs and a few old, bewildered men. Whole sections of the town had been destroyed completely, and where the houses were still standing, confronting the bulldozed spaces, the wreckers had revealed the intimate details of yesterday's veiled life. Secret cubby-holes were exposed; the blackened walls of kitchens that had never known daylight were bleaching in the harsh sun, and the lovely harem balconies where the ladies had sat discreetly only a year or two before had collapsed into the alley-ways like old, grey tea chests. Around this now devastated core, the new suburbs and shopping streets of Jeddah looked neater than before, less crazily incongruous and brazenly rich; while through the dusty corpse of the old town a new two-lane highway cleaved like an axe-stroke, with fashionable young merchants from the bazaar scudding along it in their Cadillacs and Mercedes to hit the road for Mecca.

At least, you will say, the Holy City is still there — Mecca the blessed, as the faithful have it, inviolate as ever from the infidel's touch. But the Mecca the Saudis will reach eventually, through reform or revolution, will not be the one Muhammad knew, nor will its ways be those of the puritan Wahhabis who ruled so much of Arabia for so long with their swords and self-denial. For better or worse, slowly but surely, the challenge of Dhahran will see to that.

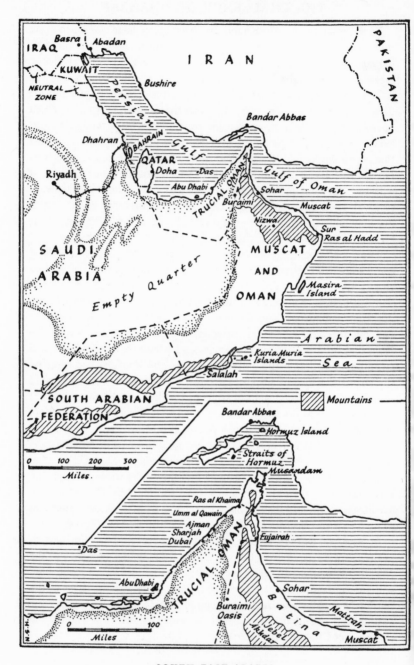

SOUTH-EAST ARABIA

10

The Last of the Raj

Every New Year's morning the British Political Resident in Bahrain has a garden party. True to the Indian traditions implicit in his title, however, he calls it a *durbar*; and although few of his guests are aware of the fact nowadays, they are invited by tradition on this occasion not to celebrate the birth of the year, but to honour the memory of Queen Victoria, proclaimed Empress of India on this day in the year 1877.

This anachronism is not altogether as absurd as it may seem, for there is a good deal of the Victorian imperial system, as well as the Victorian imperial flavour, still clinging to the little territories of the Persian Gulf over which the Political Resident exerts — or attempts to exert — his sway. Like his title, and his duties, they are relics of the Indian administration which operated in the Gulf throughout the nineteenth century and the first half of the twentieth, until India gained her independence in 1947. With him, therefore, they constitute the last, ghostly hangover of the British Raj, and their continuance in the post-imperial world has produced a situation rich in anomaly and anachronism.

Between the Shaikhdom of Kuwait and the Sultanate of Muscat and Oman, the Resident's little empire stretches the whole length of the Gulf and beyond through eleven separate states and nearly 1,000 miles, from the borders of Iraq to the coasts of the Indian Ocean. Some of the richest and some of the poorest states in the world are in varying degrees in his care. Between them they muster scarcely a million people — rather less than the city of Birmingham — and of these a half is claimed by Muscat and Oman and another third by Kuwait. The remaining nine are among the smallest — although one or two of them are still among the richest — territories in the world.

None of them is a colony, nor even a protectorate, of Britain. Both Kuwait and Muscat and Oman are fully independent states by every standard of international law. Yet all accept, by precedent or agreement,

141

some kind of British protection, and it is the principal role of the Political Resident to symbolise and when necessary discharge this traditional British responsibility. To assist him he has four Political Agents who report directly to him — one in Bahrain, one in Qatar, and two to look after the seven little shaikhdoms of the Trucial Coast. These nine states are known as 'British-protected' by virtue of a series of mostly unwritten defence obligations assumed by the British and Indian Governments in the nineteenth century. In Muscat, however, to signify the Sultan's independent status, there is a British Consul-General who does not always or necessarily report directly to the Political Resident in Bahrain, yet who accepts the Resident as his immediate superior officer on the spot; and it is part of the Resident's regular duties to visit Muscat and Oman although he is not formally accredited to the Sultan. In Kuwait, the Resident has had no diplomatic or political standing since 1961, when by agreement with Britain the state exchanged its old 'protected' status for formal independence, and the Political Agency which had formerly reported to the Resident in Bahrain was replaced by an Embassy, with an Ambassador responsible directly to London. At the same time, however, Britain formally agreed to defend Kuwait if requested to do so by the Kuwait Government, and the Resident, as chairman of the British Military Co-ordinating Committee for the Persian Gulf, is responsible for the discharge of this military function. As colleagues on the Committee and commanders in the field, the Resident has the senior British Naval, Army and Air Force officers of the Persian Gulf; and behind them stands the full, if somewhat faded, panoply of the Middle East Command H.Q. in Aden.

The Resident is, therefore, a very odd bird. Part diplomatist, part political adviser, part military commander, he seems on the whole nearer to a colonial governor than to most ordinary ambassadors. Yet he has few of the real internal powers of a governor. In Kuwait and Muscat he has none at all, and in the other states virtually his only effective power nowadays is that of dispensing justice through his Agents for all non-Muslim foreigners who would otherwise run foul of the Islamic courts which are still the basis of legal administration throughout the Gulf. Unlike the British Agents in the Aden Protectorate, he and his men have no status as advisers to the local rulers on their internal affairs. They may, and do, cajole them. They sometimes attempt to bully them. But there is nothing on paper, or in precedent, to suggest that any of the rulers need take notice of what the Resident says except in relation to piracy, the slave trade, foreign affairs and defence. These are the matters covered by the treaties and precedents of the so-called 'trucial system' on whose old nineteenth-century bones Britain hangs what is called her 'special position' in the Persian Gulf today.

Here, for a moment, we had better stop to notice a geographical fact and an historical paradox both of which are often overlooked in discussions of that position nowadays. The geographical fact is that insofar as Britain's position in the Gulf is 'special' it is confined now entirely to the Arab shore. And the historical paradox is that this implies a direct reversal of the old order of importance between the two shores. For nearly three centuries, after the East India Company established its first factories in the Gulf, at Bandar Abbas and Bushire, the Persian coast was more important to Britain than the Arab side. Persia supplied trade when Arabia offered nothing but piracy; and Persia, also, was a potential back door to India when Arabia seemed little but a barren cul-de-sac. It was only in 1948, after India was abandoned, that the Political Resident in the Gulf moved his headquarters from Bushire to Bahrain; and only about then did the Arab shore become intrinsically and overwhelmingly important with the discovery and exploitation of its massive oil reserves. Until then, the handful of petty shaikhdoms scattered upon the barren backside of Arabia, no thicker than the hairs on a rhino's hide, had been simply India's farthest outposts; and as far as most British officials were concerned they were treated with corresponding — and understandable — indifference, except when they impinged on the wider affairs of empire.

After an early flirtation with the Sultan of Muscat at the start of the Napoleonic wars, Britain's first interest in the Arab shore was provoked by the activities of the tribes of the 'pirate coast' — stretching from Qatar to the Straits of Hormuz — who were organised by the puritan Wahhabis of the interior in the first years of the nineteenth century into a maritime confederacy for systematic plunder in the Gulf. By 1810 the Government of Bombay felt obliged to send an expedition against them, and by 1820 a second was needed to protect the lawful commerce of the seas. The result was a 'General Treaty with the Arab Tribes' signed in 1820, which declared with splendid simplicity, 'There shall be a cessation of plunder and piracy by land and sea on the part of the Arabs who are parties to this contract, for ever.' Among the Arab contracting parties were the forebears of all the present rulers of the Trucial Coast and the ruling family of Bahrain.

But poverty and traditional rivalries among the tribes proved too much for this simple document, and before 15 years had gone piracy was once more the scourge of the lower Gulf. This time, the British

Resident, Captain Samuel Hennell, adopted a subtler approach by persuading the ruling shaikhs to accept a maritime truce among themselves for the duration of each annual pearling season in the Gulf. As long as the tribes concentrated on pearling, Captain Hennell assumed, they would not plunder — and with luck they would make enough money from the season's pearls to make piracy in the off-season unnecessary. Gradually the shaikhs were convinced by results, and the annual truces were extended, first to cover the full year instead of just the pearling season, then to ten years, and finally, in 1853, to 'perpetuity' with a 'Treaty of Maritime Peace' by which the shaikhs undertook to observe 'a peaceful maritime truce . . . between ourselves and between our successors respectively for evermore'.

This maritime peace was the foundation of the trucial system and the cause of the eventual translation of the 'pirate coast' into the Trucial Coast of today. Two things about it are important still. Firstly, it involved Britain in keeping the inter-tribal peace at sea, thereby committing her in practice to the defence of each of the shaikhdoms against its enemies; secondly, the truce required no specific action by Britain or the rulers in their domestic affairs. Territorially, in fact, Britain shunned all ambition as long as the maritime peace was maintained. The same principles were implicit also in the series of anti-slavery agreements which Britain forced upon the Arabian rulers at about this time. From a clause in the general treaty of 1820, forbidding the kidnapping of men, women and children from Africa or elsewhere, to a treaty with the Sultan of Muscat in 1873, abolishing the slave trade throughout the Sultanate and declaring the import of slaves to be illegal, it was the slave traffic rather than slavery as an institution that Britain sought to suppress. True, she did secure for her Agents ashore the right to manumit any slaves who applied to them for freedom, but to make a frontal attack on the problem by requiring the release of all slaves in the shaikhdoms would have involved Britain in a degree of territorial control that she was unwilling, and would probably have been unable, to assume. She preferred to hope — somewhat in vain, as it turned out — that her navy could strangle the supply of slaves and cause the institution of slavery to wither and die in consequence.

Even towards the end of the nineteenth century, when the strategic defence of India against the probes of the other great powers became paramount in British thinking about the Gulf, the governments of the day continued to avoid territorial responsibilities there as far as possible. Instead, they signed a further series of agreements giving Britain exclusive control of the foreign relations of the Arab rulers, thus converting naval supremacy into formal diplomatic hegemony. Nearly all these exclusive agreements date from the last quarter of the century, when — as someone at the time remarked — if a German sneezed in the Persian Gulf it was regarded as an attempt to shake the foundations of the British Empire. It was a particularly powerful German sneeze that caused Britain to extend her protection to Kuwait for the first time, in 1899. Until then there had been no pressing reason to include Kuwait in the British system in the Gulf. Her people were traders, not pirates, and her rulers had managed to keep other foreign powers at arm's length through most of the nineteenth century. In 1896, a new Kuwaiti ruler was specifically refused protection by the British, to whom he had appealed for help after he had secured his position by murdering the previous ruler. His subsequent negotiations with the Germans, however, changed British minds. Alarmed by the prospect that Germany might establish a terminus on the Gulf for the Berlin-Baghdad railway and dominate the whole of the Tigris-Euphrates basin, the British offered the Ruler their 'good offices' in exchange for an exclusive agreement. 'Of his own free will and desire,' the resulting document said, the Shaikh of Kuwait 'does hereby pledge and bind himself, his heirs and successors, not to receive the agent or Representative of any Power or Government at Kuwait, or at any other place within the limits of his territory, without the previous sanction of the British Government; and he further binds himself, his heirs and successors not to cede, sell, lease, mortgage or give for occupation or for any other purpose any portion of his territory to the Government or subjects of any other Power without the previous consent of Her Majesty's Government. . . .'

With this and similar exclusive agreements with the other local rulers, Britain confirmed her position by the end of the nineteenth century as the sole overlord of the Arab shore. The achievement was essentially a triumph for British naval power. Recalcitrant shaikhs were rarely pursued on shore by landing parties and no British expeditionary force of any significance set foot in eastern Arabia throughout the nineteenth century. A brusque bombardment by a sloop or two was the favourite punishment employed in these parts by the Raj — cheap, quick, and presumably convincing. There was, of course, no serious native power to challenge this form of British supremacy. The petty shaikhdoms of the coast were only occasionally touched by the Wahhabist fanaticism of the Arabian interior. Most of the time they were simply cut off from it by the desert, whose barren and apparently limitless expanse made territorial possession meaningless, and frontiers unnecessary. By nature the shaikhdoms faced seawards, towards a non-Arab world; they were the more amenable, therefore, to a non-Arab and purely seaborne discipline, such as the Raj imposed. For all these reasons the British control of the Arab shore neither required nor achieved any territorial conquest; nor did it require any landward boundaries to define its nature and extent. Above all, there was never any suggestion that Britain should assume responsibility for local government in the colonial fashion of the time. Indeed, in the absence of any economic or strategic inducement to colonial occupation of the Arabian mainland, there was every reason why Britain should avoid such responsibilities.

This policy of maritime control and territorial non-involvement was summarised by Lord Curzon, when he visited the Gulf in 1903 as Viceroy of India — the first of that title ever to do so. Appropriately, the occasion was, in its way, a naval one. To supplement their probes towards India through Persia and Afghanistan, the Russians had lately had the temerity to send the cruiser *Askold* on a tour of the Gulf. 'As the natives of the Persian Gulf then imagined that the strength of a ship depended on the number of her funnels,' a British observer commented later, 'and as the *Askold* had five, her appearance made a strong impression'.[1] The British, unfortunately, had no five-funnel vessels in the Royal Navy, so to erase the impression left by the *Askold* they sent Lord Curzon instead. Addressing a gathering of the Trucial Shaikhs on the nature of their agreements with Britain, the peripatetic Viceroy was at his most magisterial:

'Chiefs, of the relations that were thus created, and which by your own consent constituted the British Government the guardian of inter-tribal peace, there grew up political ties between the Government of India and yourselves, whereby the British Government became your overlords and protectors, and you have relations with no other power.... These engagements are binding on every one of you, and you have faithfully adhered to them. They are also binding in their reciprocal effect upon the British Government and as long as they are faithfully observed by the Chiefs, there is no fear that any one else will be allowed to tamper with your rights or liberties.... The British Government have no desire to interfere, and have never interfered in your internal affairs, provided that the Chiefs govern their territories with justice, and respect the rights of the foreign traders residing therein.'[2]

[1] J. G. Lorimer, *Gazetteer of the Persian Gulf, Oman and Central Arabia*, 2 vols., Calcutta, 1908–15, vol. I, p. 1157. This book used to be on the British Government's secret list, and is now very rare, but is freely available for consultation in the Foreign Office Library.

[2] *Existing Treaties between the British Government and the Trucial Chiefs* (1906), pp. 3–4.

In short, reject Britain's enemies, keep the peace when we are looking, and you can do what you like the rest of the time. As long as Britain's ultimate purposes were the protection of trade and the defence of India, nothing more was needed on the Arabian shores of the Persian Gulf; and for the next twenty years Britain did not attempt much more than to dot the i's and cross the t's of this existing system. She added to her domination by bringing the Shaikhdom of Qatar into the trucial system when the Turks withdrew their last garrison from Doha in 1916, and for a time she even made a protégé of ibn Saud, in return for his help against the Turks during the First World War. But the basis of British policy remained as maritime as ever. The internal affairs of the shaikh-doms continued untouched by the Raj, and their frontiers stayed undefined. Not until the 1920's was any new kind of relationship presaged between Britain and the states of the Arab shore. Three events of that period seem particularly significant now — although it is hardly likely that they were seen in the same light then — as harbingers of future trouble for Britain in the Gulf. One was the completion of a further series of agreements with the shaikhdoms, giving Britain the right to exclusive oil concessions in their territories if any oil was ever found there. The first of these was signed with the Ruler of Kuwait in 1913, when the first Persian oilfield was already in production, and the last was signed with the Sultan of Muscat ten years later. Between them they gave Britain her first potential territorial interest in eastern Arabia. A second significant event was the demarcation of Kuwait's frontiers under British auspices in 1922, which introduced the concept of a fixed frontier to these hitherto undefined territories, and implied that Britain henceforth might be committed to preserving the integrity of certain finite areas of Arabia, as well as the independence of certain coastal families or tribes. The third event was ibn Saud's conquest of the Hejaz and his subsequent recognition by Britain, in 1927, as 'King of the Hejaz and the Najd and its dependencies,' which removed him from his short-lived attachment to the trucial system and hinted at the emergence for the first time of a genuine rival power on the Arabian mainland. Taken together, these three events suggested that the maritime basis of the British system in the Gulf might not last much longer. Nor would it have done, perhaps, if oil had been as important to the British economy then as it was later, or if oil had been discovered sooner in the shaikhdoms to rivet Britain's attention upon the land at last, instead of upon the sea. But until the eve of the Second World War the only commercial strike to be made in the Gulf, outside Persia, was in Bahrain, where the smallest of all the Gulf oilfields was opened in

1932. In Kuwait, Qatar and Saudi Arabia there was no significant oil production until after the Second World War, and in the Trucial Coast and Muscat, 40 years elapsed from the day the rulers promised exclusive oil concessions to the British, until oil was discovered in their territories in the 1960's. Thus the great oil boom in the Gulf which finally lured Britain into a territorial instead of a maritime role in Eastern Arabia coincided precisely with the loss of India and the growing challenge of nationalism throughout the Middle East and the rest of the colonial world. Or, to put it another way, the need to extend the *Pax Britannica* to the Arabian mainland only arose undeniably when Britain's power to enforce peace anywhere had been irrevocably weakened. Half-a-century earlier, peace and stability might have been obtained simply by extending direct British colonial authority to the Arabian shaikhdoms. A quarter-of-a-century earlier, it might just have been possible — if anyone had foreseen the need — either to create some kind of British mandate, or to negotiate a transfer of British hegemony to the rising power of ibn Saud. By 1947 none of these courses was any longer feasible. Colonialism was ruled out by the world's new temper; and too much was at stake to contemplate any transfer of British power to Saudi Arabia, to say nothing of the fact that the British-protected shaikhs would have resisted any such disposal of their affairs with total and justifiable contempt.

Least of all was it possible for Britain to withdraw unconditionally from her obligations when at least nine of the eleven states concerned were too small and too poor to stand on their own feet in the post-war world. If some stability was to endure, therefore, the only realistic policy left for Britain was to adapt her nineteenth-century maritime system to the territorial demands of the mid-twentieth century, and accept the consequent entanglement in an unhappy web of quasi-colonial responsibility without colonial power.

Ever since India was abandoned, and the Resident moved his offices to Bahrain from the Persian shore, this has been Britain's lot in the Persian Gulf. By a series of historical and geographical accidents she has become the guardian of eleven little Arab states, but not their ruler; and while she is obliged to defend them, she has little power to change their ways or chart their destiny. She pays the piper, without being able to call the tune. Her oil is obtained from them on terms no better than anyone else's, for the exclusive oil agreements of half-a-century ago, which might once have given Britain the right to exploit nearly all the Gulf oilfields, have had no practical significance for many years. There is not a single territory in the Gulf today where a wholly British company has an exclusive concession; indeed, two thirds of the production from countries bordering the Gulf is in American, not British, hands.

Nor is there any question in the Gulf shaikhdoms, as there has been in Aden and even in the Protectorates, of directing political developments to accord with contemporary British ideas of enlightened colonialism. The shaikhdoms are, and always have been, legally self-governing, and their social, constitutional and economic development is their own affair. Much of the advice that British representatives have pressed upon them has been rejected by the rulers as unwarranted interference. The Sultan of Muscat, for example, has eagerly accepted British military and financial aid to suppress or sweeten rebel tribesmen in the mountains of Oman, but he has never allowed the British Government to supervise, or even to see, his national budget, to decide for itself what aid he really needs. The Ruler of Bahrain has been comparatively enlightened in the administration of the welfare state he inherited from his forebears, but he has firmly rejected British suggestions that he might try establishing some more representative forms of government than his own personal rule. The Shaikhs of Qatar became multi-millionaires under British protection, but they persist in grotesquely spendthrift ways to the embarrassment of every British Political Agent who tries to persuade them otherwise; and the seven rulers of the tiny Trucial Shaikhdoms, although manifestly unable to sustain their independence unaided, stubbornly object to the political cooperation that the British urge upon them in the interests of common sense and mutual survival. 'The British Government have no desire to interfere, and have never interfered in your internal affairs,' said Lord Curzon; and even in the postwar world, the rulers of the Gulf states have never let the British Government forget that fact.

These complex realities of politics in the Gulf have not often been fully understood even in Britain, and still more rarely have they been grasped elsewhere. It is easier to assume that the rulers must be British puppets, and interpret their actions accordingly. Many a British Resident and his Agents must have wished it so, for the anomalies of their real position guarantee that they endure, in my experience, about the highest rate of frustration and misunderstanding in their jobs of any members of the British Foreign Service. Most of them, in recent years, have been reasonably enlightened men, and some have come to the Gulf with high and radical reputations, anxious to make their mark by thrusting its rulers and its territories firmly into the contemporary world. But so far the system has defeated them all. A powerful historical inertia governs their every effort. The shadows of five-funnel cruisers and the ghosts of visiting Viceroys mock their wisest counsels. Willy-nilly, they must adapt themselves to a world still ruled — albeit with growing difficulty and in varying degrees — by the tenets of another age, when the Raj was great and oil had never been heard of. It is entirely appropriate, therefore, that they should still start each New Year with a genuine, Victorian *durbar*.

11

No Exit from the Gulf

The dilemma of Britain in the Persian Gulf today is rather like that of a man trapped on the sixth floor of a blazing building. If he runs down the stairs he will certainly be burned to death, and if he jumps from the window he may dash himself to death. It seems easier, therefore, for him to stay where he is and hope the fire brigade arrives before he slowly suffocates.

To translate this simile into the language of Gulf politics, we may say that Britain's main choices there are three: to head for the stairs by extending her protection of the shaikhdoms into some form of direct rule that would give her full authority to decide their short-term future; to jump from the window by withdrawing her protection and leaving the rulers to sort out their own futures as best they may; or to stay put with her present obligations and embarrassments. It is clear that the first of these is not a practical choice. Like dashing down the stairs in a burning building, it involves, so to speak, certain death, for such an extension now of British authority in the Gulf would provoke there, and elsewhere in the Middle East, just the sort of unrest that the British protection of the shaikhdoms is intended to prevent. Withdrawal, on the other hand, looks rather more tempting than leaping from a sixth-floor window, and it is seriously advocated on several grounds, both in Britain and the Middle East. Firstly, it is proposed that Britain needs to reduce her overseas military expenditure, and should anyway concentrate her forces in or near Europe. Secondly, it is suggested that the British commitments to the Gulf rulers create needless difficulties in Britain's relations with the major powers of the Arab world, especially Egypt, and that if Britain were to show herself willing to withdraw, President Nasser would have a better chance of leading his Arab colleagues into the creation of some Arab collective security arrangements that would replace the British presence in the Gulf. Thirdly, it is argued that military protection of the oilfields in the Gulf is no longer necessary, because the Arabs have as big a commercial interest as the oil companies and the consumer nations in continuing the steady flow of oil. As President Nasser once said, 'they can't drink it.' Fourthly, it is sometimes noted that the *Pax Britannica* in the Gulf has looked pretty feeble anyway, in recent years, and is now more make-believe than reality.

There is substance to all these arguments; and it is hard to imagine any British Government now that would not like to act upon them, if it could, by reducing its commitments in the Gulf. The difficulty is not the end but the means. Or, to return to the original simile for a moment, it is not that Britain does not wish to jump from the window, in preference to waiting for slow suffocation, but that she would like to think that a safety net was available to break her fall. It is when we examine the possible forms that a safety net might take, and the possible consequences of a fall without one, that a certain gloom must envelop all those who, like me, would prefer to see Britain's nineteenth-century position in the Gulf brought more into line with her contemporary loss of diplomatic and military power.

To take the second point first, the sheer enormity of what is now at stake in the Gulf must induce caution in the advocacy of any new policy there. For over a decade the Gulf region has been the world's biggest and cheapest exporter of oil, and Britain's biggest supplier in particular; and in spite of the discovery of promising new oilfields elsewhere, its importance is unlikely to diminish much over the next decade. Two thirds of the proved oil reserves of the non-communist world lie under or around the waters of the Gulf and according to estimates within the oil industry these fields will have to double their present production in ten years if they are to keep pace with the world's rising oil consumption. This is not just a matter of British concern. Although British oil companies have major interests in all the states bordering the Gulf except Saudi Arabia and Bahrain, American companies have a far higher total stake,[1] and Dutch, French, Italian, Japanese and some locally-owned companies are also participating. The destination of the oil and the distribution of the profits from it are even more international. Out of more than 350 million tons of crude oil produced in the Gulf states in 1964 — about one third of the total production of the non-communist world — half went to western Europe and the rest was shared by the Americas, Japan, India, South East Asia, Africa and Australia. To the companies and governments involved, this production was worth over £1,200 million, of which the British-protected shaikhdoms, including Kuwait, contributed one third. All the governments or rulers of the

[1] See above, p. 149.

Shaikh Rashid of Dubai

A Sharjah coffee shop

Watering a caravan in Buraimi

Omani tribesmen gathered to watch a military display

oil-producing states are committed to development programmes or personal extravagances which would be impossible to fulfil without the oil revenues, and several of the major Arab states, including Egypt, have been given a direct interest in Gulf oil production since 1962 through the Kuwait Government's Fund for Arab Economic Development, which uses Kuwaiti oil profits to finance development schemes throughout the Arab world.

What is at stake, therefore, is no longer a simple British interest, as it was throughout the nineteenth century, but the prosperity of a massive slice of the world's oil industry and the economic and social welfare of the nations and the people who depend upon it. This is sufficient, in itself, to suggest that the maintenance of a unilateral *Pax Britannica* in the Gulf is — or should be — as out of date as the Raj in India. Unfortunately, nobody so far has produced a contemporary alternative, and the difficulty of doing so seems inherent in the nature of the forces that threaten the Gulf's stability.

These derive more from the Gulf's own peculiar nature than from any long-term political plots or manœuvres. Theoretically, no doubt, there is still a Russian threat to the security of the whole region, as there used to be in the days of the Indian Empire. Militarily this is no more than a paper exercise, however, for any armed Soviet drive to the Gulf would obviously provoke a global response by the United States that would make the local *Pax Britannica* irrelevant. Politically, the Soviet threat may be more important. There have been signs in the last few years that Russia is anxious to restore her traditional sphere of influence along her southern frontiers, from Turkey to Pakistan, and the repeated tremors of political disturbance in Iran and Iraq have certainly not been devoid of Soviet influence. Since Kuwait became independent, Russia has opened an embassy there, establishing at last the sort of foothold in the Gulf that Britain successfully denied to her for over a century. But these are no more, as yet, than possible straws in the wind: they scarcely imply immediate political emergencies that Britain need be alarmed about. Much more important is the elementary fact that the Gulf itself has no natural unity. On the contrary, it is a natural line of division between the Persian and Arab cultures, with a little Indian top-dressing upon both shores. No natural focus for its disparate elements has been created among its sparse settlements, and the only unity so far imposed upon them has been provided by the diffuse overlordship of the British Raj. Among the Arab settlements, only Kuwait, Muscat and — just possibly — Bahrain are big enough and rich enough to sustain a genuine independence; yet the traditional tribal rivalries of the other shaikhdoms will not permit them to unite or federate in larger units.

At the same time, the larger states around the Gulf assert conflicting claims to the smaller territories, as we might expect when such enormous actual or potential wealth is involved and agreed international boundaries are still so few. Iraq and Saudi Arabia both lay vague claim to Kuwait's oil wealth, and Saudi Arabia and Iran each insist that Bahrain is really flesh of their flesh. Saudi Arabia maintains her claim to the Buraimi oasis on the Trucial Coast, and has not forsworn her support of the rebels in Oman against the Sultan of Muscat. Between Iraq and Iran, for good measure, there is a troublesome dispute over the Shatt al Arab and the neighbouring Iranian province of Khuzistan. There is also a general clash of interest between the Persians and the Arabs over relations with Israel, whose existence the Persians tacitly support; and a more personal clash has emerged since 1960 between the Shah and President Nasser over the forms and ideas of their respective social revolutions. Both of these have been imported into Gulf politics in the last few years, chiefly through Egyptian propaganda, and by the end of 1964 their repercussions had even reached the Yemen, where Iran had begun to help the royalist forces against the Egyptian troops.

In addition to these international conflicts, there are internal tensions in the Gulf shaikhdoms that are a permanent threat to peace. As oil discoveries and oil money have spread throughout the Gulf and political sensitivity has been heightened there accordingly, the shaikhdoms have seemed to respond to every shift in pan-Arab politics like the strings on a harp that quiver in unison with the notes struck on a neighbouring piano. When Arab unity is in the air in Cairo and Baghdad, murmurs of sympathetic ambition rustle through the Gulf from Kuwait to Dubai. When Israel is in the forefront of some dispute and there is noisy talk of shedding the last drop of Arab blood to restore Arab rights in Palestine, the mob may not be far from the streets in Bahrain. And when, as so often happens, all the brave Arab words dissolve in confusion and all the hopes of unity are dashed again, the states of the Gulf subside into a disillusioned peace.

All the shaikhdoms are touched by these characteristic Arab pressures in some degree, and the wealthier they become the more sensitive they are to the plucking of nationalist strings. At the other end of the spectrum, however, there is also a traditional tribal resistance to the encroachment of modern wealth and politics, often expressed in military skirmishes in the wilder parts of the Trucial Coast and Oman, as well as in the reluctance of many Gulf rulers to make social or political concessions to twentieth-century ways.

This list of international disputes and internal tensions is enough to suggest that the Gulf is potentially an arena of fairly general conflict, where even the powerful commercial incentive to keep the oil flowing might easily be overcome by natural centrifugal tendencies. So far, only the British presence in the Gulf has provided any guarantee of stability, and although this has not always worked — witness the Abadan crisis of 1951 and the Saudi refusal to export oil through Bahrain after the Suez crisis — it has operated often enough to indicate that without it there might have been more serious trouble. In the last decade, Britain has given military and diplomatic help to the Sultan of Muscat and the Shaikh of Abu Dhabi in the disputes over the Buraimi oasis and the rebellion in Oman; she has helped the Ruler of Bahrain to suppress domestic riots; she has protected Kuwait against the avowed threat from Iraq; and she has discouraged both nationalist and tribal disorders on the Trucial Coast. Of these, the most significant was the operation in Kuwait where, in 1961, Britain seemed at last to have broken out of her historical trap of responsibility without power by negotiating a new agreement making Kuwait entirely independent for the first time since 1899. All the local circumstances at the time seemed to favour a cautious British withdrawal. A shrewd ruler was in charge; a long native tradition of commerce had given the Kuwaitis a streak of political as well as financial sophistication; the frontiers of the shaikhdom had been internationally recognised for nearly 40 years; there was far more money available than in any other Gulf shaikhdom with which to buy off external jealousy and internal discontent; and a population of 300,000 was just about enough to make the place acceptable as a fully-fledged member of the United Nations and the international community.

But in spite of these advantages Kuwait did not abandon the old umbrella of British protection. A new defence agreement was negotiated, enabling the Ruler to enlist British aid against external threats; and within a week of the declaration of independence it was invoked, when the late General Kassem of Iraq revived an old Iraqi claim to Kuwait's territory. The result was ironic. For 62 years, while Kuwait was one of Britain's dependent shaikhdoms, no significant British land force had ever been summoned to its defence. Now, in the first month of its independence, nearly 6,000 British troops poured into the country to prove that Britain was still in earnest about upholding peace in the Gulf. It was a traumatic experience for everyone concerned: testing for the British, whose resources proved scarcely equal to the task; chastening for General Kassem, who was scared off; humiliating for most of the other Arab states who saw — not for the first time — an imperial power settling their domestic problems for them; disillusioning for the Kuwaitis, who had hoped to celebrate their independence in a burst of Arab joy and brotherhood; and profoundly frightening for all the other Gulf shaikhdoms, whose rulers have never since ceased to point out to advocates of their ultimate independence what nearly happened to Kuwait when she got hers.

Most discouraging of all, perhaps, was the inept performance of the Arab League in this sorry little crisis. Divided in their counsels, as usual, the League members refused at first to help the Ruler of Kuwait, who had turned to them even before he invoked his defence agreement with Britain. Then, although shamed into action by the British, and genuinely disturbed by Kassem's unilateral attempt to seize the richest of all Arab territories, the League took several weeks to produce a force of its own to replace the British troops. When the force arrived at last, nearly three months after the original Iraqi threat, it suffered an immediate and characteristic body blow through the secession of Syria from the United Arab Republic; and before six months were out it had collapsed, as first one and then another national unit was withdrawn for pressing domestic reasons. After this it was hardly surprising that the Ruler withstood persistent pressure from both inside and outside Kuwait to abrogate the British defence agreement in favour of an Arab pact: his Arab brothers, alas, had left him little option by their quarrelling and incompetence.

Whether General Kassem was serious in his threat to Kuwait has remained a mystery. His army undertook no large-scale movements at the time, and there is a strong school of thought which believes that the whole crisis was occasioned by a bluff — or at least by no more than Kassem's characteristically exalted belief that the Kuwaitis were ready to acclaim him as their liberator whenever he said the word. But whatever its purpose, there is not much doubt that his action retarded the development of Gulf politics by several years. The negotiation of Kuwait's independence was the first peaceful change in the Gulf's political structure since the end of the Indian Empire, and if it had been freely accepted by all parties it might have shown the other shaikhdoms that the British presence in the Gulf was no longer as necessary as it used to be. Instead, General Kassem's prompt and belligerent reaction seemed only to confirm that Britain was needed as much as ever; and nothing that has happened since has shifted the other rulers, or the British Government, from this view.

The conflicting international claims to the Gulf territories, and the persistent internal tensions, remain both potential menaces to peace and a barrier to any local collective security arrangements which could replace British protection. The wider conflicts between the major Arab states continue to render the Arab League ineffective as a peace-keeping force; and even if a valid *Pax Arabica* could be envisaged it is unlikely that it would be effective or acceptable without an Arab détente with Iran, which seems at the time of writing farther off than ever. Nor do the other possible alternatives to the British presence look much more encouraging. The international interest in the supply of Gulf oil has not so far produced any international interest in helping to maintain the Gulf's security. The Central Treaty Organisation, whose members have sometimes been urged to take a greater interest in Gulf affairs, is as near as makes no matter a paper structure, and there is no obvious reason, in any case, why any of its members except Iran and Britain should assume direct responsibility in the Gulf.[1] NATO, whose collective material interests in the region are greater than those of CENTO, has never shown any disposition to include preventive peace-keeping among its duties, except in relation to Russia in Europe. And since the dispute over the United Nations peace-keeping finances came to a head at the end of 1964, the U.N. has seemed a less likely force than ever to assume the mantle of the *Pax Britannica*.

It may be argued that discussion of all these possibilities so far presupposes the need for the Gulf shaikhdoms to be preserved as separate political units, and that such a concept is in itself manifestly absurd. There cannot be any long-term, abstract justification for the support of penniless places on the Trucial Coast, some of them with populations of less than 5,000 apiece, in the permanent trappings of statehood; and if there were some means of wiping them all from the map, the British umbrella might be withdrawn from the Gulf and the security of the oil supplies could be left to commercial common-sense. But it is hard to see what means exist except the alternatives of a brand-new federation of the smaller Gulf states, or the absorption of the shaikhdoms into one of the existing larger units of the Arab world. Neither of these looks practicable in the immediate future.

The jealousies of the rulers have defeated most of the efforts of the British so far to foster real cooperation in the Gulf, even on a modest scale. The nearest thing to an embryonic federation is the Council of Rulers on the Trucial Coast, which meets irregularly to discuss mutual problems; but no amount of British persuasion has convinced the seven Trucial Shaikhs that they should turn this into an effective administrative, let alone, political, instrument. Indeed, after oil was discovered

---

[1] CENTO's other members are Turkey and Pakistan.

in Abu Dhabi in 1960, the work of the Council was vitiated more than ever by the virtual withdrawal of Abu Dhabi from its affairs. In spite of his inability to spend all his new-found loot himself the Ruler of Abu Dhabi saw no reason to share a penny of it with his beggarly neighbours.

In Kuwait and Bahrain, where riches and education have produced more alert political thinking, a Gulf federation is spoken of with more enthusiasm, at least among the younger Arab generation who see the long-term difficulties of maintaining the *status quo*. But even there the obstacles have not been faced so far. Officials of the Kuwaiti Foreign Ministry assured me in 1963 that they had a draft plan in readiness for a federation of all the Gulf shaikhdoms under Kuwait's leadership; but they professed not to see what all the other shaikhdoms noted at once, that the disparity in finances and population between Kuwait and the others was so great that federation would probably be just another name for Kuwait's domination, or absorption, of the rest. Nor had they tackled with any conviction the sheer physical problems of communications throughout the sparsely peopled shores and islands of the Gulf, and the centrifugal tribalism that this inevitably has promoted.

In any case, there are surprisingly few genuine links between Kuwait and the states of the lower Gulf. In spite of being a British dependency for over sixty years, Kuwait was never really part of the trucial system that now ties Britain to the Gulf. With the Mesopotamian valley at her back she was less isolated from the rest of the Arab world than any of the other shaikhdoms, and far closer in the nineteenth and twentieth centuries to all the political movements involved in the decline of the Ottoman Empire and the rise of Arabism. Increasingly, in recent years, since oil has become Kuwait's *raison d'être*, she has looked westwards and northwards towards the principal centres of the modern Arab world in Cairo and Baghdad. The attempt to create a Gulf federation based on Kuwait could not be, in these circumstances, anything but artificial.

In Bahrain a federation of the lower Gulf acquires a slightly more realistic air — but only slightly. A common adherence to the trucial system has given all the shaikhdoms south of Kuwait a similar historical background. The income from the oil wells of Qatar and Abu Dhabi is substantial but not yet overwhelming, and would supplement the revenue from Bahrain's own small oil-field to finance social and economic development throughout the poorer states of the Trucial Coast. Bahrain's traditions of competent government and business expertise would help the less experienced territories and — an essential and characteristic argument for the Bahrainis — would surely make Bahrain the only conceivable site for a federal capital. It is precisely here, however, that the rifts begin to show again. There is no more liking in the other shaikhdoms for the idea of Bahrain as their new overlord than there is for the notion that Kuwait might dominate them; and among the ruling families, especially, there are endless cross-currents of suspicion and traditional hostility. The Ruler of Bahrain, for instance, is not on speaking terms with the Ruler of Qatar, to part of whose territory he maintains an ancient family claim; while the Ruler of Qatar has prudently married a daughter of Shaikh Rashid of Dubai, to the disgust of Shaikh Shakhbut, the Ruler of Abu Dhabi, who happens to be a neighbour of both of them. Shaikh Rashid dislikes Shaikh Shakhbut, the Ruler of Sharjah is suspicious of Shaikh Rashid, and the Shaikhs of Ajman, Fujairah, Ras al Khaima and Umm al Qawain, being the rulers of the four smallest and poorest territories of the lot, are steeped in suspicion of practically everybody.

In short, there is no realistic possibility of the present Gulf rulers coming together of their own accord in any political grouping worth talking about. There remains the prospect that Britain might somehow bully them into it; but the precedents and the circumstances for this seem equally discouraging. British political power in the Gulf, as we have seen, is severely limited, and its exercise tends to excite hostility not only among the rulers, who object to British interference in their internal affairs, but also among the nationalists within and beyond the Gulf. A British-inspired federation, indeed, would be still-born — so one Bahraini nationalist assured me — simply because Cairo would never accept it. Nor, I suspect, would Saudi Arabia without some handsome *quid pro quo*. To thrust a federation into being in spite of these hostilities would be to risk repeating the British experiences in Malaysia and South Arabia, where the creation of federations as a means to colonial disengagement resulted in greater British military commitments than before. It is a course Britain may yet feel forced to attempt in the Gulf for lack of any alternative, but the chances of success seem to me less than they were in the other two cases, and the penalties of failure potentially higher.

Only one further obvious possibility remains — the absorption of most of the smaller shaikhdoms by one of the large states bordering the Gulf. This immediately raises the problems of Iranian-Arab and inter-Arab rivalries that most need to be solved. For Kuwait to be absorbed by Iraq, for instance, would be no more acceptable to Saudi Arabia now than it was in 1961, nor to Egypt, either, for that matter, unless Iraq were also politically united with Egypt. For Bahrain to be taken over by Iran would be unacceptable to all the Arabs, and for Saudi Arabia to annex it instead would be unacceptable to Iran. To hand over the shaikhdoms of Qatar and the Trucial Coast to Saudi Arabia would displease Egypt; and their rulers, in any case would resist to the hilt any attempt to force them into Saudi arms. They are — aside from a few small irritations — all too happy in the arms of Britain. Nor would the people of the Gulf states — supposing they could somehow be consulted — welcome their inclusion in the Saudi state in its present phase of social and political immaturity. Moreover — and one is forced to return again and again in the Gulf to this elementary but crucial objection to many of the hypothetical changes I have mentioned — Britain is in no position to take unilateral action in the Gulf to initiate any of these courses. Her obligations of precedent and treaty exist and cannot be brushed aside without endangering the stability that she and a good many other powers and people wish to see preserved. In fact, as some British commentators have pointed out, and as this morass of futile hypotheses must indicate, the most serious immediate threat to the stability of the Persian Gulf and its oil industry, might be the actual or threatened withdrawal of Britain's military and political presence.[1]

To say that no initiative is open to Britain at the moment does not mean that others will be inhibited from trying to change things in the Gulf. The young nationalists of the Gulf, in particular, are slowly but surely growing in numbers and are persistently inflamed by Egyptian propaganda against both the rulers and the British. They surely will not be deterred forever from pursuing their dreams of revolution and Arab unity by negative arguments, however rational. In Kuwait they already give the impression of being the tail that sometimes wags the dog of government. In Bahrain they simmer in permanent discontent. Even in Qatar and on the Trucial Coast there have been minor stirrings of nationalist unrest in the last few years. Theoretically, we might suppose from this that popular nationalism would provide eventually a common cause sufficient to knit together some unity on the Arab shores of the Gulf. But even that seems a faint hope for several years ahead. Except for Kuwait and Bahrain the smaller Gulf territories may have to wait another generation before the nationalists are likely to become a real menace to the existing structure; and for the next few years at least it seems probable that the chronic divisions of the wider Arab world will continue to paralyse concerted nationalist action in the Gulf. Even if any such action could be mounted a revolutionary regime anywhere in

[1] See e.g. D. C. Watt, 'Britain and the Future of the Persian Gulf States,' *The World Today*, vol. 20, no. 11, November, 1964, published by the Royal Institute of International Affairs, London.

the Gulf would have to reckon with the hostility of Saudi Arabia as long as that country maintains its present attitudes — and the history of the Yemen since 1962 does not encourage the belief that Saudi hostility would easily be overcome.

Short of a nationalist revolution in Saudi Arabia, which would change the balance of power throughout the Arab world, and might — although not at all certainly — put Egypt and Saudi Arabia into a common harness in Gulf affairs, it is impossible to see how many of the conflicts of the Gulf can be resolved for some years ahead. Even that would not reduce all the local tensions, for apart from the rearguard action of Arab tribalism it would still leave the role of Iran to be negotiated, and perhaps of Iraq, too. Besides, such a drastic cure for inter-Arab quarrels might prove worse than the disease, for if — as I suggested earlier — a Saudi revolt resulted in the division of the Saudi state and a further inflammation of Arabian tensions, American intervention would be difficult to avoid. The Russians, no doubt, would follow, and the Yemen war might be succeeded in Arabia by something more like a Congo débâcle, from which the Gulf states could scarcely hope to escape.

That is possibly too much of an apocalyptic vision, yet with so much at stake around the Gulf, it would be a rash British Government that did not reflect occasionally that reality just could take such a shape. It seems unlikely, therefore, that any British Government will be in a hurry to throw itself from the window in the Gulf by staging an early withdrawal, however hot the fire may be from time to time. Yet there are many reasons why the search for a fire escape — or a safety net — must still be ardently pursued. The impending loss of the Aden base, which now seems highly likely, will leave Britain's military presence in the Gulf more shadowy than ever, and must stimulate eventually either new military arrangements — such as are implied in the Anglo-American search for an island base in the Indian Ocean — or new political arrangements that will serve instead. It is axiomatic that the second of these, or a combination of the two, is preferable to the first alone. The sheer cost of maintaining a *Pax Britannica* by military means is steadily becoming less bearable for Britain, and, although the United States may perhaps be induced to bear a larger share of the burden in the future, it will become increasingly true in the Persian Gulf, as much as elsewhere, that military action by external powers tends in the long run to create as much trouble as it suppresses. Moreover, as time goes on and the nationalist movements in the Gulf territories increase in strength, it is likely that a purely military umbrella will be forced to take the form, under the present political system, of intervention on behalf of the traditional rulers against the discontented nationalists. If Britain and America, singly or together, are to avoid this embarrassing requirement in the future they must seek a political complement to their military guarantees.

Their own military co-operation would be a valuable beginning, for it would imply not merely an infusion of real strength in the somewhat bloodless arteries of the old Raj, but also a widening of political horizons in the area. For the moment this may be the best anyone can hope for; but in the longer view, it will also prove inadequate. The Gulf cannot be fossilized forever in its nineteenth-century pattern, and if a *de facto* Anglo-American alliance were formed in the area, other lines of diplomacy and experiment would still need to be explored — in spite of existing discouragements — through the Arab League, the United Nations and possibly other *ad hoc* international groupings, in the hope of discovering some orderly means of restoring fluidity to the territories of the Gulf.

It would be agreeable, of course, to be able to predict that this might be accomplished in the next few years, so that the last relics of the Raj could be cleared away to permit Britain and Arabia to enter a new and less ambiguous relationship at last. Agreeable, but — I fear — futile. In the nature of things, people and history in the Persian Gulf, fire escapes are hard to come by and even safety nets take time to improvise. There is no point in being sanguine where the grounds for hope are small. For the foreseeable future, perhaps even a decade or more, there may well be little choice for Britain — and the Arabs, too — but to grin and bear the burdens of the past.

12

Faster, Faster, in Kuwait

Two images of Kuwait tell a story of success. The first dates from 1957, when I sat cross-legged on the floor of a gaunt little room above a shop in the Kuwait *suk*, nursing a bottle of Pepsi-Cola, and listening to the grievances of a dozen members of a local youth club. The Suez crisis was not long over, and as an Englishman I was a fair target for Arab resentment of every kind. The British Government, I learned, for the umpteenth time that year, was not only imperialist and pro-Zionist, but (which seemed to vitiate the argument for the sake of rhetorical emphasis) demonstrably and irrevocably mad. Furthermore, as worthy sons of the Arab nation my hosts rejected with contempt the British protection extended to Kuwait, and condemned their own Ruler who continued to accept it as a traitor to the Arab cause. Revolution, undoubtedly, was on the way, and when it arrived they — the worthy sons, etc. — would join hands in brotherly union with Gamal Abdul Nasser, and with their revolutionary brothers in Iraq, too, just as soon as those dear brothers and neighbours had thrown off the yoke of imperialism and reaction.

Cliché after cliché dinned upon my weary ears, and the temptation was strong to dismiss them all intolerantly as a lot of exaggerated nonsense. Yet the passion with which they were delivered was impressive; and one remark in particular stuck in my mind long afterwards as a symbol of youthful frustration in Kuwait. 'Do you know?' I was asked by one young malcontent, with a shocked earnestness that suggested some great scandal in the offing, 'what our Ruler does all the time?' I said I did not, but would be glad to learn, and was told that in his palace he had a salon whose ceiling was decorated with high-bosomed ladies of the imperialist past, like Queen Alexandra and Lily Langtry, upon whose charms the ageing Shaikh dwelt in secret satisfaction. 'He sits there all alone,' said my ardent young informant, 'and looks at them; and he imagines that at the end of every day they all come down and dance for him, as if they were women of his harem!' It seemed to me, if true, a harmless and even appropriate foible in an elderly Arab gentle-man — better, surely, and more imaginative than the common practice among the Ruler's peers around the Gulf of importing cabaret girls from Beirut — but I was assured very firmly and puritanically that it would not do. Indeed, it was an insult to the Kuwaiti people. 'Our Ruler,' said this fierce youngster, in effect, with a face like a Muslim Savonarola, 'is nothing but a dirty old man!'

The second image dates from some seven years later, when I was visiting Kuwait once more. I sought in vain then for those old acquaint-ances from the youth club. Their meeting place had vanished, brushed aside by the bulldozers like most of the rest of the Kuwait *suk*, and replaced by an air-conditioned box of glass and ferro-concrete, in whose offices smart young Arab girls rattled away on typewriters and tabulators like the model young secretaries they clearly were. This time I found myself with another sort of party, not sitting on the floor of a dingy little club-room, but lounging in an armchair in the bachelor flat of a young executive of the Kuwait Planning Board, recently returned from some years of study in England. One wall of his living-room was lined with books in English, German and Arabic, and the others were hung with reproductions of paintings by Gauguin, Klee, Modigliani and Soutine. There were five in the company besides the host and myself. They had all been to universities in Britain or America on Kuwait Government schol-arships, and they had all returned to good jobs. One was an executive of Kuwait Airlines, three were senior government officials, the fifth was headmaster of the biggest secondary school in the shaikhdom. Not one of them was over thirty, and most of them, I gathered, were making more money than me. The passion and frustration that my acquaintance in the *suk* had managed to express over a bottle of Pepsi-Cola found no echo in their behaviour. They all drank whisky, gin or beer, and their conversation was relaxed and sceptical. About Arab unity and brother-hood they were firmly realistic: 'Kuwait is very rich,' they said, 'and Kuwait is very small. So Kuwait must be very suspicious.' And besides, what country and what brothers could they possibly unite with? Iraq was too unstable, Saudi Arabia too backward, Egypt too poor and much too far away. Unity must wait, therefore, until a better day. Meanwhile, they called themselves Kuwait's 'new blood' and took a complacent pride in their position as the first generation of home-grown intellectuals and administrators. Remembering the old story of the Ruler and his painted ladies I asked these new bloods what they thought of the old man now. The answer was almost a paean of praise. 'He is,' they declared, without a dissenting voice, 'the wisest man among us all.'

With certain local variations, the first of these two scenes might be as true in the middle 1960's of Bahrain, Qatar, or even Dubai, as it was of Kuwait in the middle 1950's; and in a little while, I do not doubt, it may be true of Abu Dhabi and Muscat, too. But the second scene, so far, is exclusive to Kuwait and there is not another of the Gulf Shaikhdoms which looks like repeating it in the near future. To account for this apparent transformation in Kuwait when the other Gulf territories are still festering in frustration, or have not yet left their old tribal state, we must look first at the role of money. The new bloods of Kuwait are the first to admit that they are the beneficiaries of the social revolution of sheer wealth. Other territories in the Gulf have enjoyed, and will enjoy, comparatively large oil revenues, but none so far has had the overwhelming riches that Kuwait has known since 1950. In that year, Kuwait's income from oil was about £5 million. By 1956, it was £100 million, and by 1964 it was nearly £200 million. In fifteen years the shaikhdom received altogether almost £1,700 million from its oil production, which works out at a minimum of £6,000 per head of the shaikhdom's population over the period, and probably — at a guess — more than £20,000 per family. Of course, only a minority received anything like as much as that in cash, but the sheer enormity of the total sums involved guaranteed that the impact upon a small and compact population would be revolutionary.

At first, as in Saudi Arabia, the impact seemed merely destructive and confusing. The new wealth struck at the old structure of society as the new bulldozers thrust through the old mud walls — without thought, restraint or plan. As late as 1950 Kuwait was still essentially the same traditional pearling and trading port of the Gulf that it had been for many centuries, with several handsome Turkish villas, a rambling old *suk* and a fine mud wall. Its Ruler, Shaikh Abdullah as-Sabah, was the only source of authority. His only lieutenants were drawn from among his many relatives, and his sole guides and protectors were the British. But the oil industry brought in, besides its enormous wealth and opportunities, tens of thousands of Arab immigrants, from Iraq and Egypt, Jordan and Lebanon, including many Palestinian refugees with a violent sense of grievance, who captured most of the new skilled jobs. Even when they were not engaged in overt political propaganda — as some of them were — the immigrants radiated an aggressive confidence in their modern ways and a corresponding contempt for the traditional outlook of the Kuwaiti ruling class and its British supporters. The young, and so far disinherited, Kuwaitis quickly picked up these attitudes. As the shaikhs suddenly acquired Cadillacs and villas in

Lebanon, or flew off with their new millions to explore the wilder shores of Europe, the young men at home muttered fashionably of rebellion. Theirs was the voice of 1957 — frustrated, envious, adolescent and idealist — the expression of a generation for whom the old ways were already dead or dying but for whom the new ways, as yet, provided no satisfaction. That this strident voice seemed muted a mere seven years later was due partly to sheer affluence. The money whose first impact had produced young rebels went on, in ever-increasing quantity, to turn them into reasonably contented new bloods. The man who drove me to the new blood party had a large Mercedes; the one who drove me back again to my hotel had the latest M.G. Such comforts are not lightly brushed aside by anyone, and they went surprisingly far down the social scale in Kuwait in 1964. Shaikh Abdullah and his relatives, assisted before 1961 by the British, had set up a welfare state more generous and comprehensive than anywhere in the Gulf, and perhaps more opulent than anywhere in the world. There were social security and unemployment benefits, subsidised housing and free work training. There were children's homes and free medical treatment for all, youth clubs and magnificent hospitals, culture clubs and holidays with pay, sports grounds and a forty-hour week, no income tax and free telephone calls — you name it, Kuwait could supply it. Above all, it supplied free education, for boys and girls, children and adults, at home and abroad, at a cost to the State treasury of over £500 a year for every pupil. This was not a new concept in the Gulf: Bahrain had been running a welfare state similar in principle for a quarter-of-a-century. But Kuwait's effort was on a scale that was never within Bahrain's reach, setting standards of social care and financial security hitherto unknown in the Arab world; and it helped to deflect a sizeable current of discontent.

The affluence distributed by the welfare state was complemented by the general boom in the Kuwait economy, which accelerated swiftly in the second half of the 1950's. Until then, although the oil revenues had practically doubled every year for five years, the weight of money in the pipeline, so to speak, had not made itself felt fully in Kuwait. Much of it was invested in London where, by 1957, reliable estimates of Kuwait's holdings ranged between £400 million and £600 million; and the thought of their importance to the strength of sterling caused nightmares in the Treasury and the Bank of England. In Kuwait itself, the old Gulf town and the old Gulf ways were still very much alive, to the irritation of the young rebels who were growing up in the consciousness of a financial and political fortune all around them, only waiting to be seized. The city wall had gone, and the Turkish villas had disappeared, but a traveller who had left the local pearl merchants ten years before, swopping their yarns and prices over coffee in the *suk*, could have returned then to find them in the same places, and probably telling the same stories still. The corrugated iron roofs and gloomy little caves of the shopkeepers in the old bazaar still looked more secure than the stucco façades of the new streets that were beginning to surround them. The old town spoke of roots and established certainties, the new seemed to have nothing but its novelty to sustain it. In their raw, ill-finished opulence, with the rubble piled high at the back doors and the electricity wires looping untidily across the unpaved streets from one naked light bulb to another, the new buildings had the impermanent air of an international fairground, here today and gone tomorrow, as if in a year or two they would all crack and crumble and return to the dust from which they had come so lately. They looked, and were, the material equivalent of those argumentative members of the youth club — dynamic but undisciplined, with both the boldness and the pimples of adolescence.

Seven years later most of the pimples had disappeared and the new Kuwait had emerged in something like maturity, after the most intensive material and political reconstruction of any country in the Middle East. The ragged old *suk* had almost vanished, and in what little was left of it the old pearl kings seemed poised for instant flight. There was not a single Kuwaiti pearling dhow left sailing in the Gulf, and not a reason in the world, except nostalgia, why the merchants should have bothered with the paltry rewards of their old trade any longer. They had made far bigger profits out of the rocketing land rents that had accompanied the oil boom, and now they sat over their coffees, with the dust gathering on their cabinets and the whitewash flaking down from between the mangrove poles that held up the old mud roof, and waited for the bulldozers to finish their inevitable work. All around them the new streets were not merely broad but paved from side to side. The piles of rubble had gone, the electricity wires had been hidden, and the naked bulbs were clothed in globes and chandeliers. There was still an air of the *nouveau riche*, especially about the miles of residential suburbs on the desert fringes, where the architectural exuberance of the new villas expressed the understandably boundless satisfaction of their owners. But at least — so I was told — the lavatories worked. Money had indeed worked a miracle. It had given Kuwait the face and attributes of a new security; and not one of the shaikhdom's inhabitants, down to the poorest labourer on the building sites, had failed to feel its beneficent impulse.

But it was not money alone that transformed Kuwait in these few years. By a piece of rare good fortune for all concerned, this richest of all the Arab shaikhdoms was also better endowed than any other to handle its enormous wealth. Had Qatar, for instance, or any one of the petty shaikhdoms of the Trucial Coast, enjoyed Kuwait's income throughout the 1950's, there might have been a more turbulent story to tell. As it was, Kuwait had its difficulties; but it also had some advantages that enabled it to survive them — especially, perhaps, a Ruler of considerable shrewdness and adaptability. Shaikh Abdullah was already elderly when he succeeded his brother Ahmad in 1950, but he did not, like some other ageing Arab rulers, spend his late years trying to play a political Canute holding back the tides of change. Instead, he pursued a calculated policy of reconstructing Kuwait's economic and political alignments, to strengthen the shaikhdom's independence and buy off opposition. His policy had both a foreign and domestic face, and was generally supported — and to some extent even inspired — by consistent British advice, especially in the post-Suez years, intended to give Shaikh Abdullah a new image in the Arab world. At home, the welfare state was only the first step. The second was the well-known expedient of finding jobs for the boys in an expanding national administration, when the Ruler accepted that if his welfare state was going to educate everyone it had better also give everyone suitable jobs to do — or risk a white-collar revolt. This had the treble advantage of keeping Kuwait's educated youngsters quiet, of building up an efficient civil service and of removing some of the most influential posts from the jealous grip of British expatriates or Arab carpet-baggers who had cornered them before Kuwait had any properly trained men of its own. The third domestic step was more daring, but no less justifiable — the creation of an elected National Assembly which diluted the Ruler's personal authority for the first time. In essence, this was an extension of the principle of jobs for the boys, from the safe field of administration to the more dangerous one of legislation, where Kuwait's rising new bloods might learn to exercise power as well as responsibility.

The Assembly was not, by western standards, a spectacular exercise in parliamentary democracy, for executive authority remained in the hands of the Ruler's cabinet, which he continued to appoint himself as before, mostly from among his close relatives. Yet it was, and has remained so far, one of the few genuinely functioning assemblies in the Arab world, and the only attempt in the Arabian peninsula, outside Aden and — more recently and erratically — the Yemen, to create a contemporary alternative to the *majlis* of the tribal chieftains. At its outset, in 1962, it was commonly expected to be no more than a rubber stamp, but within twelve months its members had shown their critical mettle by knocking 20 per cent off the Ruler's defence budget, and within two years they were attempting to call still more important tunes, such as the terms which Shaikh Abdullah should negotiate with the international oil companies.[1]

While these concessions introduced a new and more popular radicalism at home, Shaikh Abdullah steadily consolidated Kuwait's position abroad, especially in the Arab countries. The formal declaration of Kuwait's independence in 1961, with the termination of its special relationship with Britain, was the indispensable initial step in the process. In spite of General Kassem's arrogant response, the rest of the Arab states agreed to recognise the shaikhdom as an independent state, and Kuwait was admitted as a member of both the Arab League and the United Nations. The price for these pan-Arab mercies, however, was a share in Kuwait's oil revenues. The Kuwait Fund for Arab Economic Development, which began in 1962 with a capital of £150 million, provided an entirely new source of investment capital for development projects anywhere in the Arab world. Unofficially, but with perfect clarity, it was understood everywhere from Casablanca to Baghdad as the first instalment of Kuwait's protection money. Other and more naked forms of bribery supplemented it, such as interest-free loans for unspecified purposes direct from the Kuwait Treasury. The more immediate the menace, the higher the cost of this protection. £25 million went to Egypt; and £30 million were required, interest-free, to buy off Iraq in 1963, when General Kassem's successors formally agreed to abandon his claim to sovereignty in Kuwait and to recognise the shaikhdom's independence.

With concessions at home and bribery abroad, Shaikh Abdullah managed better than most other Arabian rulers to keep abreast of his critics, and even occasionally to outpace them. But even Shaikh Abdullah might have failed, or at least have experienced greater difficulties, if his critics had not been partially silenced by their own disillusionment. Their strength rested not only upon inequalities and frustration at home, but also upon leadership and example abroad — and from 1958 onwards these conspicuously failed them. After General Kassem overturned the old regime in Baghdad on July 14th of that year, and Arab revolution seemed about to triumph everywhere, the young Kuwaiti nationalists began a long and involuntary slide into a trough of

[1] In January 1965, the Assembly refused to ratify the Kuwait Government's acceptance of new, compromise, terms for oil payments negotiated through the Organisation of Petroleum Exporting Countries (OPEC).

despondency. Kassem's failure to bring to Iraq any of the supposed benefits of revolution, his immediate and acrimonious quarrel with Nasser, and his encouragement of the Iraqi communists against the nationalists, fell upon the young Kuwaitis like so many buckets of cold water. My acquaintances in the youth club, for example, were still meeting in their dingy little room over the shop when I visited Kuwait again in 1959, but they no longer harangued me with one voice as they had done two years earlier, as if they were an individual demagogue and I were a public meeting. They quarrelled among themselves instead. Bitterly, they had discovered that their ideals had been betrayed; unity and brotherhood seemed farther off than ever; and life in Kuwait held more blessings than before. This disillusionment was deepened by the crisis that accompanied Kuwait's independence two years later; and even after that was settled the general inability of the Arab states to agree about anything except Israel for very long, and the Egyptian failures in Syria and the Yemen in particular, discouraged Kuwait's aspiring nationalists. Through at least five crucial years of Kuwait's development, in fact, they had no incentive to turn their old rebellious sentiments to action. Sensibly, if sometimes reluctantly, they counted their blessings instead — until, by the middle of the 1960's, it seemed to many of them, like my new blood friends, that no forcible revolution could have achieved for them what Kuwait's peaceful evolution had already accomplished.

As a result Kuwait looked more secure than ever before. When the British troops landed there in 1961 in response to Shaikh Abdullah's appeal for help against Iraq, one young nationalist told me, in tones approaching anguish, 'It broke the Ruler's heart to ask you to come back — but what else could he do?' The answer then was probably nothing: whatever their intentions, the actions of General Kassem and the other Arab states had driven Shaikh Abdullah back into Britain's arms. But by 1964 his policies of re-alignment had made it less likely that Britain would ever be asked to intervene again. The prospect of an external take-over by a jealous neighbour had been reduced by buttressing Kuwait's sovereignty with international recognition and hard cash; and revolution within the shaikhdom seemed to have been averted by prosperity and an embryonic parliament.

It is a frequent rule of politics, however, as much as of love, that the appetite grows by what it feeds on; and both inside and outside Kuwait new demands are gathering now to test Shaikh Abdullah's acumen and his state's stability. As the first wave of new blood is succeeded by a second and a third, the orderly transfer of power from the Ruler to his subjects becomes more necessary and perhaps more difficult. The present young men in their well-paid jobs may be content with their administrative authority, but their juniors — to whom the best posts are already closed by seniority — may insist upon more political power as well. The National Assembly in its present, limited form, is not likely to satisfy them for long, and if they cannot enlarge its authority peacefully they could, in a few years, decide to do so by force. Since 1961 both the army and the police force have been rapidly expanded, in keeping with the dignity of a sovereign state, and to the youngsters who are captains now and will shortly become colonels, ambition may prove a sharper spur than loyalty and the rewards of power more tempting than a substantial pay packet. If so, they will only be confirming the common experience of the Arab world so far, where so many revolutions have been accomplished or attempted by military cliques.

Behind this incipient menace to the present regime lies another, and possibly more intractable, problem: what is to become of the Arab immigrants? Until now Kuwait's prosperity has been based almost as much upon immigrant skills and labour as upon the oil resources they have helped to exploit. The Palestinians and Egyptians who run the schools and hospitals; the Lebanese and Syrians who are prominent in Kuwait's international commerce; the Iraqis who have provided a great part of the unskilled work force in the oilfields; and the Arab clerks and artisans of all nationalities who are still the backbone of the economy and administration; these are the eunuchs in the shaikhdom's golden harem. They have prosperity without power. They are denied any voice in local politics, and as more young Kuwaitis acquire an education they are increasingly denied the best jobs as well, for the law gives priority to Kuwaiti nationals in every walk of life. Steadily, therefore, Kuwait is becoming two nations divided along potentially explosive lines — a power-élite of citizens anxious to protect their privileges, and a rootless, voiceless mass of expatriate underlings who will be ready to use any instrument to improve their status.

The most likely instrument is pressure from outside, exerted through subversion and a revival of militant pan-Arabism. The faith in ultimate Arab unity is one that never dies, however often it is subdued or disappointed, and among the gritty discontents of the Kuwait immigrants it sprouts like a weed: crushed here, uprooted there, it still pushes up through a crevice somewhere else whenever it receives encouragement. To President Nasser in particular this provides a standing opportunity for putting the squeeze upon the Ruler of Kuwait. He, more than anyone, can still stir the Arab world with the call to unity, for all the tarnish that recent years have added to his shining armour; and he, more than anyone, has a built-in-system of agents in the Palestinians and Egyptians in Kuwait who accept him as their natural leader. In the confusion of pan-Arabism after 1958 he became cautious in his advocacy of outright political unity; but five years later, when he was thoroughly embroiled in the Yemen war, both events and his temperament seemed to be thrusting him towards a modified policy of militancy that evoked some of the old *frisson* of unrest in Kuwait. In 1963, when Syria and Iraq joined briefly under Baathist governments to proclaim a new political federation with Egypt, 12 deputies in the Kuwait Assembly voted for a resolution demanding 'closer ties' between the shaikhdom and its sister-states and the abrogation of the British defence treaty. Neither the Federation nor the resolution lived; but a year later, in a May Day speech in Cairo, Nasser coupled an attack on the British in South Arabia and their alleged attempt to persuade the United States to withhold aid from Egypt, with a reference to the profits Britain received from Arab oil: 'If Britain believes she can intimidate us,' he added ominously, 'I have this to say: We also can apply economic sanctions against Britain.' Being a shrewd statesman he did not elaborate; but the remark in its context reminded some observers[1] of the passage in Nasser's book, *The Philosophy of the Revolution*, which speaks of oil as one of three main sources of strength in the Arab world — 'a sinew of material civilisation without which all its machines would cease to function.' In spite of Sir Anthony Eden's nightmares at the time of Suez, when he saw President Nasser laying greedy hands on all Arab oil and holding Britain to ransom, the vague menace in such suggestions has never yet been fulfilled.[2] But the temptation to invoke the menace is always there, as long as a responsive audience exists in Kuwait among the disgruntled, but essential, Arab immigrants. Shaikh Abdullah and his government have tried to outflank this danger in recent years by adopting an increasingly militant pan-Arab tone themselves. In the early months of 1965, for example, when President Nasser led the Arab nations into a diplomatic crisis over West Germany's intention to recognise Israel, and renewed his talk of using Arab oil as a political weapon, Kuwait was one of his firmest supporters in a somewhat wavering Arab front against Bonn. Such attitudes may not be entirely serious or practical as yet, but they tend to create their own momentum, so that with every renewal of

[1] See e.g. 'Oil in the Persian Gulf', an anonymous article in *The World Today*, vol. 20, no. 7, July, 1964. Royal Institute of International Affairs, London.

[2] *Full Circle*, The Memoirs of Sir Anthony Eden, pp. 465–6. Cassell, London, 1960.

tension the postures need to be struck with still more emphasis until — quite possibly — they become the only reality.

In short, like the Red Queen in *Alice Through the Looking Glass*, Shaikh Abdullah finds himself running faster and faster just to stay in the same place. When I think of those ardent and embittered boys in the Kuwait youth club years ago, it seems to me remarkable that he has stayed the pace so well, so far, bringing his shaikhdom through a period of perilous potential turmoil with less fuss and insecurity than once seemed possible. As long as he lives, no doubt, he may keep up with the running, for he is widely and deservedly respected by his people now. But he is already an old man who cannot reasonably expect many more years of grace; and there is no-one obviously qualified to succeed him. Like the end of the Imam Ahmad's rule in the Yemen, Shaikh Abdullah's death may release a struggle for power in Kuwait which would reveal the many changes since 1950 as only the first phase of the political and social evolution required to meet the new demands that exist inside and outside the shaikhdom. On that reading, it will be surprising if Kuwait survives the next 10 years with no more alarms than it has suffered in the last decade. Unless, of course, sheer wealth performs another miracle.

13

Ghosts in Bahrain

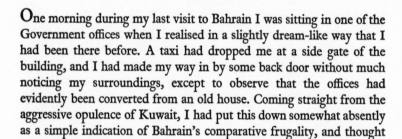

One morning during my last visit to Bahrain I was sitting in one of the Government offices when I realised in a slightly dream-like way that I had been there before. A taxi had dropped me at a side gate of the building, and I had made my way in by some back door without much noticing my surroundings, except to observe that the offices had evidently been converted from an old house. Coming straight from the aggressive opulence of Kuwait, I had put this down somewhat absently as a simple indication of Bahrain's comparative frugality, and thought no more about it.

Upstairs on the first floor, I sat down in an office partitioned from a larger room with beaver-board, before a middle-aged Palestinian in Arab robes. He offered me a joking welcome. 'You must be a bad sign,' he said, 'We haven't had enough trouble to bring journalists here since Suez.' There was, in fact, no trouble; and I was about to reply that only curiosity brought me to Bahrain on this occasion when I suffered a mild hallucination. The air conditioning stopped humming for a moment in the office, and I seemed to hear instead the rhythmic flutter of a ceiling fan. The partitions fell away, the grey metal filing cabinets against the walls were replaced by mahogany tallboys displaying English china. The plain office desk vanished and the piles of dusty folders with it, and in place of the Palestinian in his robes there was a tall, grey Englishman in a fawn summer suit and spotted bow tie sitting at a polished dining table. He was telling an inconsequential story about his impending retirement and said, 'After all, I've been here over thirty years. I suppose I've earned a rest.' As with all such visions it was over in a second, while the Palestinian was still chuckling at his little joke. But as I looked about his office now, at the hole in the ceiling where the fan had once been connected, at the windows that were closed for the air conditioning but through which I could just see the sea, beyond the overgrown shrubbery,

174

I knew where I was. 'You know,' I said, 'I've been here before. Wasn't this the Belgrave dining room?'

It was. Seven years had gone since I had sat in it at a luncheon party, not long after the Suez crisis had provoked riots in the Bahrain streets, and superficially there was nothing left to show that Sir Charles Belgrave, personal adviser to successive Rulers of Bahrain for thirty-one years, had eaten and entertained there throughout most of his working life. The other rooms in the house had changed their personalities, too. The broad verandah where I had once sat with a gin-and-tonic, savouring the light sea breeze rustling through the palms, was now walled-in, air-conditioned and filled with office furniture. Where bookshelves had once lined the central hall there were only bare walls, and where Persian rugs had covered the floors there were bare boards. It was neither a convenient office nor a home any more, but a makeshift conversion peopled by old ghosts.

They were not grand ghosts, for Bahrain has never been a very grand place. Even Lord Curzon, on his undeniably grand tour of the Gulf as Viceroy, in 1903, made a rather less than Vice-regal arrival here. There being no sedan chair in which he might be carried through the shallows from his launch to the shore, in a manner fitting to his exalted status, he was slung aboard a plain kitchen upright with two carrying poles slipped beneath the seat and dumped unceremoniously upon the beach from that. Sir Charles Belgrave, likewise, lived here in relatively modest style. His house had the quality of a well-to-do English country rectory — correct, yet relaxed, with just a touch of genteel shabbiness in the upholstery and a hint of parish politics in the visitors who were usually waiting in the downstairs hall. While Lady Belgrave did the flowers and organised women's meetings (bringing a measure of female emancipation to Bahrain in the process, far ahead of the rest of Arabia) Sir Charles attended to higher matters of state. He belonged to the last, paternal period of Empire — the twilight of the Raj that settled upon British India and its dependencies after the First World War; and it was characteristic of his period that he should have got his job by answering an advertisement in the personal column of *The Times* that sought a 'young gentleman' of public school education 'for service in an Eastern state.'[1]

Belgrave was never a servant of the Raj himself, in the strict sense of the word. Although his appointment was negotiated by the British India Office he was in the pay of the Ruler of Bahrain, not of the British or India Governments. But because he stayed in Bahrain for so long as the

[1] See Sir Charles's autobiography, *Personal Column*, Hutchinson, London, 1960.

Ruler's personal adviser while other British officials came and went as London or Delhi directed, Belgrave became in the end a living symbol of Britain in the Gulf. In the Arab world after the Second World War this made him inevitably a figure of growing suspicion; and it was fitting, if slightly cruel, that the moment of his final retirement was possibly hastened and certainly tarnished by the aftermath of the Suez débâcle.

And yet his ghost lingers. Unlike Kuwait, Bahrain has not changed much in the passionate post-Suez years. As the seat of the British Political Resident it remains the centre of the trucial system in the Gulf, and like Sir Charles Belgrave himself the Raj maintains here a slightly phantasmal sway. The Indian rupee is still Bahrain's official currency, and in the influx of Indians and Pakistanis that came in the British wake nearly every shop seems to have been opened by a Jamshid or a Jashan-mall, and every clerk seems to answer to Singh, or maybe Mukerjee. In BOAC's Speedbird House Hotel, itself a relic of thirty years ago when the Empire was still the Empire and Imperial Airways made Bahrain an overnight stop on the route to Bombay, a visitor from the Arab world catches echoes of an old Indian Army mess. The servants are all 'bearers', the laundryman a 'dhobi', and the watchman a 'chow-kidar'; and on Sundays the guests are confronted with the ancient, and agreeable, Anglo-Indian ritual of a mountainous curry lunch. When the Ruler of Bahrain has a ceremonial parade his escort is a squadron of mounted lancers, better fitted to the retinue of a small Indian prince than an Arab chieftain; and in the Gulf world of status-symbol Cadillacs, there is something endearingly imperial and old-fashioned about his preference for a Rolls-Royce. Only a little more substantial than these old ghosts are the British forces which help to preserve the trucial structure. They are not many — a couple of corvettes of the Royal Navy, two or three battalions of soldiers in barracks around the Resident's compound, and a few RAF aircraft sharing the civil airport. Indeed, they are hardly more than a token of the *Pax Britannica* on its last legs, yet they give to Bahrain a faint but perceptible flavour of a genuine imperial base.

Perhaps it was the island nature of Bahrain that enabled the Raj to stamp its image more clearly here than in most other parts of the Gulf. By that short stretch of sea that isolates it from the mainland of Arabia Bahrain must have been brought appreciably closer to the shores and influences of India. This little archipelago of islands even looks less Arabian than anywhere else around Arabia's shores. As you fly in over the royal blue waters of the Gulf you can sense the change at once when the network of fish traps comes into view beneath your window.

Nowhere else on the Arabian coast are these as prominent as around Bahrain, where the V-shaped lines of wooden stakes driven into the shallow seabed form a lacy frill along the shore and speak of a community that is used to living with and off the sea. Among them too, you may spot occasional rings of silver in the blue where springs of sweet water gush even from beneath the sea; and beyond them, around still more springs, the date palms and fruit gardens splash the islands with unaccustomed green. There is none of the barrenness of Kuwait — still empty of trees, for all its money — nor the arid, glaring greyness of Abu Dhabi's sandy wastes, nor the sharp, naked cliffs of Muscat. Bahrain is green, at least in substantial patches, and often as humid as a hothouse. On summer mornings the roads are as wet with condensation as they might be after a shower of rain.

Immediately, therefore, these islands establish a distinctive character, softer and more maritime than their mainland neighbours and possibly more amenable to non-Arabian influences. Britain's Indian Empire is not the only one of these to have left its mark, although it is the last. There is still, for example, a significant Persian legacy in Bahrain which makes Teheran's persistent claim to sovereignty there just a trifle less absurd than it might seem otherwise, 200 years after the last Persian occupation. A strong strain of Persian blood among Bahrain's people and a majority of Shiite over Sunni Muslims both derive from the Persian years. But the presence of Arabia has remained the most consistent influence, and having outlasted that of Persia it is now, in due time, re-asserting itself against the slowly fading image of the Raj.

The process is far slower than in Kuwait, however, not only because Bahrain's historical ties with Britain are stronger and her geographical and racial links with Arabia slightly weaker, but also because it has never had anything like the same resources in recent years. This was not always so. In 1926 when Belgrave arrived as adviser to Shaikh Hamid bin Isa al-Khalifa, he found a ruling family at least as rich and sophisticated as anywhere in the Gulf. Even more than Kuwait, Bahrain was a flourishing port, with lively pearling and boat-building industries and the additional advantage — unique in the Gulf — of her plentiful fresh water. Within six years Shaikh Hamid was also the happy owner of the Gulf's first producing oilfield, and on the proceeds of commerce, agriculture and a few modest oil wells he and Belgrave, and later Hamid's son, Shaikh Sulman, constructed the first of the Gulf's modern welfare states. Belgrave's contribution was both technical and inspirational — he knew what was needed and, within limits, how it might be done. Free schools, free hospitals, and an organised police force, a new port, new roads, and properly managed finances were all parts of the Belgrave legacy; and — as is the way of empire — Belgrave ended by working himself out of a job. By the time he left, the pupils who had been educated in the schools he helped to create were among those most loudly demanding his removal as an agent of imperialism.

Yet still the pace of Bahrain's progress was comparatively slow. Although her oilfield was the first to be discovered in the Gulf and was in production nearly fifteen years before Kuwait began to make much money out of hers, it remained the smallest of them all. A new marine field shared with Saudi Arabia is now under development, but from present production Bahrain only makes in a year what Kuwait earns in less than a week. Even with the revenue from its big oil refinery, processing Saudi oil from the mainland, Bahrain's Government still has less than £6 million a year from all sources. Spread among the whole population of nearly 150,000, this is not much more than one twentieth of Kuwait's *per capita* income. Where Kuwait spends £500 a year on the education of each child of school age, Bahrain makes do with a modest £35, and must scale down her other services in proportion.

By the standards of the old Arabia, still prevalent in most of the Trucial Shaikhdoms, even this makes Bahrain rich. There are, I am told, at least four sterling millionaires among her merchants, and probably a score or more who count their millions in rupees. She has her share of Cadillacs and Mercedes, and her Ruler, sedate and un-flamboyant as he may seem in his Rolls Royce, disposes of a pretty line in expensive, jewelled gifts. But there has been no irresistible flood of money to sweep away the old world and replace it with the new in a single generation. Instead the two have co-existed for 40 years, with the twentieth-century world of oil and Arab nationalism only gradually overcoming the traditional responses of pearling and paternalism. Bahrain's old boat-builders, for example, have not yet vanished like those of Kuwait. Hammering and caulking along the waterfront under the hulls of their high-pooped dhows, they offer pretty much the same face to the world now as they must have done to Lord Curzon when he was tumbled among them, sixty-odd years ago. A dozen pearling vessels still carry on their old trade, too — fitfully, and less profitably every year, but not yet utterly abandoned for the easier rewards of oil royalties and property rents. As yet the bulldozers have not flattened all Bahrain's old mud and coral houses; nor are the shaikhs too rich or too sophisticated to squat hour by hour at the gates of the Ruler's palace, each with his favourite falcon on his arm. The wilder shores of Europe are not yet their more natural domain.

Equally, the twentieth-century's political pressures have not yet proved irresistible. The present Ruler, Shaikh Isa al-Khalifa, retains nearly as much personal authority as his father or his grandfather. There is no National Assembly in Bahrain to compare with Kuwait's, and few Bahraini 'new bloods' have been given their heads in the Civil Service. In foreign affairs the relationship with Britain remains dominant and unchanged. No declaration of Bahrain's formal independence has been seriously considered, nor any application for membership of the Arab League or the United Nations. Under the nineteenth-century agreements Britain maintains her monopoly of diplomatic representation in Bahrain, although India and Australia have been allowed to open trade missions. To all hints that other interested nations like the United States — to say nothing of brother Arab states, like Kuwait, Saudi Arabia or Egypt — might safely and even profitably be allowed to open embassies now, Shaikh Isa replies cryptically but finally, as he once replied to me: 'A nation, like a man, must have only one face. Two faces means that one face must cheat.'

A sorry look-out, we may think, for the governments of the great powers, with embassies of 100 sovereign nations in their midst and — presumably — ninety-nine cheating faces to keep supplied with prevarications. But nobody so far has persuaded Shaikh Isa that such a response is inadequate in the contemporary world. This is not altogether for want of effort by the British, who have been trying to convince him for some years now that a broader vision in foreign affairs and a little more liberalism at home would both ease their conscience and improve his prospects of a long and happy reign. 'Why should we change?' the Ruler asks. 'We are happy as we are. The trouble with you British,' he once added to me as an afterthought, 'is that you like change too much for its own sake.' This odd view of the British character is held by Shaikh Isa and many of his relatives with apparent conviction; but there are plenty of other Bahrainis who hold, with equal conviction, that the trouble with the British is that they do not like change enough. 'Why,' I have been asked more than once in Bahrain, 'do you British not force the Ruler to change his ways?' One answer, as we have seen, is that Britain does not have the authority to force changes upon any Ruler in the Gulf. Another explanation is that, with her usual instinct for the middle course, Britain has tried to compromise between the Ruler and his critics, first persuading one to move forward and then restraining the others from trying to move still faster. Predictably, this has failed to satisfy either side.

To begin with, Britain supported Shaikhs Hamid and Sulman and their adviser, Belgrave, in creating the welfare state — an exercise in benevolent paternalism which resulted, as usual, in a demand for more benevolence and less paternalism. This demand, also, the British supported, with new proposals for democratic institutions. But the ruling family was unwilling to surrender any of its traditional authority, and from about 1952 onwards, when Nasser and the Egyptian revolutionaries began to show the Arabs how to deal with indigenous monarchs and foreign overlords at the same time, Bahrain seemed to simmer and occasionally to seethe in unison with the rest of the Arab world. By 1954, when the British Government was still wrestling with the Egyptians over the fate of the Sudan and the Suez base, the underemployed, educated youngsters of Bahrain were demanding a trade union, a modern code of law and the removal of Belgrave. In 1955, after a general strike, the Ruler gave in to some of their demands — but too late, for they had already grown again. Now it was an elected legislative council the Bahrainis wanted; and as the tensions of the wider Arab world mounted throughout that year, with loud denunciations of the Baghdad Pact, and President Nasser's triumphant new arms agreement with the Russians, the discontent in Bahrain mounted, too. When General Sir John Glubb was suddenly dismissed from his command of the Jordan Army by King Husain in the spring of 1956, the Bahrainis took to the streets again, eager to show that they also could strike a blow against imperialism and reaction; and they contrived to do so, more literally than they might have dared to hope, by stoning the luckless Mr. Selwyn Lloyd, then Britain Foreign Secretary, who had unhappily chosen to visit Bahrain that day. Up to this point the British were still trying to keep the Ruler abreast, if not ahead, of the burgeoning demands of his people. But six months later they turned back in their tracks, when their attack on Egypt provoked the worst riots Bahrain had ever known. British troops were landed to help the Ruler restore order, the ring-leaders were arrested, and three of them were shipped off — without benefit of legal formalities — to exile in British custody on the island of St. Helena. Abruptly, a firm repression replaced the cautious liberalism of the pre-Suez era.

Wonderful to relate, there was no serious disturbance in Bahrain for the next eight years. To the young Shaikh Isa, who became Ruler only in 1961, five years after the Suez riots, at the age of twenty-six, this has seemed evidence enough that a firm and fatherly hand is, after all, the source of all happiness for his people; and the coincidence of this long period of relative calm with the continued turbulence of the rest of the Arab world has strengthened his determination to make no more concessions to their political aspirations. He has maintained, and even extended, Bahrain's welfare state in the tradition of Belgrave and his own forebears. He has continued to avoid the debilitating extravagance and corruption that have so often accompanied the easy money of oil royalties elsewhere. He has cautiously relaxed the heavy post-Suez hand of political repression. The exiles of St. Helena were rescued by Opposition pressure upon the British Government in the House of Commons, and have settled comfortably in business in Lebanon and Iraq with £15,000 apiece of British money to compensate them for their wrongful detention. The other prisoners of 1956, held with less publicity in Bahrain's own gaols, have been freed again. But of political advancement there has been no further sign. Bahrain has remained stuck in the paternal rut under the attenuated shadow of the Raj.

To the young men and women educated in the schools of the welfare state, now reaching into the third generation, this is not a happy state of affairs, whatever the Ruler may say about it. Characteristically vague but heated aspirations fire them. Socialism, democracy, independence and Arab unity are their idols. Nasserism and Baathism, the two conflicting theologies of the Arab revolution, are their principal ways of worship. Egyptian schoolteachers and Palestinian civil servants are their priests. If their movement had only been united Bahrain probably would not have enjoyed its recent years of comparative stability. Arab disunity at large, however, has been faithfully reflected among the young Arabs of Bahrain. In 1956 the enemy was easily identified by all Arabs as Britain and her reactionary stooges, coupled with the abominable name of Israel; and from the Atlantic Ocean to the Persian Gulf, as the Arab propagandists never tired of declaring, they united against that combination with a common will. But never since then has the pattern seemed so clear. With Baathists and Nasserists divided; Baghdad, Cairo and Damascus dancing a three-cornered jig of alternate abuse and reconciliation; Saudi Arabia and Egypt carrying their enmity to the brink of open war; Iran continuing to claim her ancient rights in Bahrain; and Iraq setting an alarming example by her attempt to annex Kuwait, there has been no agreed, or agreeable, future for the young Bahrainis to anticipate and no coherent policy for them to espouse, save to wait and see. They have subsided, in consequence, into confused and sullen acquiescence.

This unhappy attitude may not last much longer, not because the long-term answers to the problems of Arab unity are any clearer, but because frustration cannot be contained forever. There were signs in 1964 that Bahrain's suppressed emotions might be approaching a new explosion. Even the merchants, I discovered on my last visit, were beginning to grow restive. Previously united behind the Ruler's paternalism, they were tending to divide — as their counterparts did in Aden some years earlier — between Arabs and the rest. As in Aden, the Arab traders were anxious to insure themselves with the discontented nationalists, while Indians, Pakistanis and Persians preferred to remain under the combined protection of the Ruler and his British friends. The pressure was also growing again for more and better jobs for Bahrainis in the civil service and the police, where not only Palestinians, but some faded old British officials, too, still held many of the senior posts. And although some of the consequences of Kuwait's independence might have been chastening to young Bahraini visions of perfect Arab brotherhood, the rapid development of Kuwait's administration and national assembly was beginning to wound Bahraini pride. After all, Bahrain had set the pace of modernisation in the Gulf for a quarter-of-a-century: was she now to be left standing by those northern parvenus? Anger mounted at the humiliation of it. 'Look,' said one young man whom I encountered by chance in a Bahrain bookshop, thumbing rather furtively through a back number of the *New Statesman*, 'we are treated like children. Children, I tell you!' And he listed in an indignant whisper the trappings of modern manhood to which he aspired in vain. 'We have no parliament. No newspaper. No trade union. No modern law courts, and no modern laws. We can't even please ourselves whether we drink or not — if we want a glass of whisky we must come and ask people like you for it. I know I'm a Muslim,' he added, 'but is this modern? Is this fair? I ask you, as an Englishman, is this fair?' He was, so he told me, a graduate of London Univeristy. 'And what am I doing?' he hissed rhetorically, growing more fierce at the thought of each new injustice, 'I teach in a school. Teach!' he snorted, as if it were the last indignity, 'If I were in Kuwait, I would be an under-secretary. But here all those jobs are for cousins of Shaikh Isa!' No doubt some of his scorching indignation was assumed for my benefit, for Arabs have a natural capacity for histrionics that never seems to desert them, however many foreign universities they may go to. Yet his grounds for frustration were surely real enough, and they are shared by hundreds of young Bahrainis who have inherited the Belgrave legacy but have not yet been allowed to spend it in their own way.

Only a fool would predict when they might try again to force the ruler's hand. But not even a fool could deny that eventually they will — and must, if he does not offer them something first. It could be tomorrow, or the day after. It is perhaps more likely to be next year or the year after that. The day will certainly be hastened if the Arabs as a whole appear to be advancing towards unity again, and delayed if they seem to be continuing in their quarrelsome disarray. But it scarcely seems within the bounds of possibility that the young men of Bahrain should bottle up their frustrations for another ten years, as they have done during the decade since Suez. Whether they will achieve much when they do explode again is far more questionable. Unless the Arabs have genuinely settled some of their differences, they might achieve nothing but to bring the British more firmly to the Ruler's aid, and so harden the divisions that already exist between the young nationalists and the old order in the Gulf. On the other hand, they might persuade the Ruler that the British mania for change is as nothing compared to the demands that are growing among his own people. Shaikh Isa, after all, is still young. He might still be capable of learning.

Meanwhile, politics in Bahrain seem to be walled-up, as it were, inside an old house, with no obvious means of escape. The walls are good, nineteenth-century constructions, valuable and cosy in their day but unlikely ever to make a desirable modern residence, for they are manifestly clumsy and out-of-date, cramping the contemporary energies and ambitions of both Britain and the Arabs. Like Sir Charles Belgrave's old home, they were built in other days for other ways, and the ghosts of the past haunt their confines still. They would be better torn down and replaced by something new, if only someone could find a way to do it. Alas for us all, it is extraordinary how tenacious some old walls — and ghosts — can be.

14

Cancer on the Coast

The farther south you go in the Gulf, the more the old Arabian world asserts itself. In Kuwait the old world is virtually dead. In Bahrain it is clearly dying — although it is taking an unconscionable time about it. But on the Trucial Coast of Oman the ancient life of Arabia persisted almost unchallenged until the other day, and its rhythms and customs still seem paramount.

It was only at the end of 1962 that the shaikhdom of Abu Dhabi shipped its first load of crude oil from Das Island, a rocky speck in the Gulf between Qatar and the Trucial Coast; and another year elapsed before the first tanker was loaded from the wells at Murban, on the Abu Dhabi mainland. In the other six tiny principalities of the Coast — Dubai, Sharjah, Ajman, Ras al Khaima, Umm al Qaiwain and distant, rocky Fujairah on the shores of the Indian Ocean — there is still only hopeful exploration; and although in all of them shaikhly nostrils are distended now to catch the heady scent of Abu Dhabi's unearned income, the old preoccupations of tribal life maintain a tough supremacy over newer ways.

Stern and jealous those preoccupations are, for the Trucial Shaikhdoms waited a long time in poverty, neglect and savagery before even the smell of prosperity came their way. Pursuing her traditional maritime interest, Britain left their internal affairs to fester unchecked for a century after she had established her control of the sea, and what pugnacity their people were prevented from discharging in piracy in the Gulf, they devoted to banditry and murder ashore. Fratricide, parricide and constant warfare were their normal modes of political argument. A British report of the second half of the nineteenth century hints eloquently at their benighted state:

'The mania for fighting that seems to possess the Arab mind in general appears to have lost none of its intensity among the warlike

The Sultan's palace and the waterfront at Muscat from Fort Murani

A slave has his head shaved in Nizwa

British troops arrive in Nizwa, 1957

The Sultan of Muscat and his slaves

Chieftains of the tract of country on the Western shores of the Gulf, and formerly known as the Pirate coast, during the year under review. The limits of this Report do not permit, nor indeed would the interest of the matter warrant an account in detail of all the petty skirmishes and engagements, the night attacks, and plundering raids, that form the events of their guerrilla-like system of warfare. . . . It is to be regretted that the friendly offices of the British Agent and the Residency to procure an amicable settlement of these differences have hitherto been unproductive of successful results.'[1]

British 'good offices' rarely did produce results; but as long as the seaways were clear and the coasts free of other foreign interference, little else was attempted by the British or Indian Governments for another 70 years. An account of the remarkable state of affairs in Abu Dhabi half-a-century later by a former Political Resident confirms that nothing much had changed there then, either in the violent circumstances of local life or in the British attitude towards them:

'Some few years ago the Sheikh of Abu Dhabi, at that time the chief Sheikhdom of the Trucial coast, died and left several sons. The eldest son inherited. After some years of his Sheikhdom a brother asked him to dinner; as the Sheikh left after dinner his brother followed him down the stairs, and, having incontinently shot him in the back, reigned in his stead. After a short interval a second brother asked the new Sheikh to dinner, and, as the Sheikh left after dinner and proceeded down the stairs, his host also seized the happy occasion, and, having shot him in the back, reigned in his stead. This brother was the Sheikh when I took over the appointment of Resident, and I have never seen a man with fear so written in his face. I gave him a year at most to live; he proved me wrong, he lived eighteen months. He was also asked to dinner by a brother, who, however, did not shoot him in the back; the Sheikh came upon an ambush on his way home and was shot in the front. The last brother was a wise man and put his nephew on the throne, and now the sons of the last murdered man are already maturing their plans to murder the new Sheikh.'[2]

The new Shaikh, however, survived longer than the Political Resident expected. At the end of 1964, in fact, he was still there — Shaikh Shakhbut ibn Sultan, Ruler of Abu Dhabi, the first man in nearly two centuries to enjoy that title for so long, and the direct inheritor of as

[1] Administration Report of the Persian Gulf Residency, 1874–5, quoted in the *Memorial of the Government of Saudi Arabia* submitted to the International Tribunal on the Buraimi dispute; 1955: Sect. IV. Para. 241.

[2] Sir Lionel Haworth, 'Persia and the Persian Gulf,' *Journal of the Central Asian Society*, vol. 16 (1929), part 4, p. 501.

bloody a sequence of family murders as was ever tolerated by the British Raj. Why was it tolerated? The Resident also asked that question, and provided the definitive answer. To put a stop to it, he wrote, 'would entail a control on the mainland that we have no desire to assume, it would mean an extension of the British Empire; in such a work you cannot stop halfway, however much you may desire to do so.'[1]

So Britain not merely stayed her hand, she effectively turned her back on the Trucial Shaikhdoms until after the Second World War. Except for building a primitive airfield at Sharjah and a flying-boat base in the creek at Dubai for the use of Imperial Airways on the route to India, she did nothing to assist their development. There was little practical reason why she should. In their unprofitable Arabian sands what the British Government wanted was not a new colonial responsibility to stretch its administrative resources further, but the maintenance of what Lord Curzon called 'loyal feudatories' — chieftains who acknowledged British external supremacy and could safely be left thereafter to get on with their local wars and misgovernment undisturbed.

They did. As late as 1948 Dubai was still at war with both Abu Dhabi and Sharjah. A friend of mine, Mr. Ronald Codrai, newly arrived then upon the coast, has described to me, as he saw it, the last of this action on the Sharjah side. The armoury of the warriors consisted chiefly of ancient muskets and naval cannon captured by local pirates as much as 300 years before. In the absence of proper wadding they were usually plugged with old rags, and one old Portuguese cannon was used to fire pistons plundered from abandoned motor engines. Cannon balls generally were in such short supply that a truce was declared after sunset prayers every night to enable both sides to comb the battlefield for old balls that might be used again next day. Such makeshift hostilities were all of a piece with the black comedy of politics in the shaikhdoms throughout the previous century; but the comedy was about to end at last — and Codrai, as it happened, was the symbolic reason why. He represented the Iraq Petroleum Company.

Since the first oil agreements on the Coast had been negotiated in the 1920's between the local chiefs and the British Government, little had been done to follow them up. The first concessions were not leased to oil companies for more than ten years, and the Second World War delayed any serious exploration. When the oil companies began to display a real interest in the Trucial Coast, after 1945, they immediately encountered two problems which have dogged the politics of the region ever since — the absence of internal security and the lack of fixed

[1] ibid.

frontiers. The first was vital to the safety of their prospecting teams, and the second was needed to establish the limits of their concession areas. Yet so foreign to the Trucial Coast were these normal attributes of modern statehood that the very existence of some of the shaikhdoms was in doubt. Sometimes in the heat of war or the aftermath of assassination there had been only four or five of them. At other times, there were eight or even nine. In none of them had security ever been assured for oil prospectors, or anyone else. The arrival of the oil-men, however, forced the British Government to accept responsibility for establishing peace, security and a recognisable *status quo*. Thus, while the Empire elsewhere was dead or dying, here it acquired, suddenly, a new lease of life as the principle of non-interference in the internal affairs of the shaikhdoms was abandoned, willy-nilly, and the Raj bestirred itself at last upon the land as well as the sea.

Appropriately enough, Ronald Codrai was not only a symbol of this belated change but also, in at least one bizarre incident, an agent of it. One day in 1950, having made his way over the mountains of the Musandam peninsula to the village of Fujairah, just south of the Straits of Hormuz, he was set upon by the local shaikh, who demanded to know why he had shelled Fujairah 'yesterday' and destroyed the local fort. Codrai, who had never seen the place before, requested an explanation in his turn, and discovered that — as so often happens in Arabia — the shaikh's measure of time was more poetic than precise. In fact, he harboured a grudge from some twenty-five years earlier when, in an obscure difference with his father, the British Government had sent a sloop to lob a few admonitory shells into the village. Unfortunately, the captain had either omitted to put anyone ashore to explain his action or had been unable to find the shaikh or his son, both of whom had prudently fled to the mountains. Codrai was the first Englishman to have set foot in the place since then, and the son — by that time ruling in his father's stead — thought it reasonable to seek an explanation from him.

Such was the prevailing ignorance at the time in the British Government of the petty affairs of the Trucial Coast that Codrai's report of this incident appeared to be the first confirmation it had received for many years that Fujairah still enjoyed some independent existence. But another year went by before, on a second surveying expedition in the same area, Codrai established some idea of the extent of Fujairah territory. Encountering tribes in the Musandam interior who acknowledged loyalty to the Fujairah shaikh he realised that his indignant interlocutor of the previous year must be more important than anyone had supposed; and a further report from him persuaded the British

Government to seek treaty relations with the shaikh. Still another year later, in 1952 — seven years after the Second World War, let us remember, and five years after the Indian Empire had gone — Fujairah was formally incorporated as the last Trucial Shaikhdom of Oman. Even then the British system in the lower Gulf was not quite complete, as we now know it, for with the addition of Fujairah there were then eight shaikhdoms instead of seven. Only when one little territory called Kalba was absorbed by its slightly larger neighbour, Sharjah, a few weeks later, was the present outline established at last.

By then the mechanism of British intervention had begun to creak into tardy action. In 1952 the Government raised a small group of local levies to act as a police force throughout the Coast. Known at first as the Trucial Oman Levies, and later as the Trucial Oman Scouts, the force was based on the principle often employed by the Raj among the tribes of the North West Frontier, and later adapted to Arabia in the Aden Protectorate Levies and the Jordan Arab Legion, of turning poachers into gamekeepers by giving them British officers and a regular wage. Local tribesmen who had spent most of their lives fighting and robbing each other were recruited expressly to prevent their cousins from continuing to do the same — and thus to establish, at the same time, a minimum of physical security for the oil-prospecting teams. Almost immediately, however, they were involved in another task, when Saudi Arabia laid claim to the oasis of Buraimi and established a police post there in 1952, in the hope of extending her oil-bearing lands at the expense of the Sultan of Muscat and the Ruler of Abu Dhabi. Here was a direct threat of external aggression — even though a confused and minuscule one — to which Britain was obliged to respond under the terms of her old agreements with the rulers; and in 1955, after an abortive attempt at international arbitration, she used the new Trucial Scouts to expel the Saudis from Buraimi by force. The details of the Buraimi dispute will be examined later, but the point to be made about it now is that — as the Saudis might have expected, but apparently did not — it resulted in strengthening, not weakening, Britain's commitment to the Trucial Shaikhs. In effect, it caused Britain to serve notice that, for the first time in 150 years, the frontier she was ready to defend had moved from the Gulf coast to the deserts beyond; and that just as she had previously policed the seas to protect her commerce and her Empire, so now she was prepared to police the land to protect her potential or actual oil supplies.

Oil, indeed, although still undiscovered in the Trucial Shaikhdoms, had become their new *raison d'être*. Within a few years after the Second

World War, the promise of oil had caused Britain to stabilise their form and numbers, inspired pacification of their eternal tribal warfare, created a demand for their territorial definition, and provoked a direct external challenge to their existence. From being fluid, tribal backwaters of empire, largely unknown and uncared for, they had become territorially and diplomatically immutable — seven tiny principalities, whose joint population did not, at a generous estimate, exceed 100,000 souls, but to whose individual and collective security Britain was now totally committed. The 'loyal feudatories' had never had it so good. What was more, they knew it; and stoutly as successive British Agents pressed upon them all the wisdom of increasing mutual co-operation, the Rulers were even stouter in their resistance. Conscious of the manifest absurdity of these territories as potentially independent states, and anxious to prepare the way for a more rational future, the British toyed with the notion of a federation. Conscious of the strength of their position as long as the British umbrella was held over them, and of the lack of any other alternatives acceptable to Britain, the Rulers simply ignored such ideas. The new hopes of oil were as divisive as ancient jealousies. No Ruler would surrender to his cousins even a putative share in a possible income from a prospective oil discovery. The most that the British could do was to persuade them to meet now and then in a Trucial Council; and since oil was found in Abu Dhabi even the Council has been weakened by the absence of Shaikh Shakhbut. He is keeping his money strictly to himself — and his fellow rulers are looking forward still more avidly to doing precisely the same thing.

For all their new security and their dreams of oil, therefore, the Trucial Shaikhdoms seemed still to languish, even after 1952, in a romantic, anachronistic limbo. Their rulers had little conception of the changing world beyond their shores, and their people had less. Shaikh Shakhbut, for instance, had never used a bank, although his income from the oil companies, for their exploration rights in his territory, was more than £100,000 a year after 1952. The money was paid, at his insistence, in brand-new Indian rupee notes which he carried off in one of his voluminous under-skirts to the strong room of his little palace. There, with great labour and much suspicion, he counted every note himself, thrust them into old petrol tins and suitcases, and locked them out of sight and use. When at last Shaikh Shakhbut was persuaded to open a bank account and permitted a British bank to open a branch in his town, it was some years before he was reconciled to losing sight of his money. More than once he asked to be shown his cash, to reassure himself that it was still there; and great was the relief of the manager when he was discouraged from counting for himself every rupee in the place. Cheques were a special cause of suspicion and bewilderment. Once when he had flown to London for the first time for a holiday he sent his Arab secretary back to Abu Dhabi again to get him some more money. 'But why,' asked the local bank manager, 'didn't the Shaikh write a cheque in London?' 'He did,' the secretary replied, 'Do you take him for a fool? I have brought it with me, of course!'

Even in 1957, when I saw the Trucial Coast for the first time, there was only one bank in Dubai and a branch ten miles away in Sharjah that was open twice a week. Nowhere else along the Coast was there any bank at all. Kuwait by then had been causing fainting fits in the British Treasury for a full five years, the Shaikhs of Qatar were daubing the night clubs of Europe and the Middle East with gold, and Bahrain was simmering with the aftermath of her Suez riots. But on the Trucial Coast both affluence and nationalism still seemed far away. Along Dubai's stinking creek, where the dhows lay bow to stern under ragged and piebald flags, and the boatmen heaved their passengers under white awnings from shore to shore, like Venetian gondoliers, the air of romantic isolation was like a shroud. This, surely, was the end of the imperial line. The creek was all too clearly a public lavatory, the harbour bar was undredged, and for ten miles inland there was no way of crossing from side to side except by ferry. The *suk* was empty of all but the cheapest goods from India and Hong-Kong, and except for a couple of pictures of President Nasser and a painted tray that seemed to be a stray Asian relic of Bandung — with portraits of Nehru, Sukarno and Mao Tse-tung — there was no sign of political thinking or agitation.

Yet Dubai was by far the biggest town on the coast. Perhaps 40,000 people were gathered there then; and it was a measure both of its importance compared to the rest of the Trucial Shaikhdoms and its insignificance in most other contexts that seamen in the Gulf knew it simply as 'the light' — after the solitary electric illumination in the middle of town, over the offices of Gray, Mackenzie, the British shipping agents. It was the only place on the coast with a substantial centre of permanent buildings, which threw up crenellated, shimmering ranks of wind-towers on either side of the creek to catch the breezes and carry them down into the rooms below in a primitive form of air-conditioning. The poorer houses erected towers of straw and sacking, like tattered box-kites; but the better towers were made of mud and stone, with two or three decorated louvres on every side, like narrow renaissance windows, confirming the incongruous impression left by the boatmen that Dubai was a sort of decrepit, Arabian Venice.

Although Dubai had a bank, it had no hotel. Alone among the Trucial Shaikhdoms, that privilege belonged to Sharjah, where the inhabitants' chief pride and joy — apart from a Ruler who combined a reputation as a poet with a taste for Indian astrology — was a curious building known as 'The Fort'. Square, solid and white-washed, with a courtyard within and battlements without, The Fort was built in the wild and lawless '30's, when Imperial Airways began to use the Sharjah airstrip and required some safe overnight accommodation for their passengers and crews, as well as an airfield operations centre. No doubt The Fort fulfilled these functions admirably. Its stone walls and iron-clad gates must have foiled any marauding beduin. But no-one could have described it as a comfortable or convenient place to stay for visitors who wanted to do business on the Coast. Except for an occasional aeroplane to Abu Dhabi the only means of getting anywhere from The Fort — even into Dubai — was to walk or hitch-hike on what few vehicles were available. Its air conditioning units, installed as a well-meaning salute to the modern world, stopped every night when the local power supply failed; and its solitary shower never, while I was there, produced anything but salt water. Outside, R.A.F. jets screamed off the airstrip in thundering clouds of dust, while a poor, deranged negro in a naval cap and red sash strutted indefatigably round the walls all day controlling imaginary air movements at the top of his voice. 'Sharjah callin', Sharjah callin', ovah to you, ovah to you, Rojjah!' he would cry, in a passable imitation of the signallers' jargon, while the local beduin squatted at the gates, scraping their teeth with twigs and spitting in puzzled but respectful incomprehension.

Elsewhere along the Coast there was nothing but an occasional scatter of palm-thatch huts along the shore and sometimes a 'palace' of white-washed mud occupied by a local ruler. This unrelieved poverty and barrenness was, and to a great extent still is, the most characteristic aspect of the Trucial Shaikhdoms. At heart they are still those same lawless little places where that 'mania for fighting that seems to possess the Arab mind' so impressed the British Agent a century ago. Outside the larger settlements like Dubai, few of their inhabitants are ever seen without a rifle and a belt full of bullets; and in spite of the efforts of the Trucial Scouts travellers are still ambushed in the desert, and blood feuds and tribal wars are still pursued in the mountains of Musandam. Piracy on the Coast may have been dead for a century, but smuggling is more alive than ever. From isolated beaches, guns are run to the rebels against the Sultan of Muscat's authority in the interior of Oman; and from the waterfront of Dubai gold is smuggled every month into the rickety economies of India and Pakistan. Several comfortable Dubai fortunes have been built on the latter trade in the last ten years, for gold that is freely and legally bought there can be sold across the water at a profit of 100 per cent or more, and there is hardly a dhow captain in the creek who has not tried his hand at the game.

The return cargo can be lucrative, too, and far more offensive, for it deals in human lives and hopes as well as in simple avarice. Unscrupulous boat-owners on the Coast maintain agents in Pakistan and India to encourage Muslim peasants to make the pilgrimage to Mecca by taking a cheap passage to Arabia on their dhows. Thousands of peasants every year swallow this swindle. Eager for the solace and glory of the Haj, they sell all they own to pay for their passage and crowd upon the boats already destitute of everything but their faith. A few days later they are put ashore at some uninhabited cove in Oman and told that Mecca is just over the horizon. It is, in fact, 1,000 miles away across some of the worst desert in the world.

I saw some of these poor souls once, outside a tiny British hospital in Ras al Khaima, to which fortune had guided them out of the killing desert. It was night, the electricity generator had failed, and the solitary British doctor was using hurricane lamps. At the edge of their white glare as we walked across the little hospital compound we saw a row of ghostly figures beyond the wire. Patient and emaciated, they squatted there upon their haunches — two old grey-beards, two younger men, two women and some children. Their bony knees each supported an elbow, with the forearms thrust outwards and the palms turned upwards in supplication, and eight or ten pairs of opaque eyes gazed at us through the lantern-light. We took them inside and they were fed. One of the children was almost dead, another seriously ill. They spoke no language that any of us knew, they had no money and no possessions. They were literally castaways, flung upon this coast like flotsam to make their way to Mecca or die. Many like them do die. In the winter season, from September to May, when the winds are favourable for the dhow traffic, two or three hundred of them may be dumped upon the Trucial Coast every week. A few may find jobs, many exist by begging, others eventually are rounded up and sent home, and a lucky handful — richer, brighter or fitter than the rest — may somehow get through to Mecca. The rest die. Where the sand desert begins in earnest on the western fringes of Abu Dhabi, the Trucial Scouts bury two or three of these pilgrims on every patrol through the winter season, and many other bodies probably are never found. In its callousness and profitability this is the modern equivalent of the slave trade, but it is more difficult to suppress because the victims come of their own free will, ready accomplices of the merchants and their agents.

Some critics have insisted that the slave trade itself is not yet dead on the Trucial Coast, and there are even a few who profess to believe that the British authorities do not really want to end it. This is not my own experience. In most of the British-protected territories of Arabia, the traffic in slaves has been banned officially for a century or more, and although in practice the traffic certainly continued in many places for as long as the British exercised no territorial control, I have never seen any sign of it in the last ten years, and I have never met anyone who could give me first-hand evidence of it, either. Most of the isolated cases of slave trading that are reported nowadays are somewhat ambiguous. There is an unscrupulous practice among some men on the Trucial Coast, for example, of marrying young girls and taking them to Muscat where the brides are divorced by Muslim custom and remarried to other men for a suitable consideration. Some may see this as a form of slave-trading, others may find it a logical result of the inferior position of women in an orthodox, Islamic society. Short of disrupting the entire social structure, however, it is hard to see what any external authority like the British can do about it. Apart from this sort of traffic, and a few cases of kidnapping, I do not believe there has been any active slave trading on the Trucial Coast since the Scouts occupied Buraimi. Before that, when no effective control was exercised in Buraimi by Britain — and not much by the local rulers either, for that matter — Saudi slave traders ran a flourishing market there, asking anything from £150 to £300 a head for their merchandise.[1] But since 1955 that traffic has been stopped, and the three known Saudi slavers in the oasis have all been compulsorily retired.

This is not to say that slaves have ceased entirely to exist upon the Trucial Coast. Slavery as an institution is permitted, with certain qualifications, under the *sharia* law of Islam, and it has always been, therefore, one of those 'internal affairs' of the Arabian rulers with which Britain chose not to concern herself officially, however much her representatives might deplore it unofficially. In consequence, it was 1956 before the British managed to persuade six out of the seven Trucial Shaikhs to declare that 'anyone who was formerly a slave is now free'. The seventh was the stubborn Shaikh Shakhbut, who was not cajoled into a similar declaration until June, 1963, when the Yemen revolt and the Saudi example had frightened him into action. Now, in all

[1] See e.g. Wilfred Thesiger's account of Buraimi in *Arabian Sands*, Longmans Green & Co., London, 1960, pp. 224–5.

Arabia, the Sultan of Muscat is the only important ruler who maintains unchanged the permissive *sharia* law on slavery. There is not much doubt that the 'retainers' in his palaces are what the rest of the world would call slaves. Yet even in Muscat the slave traffic has been forbidden for nearly a century, and the British Consul-General, who is empowered under the nineteenth-century treaties to manumit any slaves who come to him for the purpose, sometimes grants 'freedom' to a score of persons in a single year.

On the Trucial Coast also, this ancient procedure of manumission continues. The Political Agent in Dubai still wakes up half-a-dozen times a year to find some man or woman clutching the flagpole in his garden — where, by tradition, a slave is acknowledged to be safe. But neither he nor they can be certain nowadays whether such people are slaves or not. Legally, after the Rulers' declarations, they cannot be; but they may well be former slaves who have only just grasped that they now have a right to their freedom and have come to claim it in the traditional way, from the father-figure of the Raj. Often, however, they are not and never were slaves in the ordinary sense of the term, but disgruntled servants who hope to use a certificate of manumission to squeeze better terms out of their employers. Some of them are regular supplicants at the flagpole, arriving once a year to have their certificates renewed like passports — and offering, in the process, a touching reminder of the former authority and somewhat arrogant assumptions of British power. Like that message from the Foreign Secretary which still adorns British passports, to 'request and require in the name of Her Majesty' that the bearer shall pass without let or hindrance, the manumission certificate speaks to us from a simpler and more optimistic age. 'Be it known to all who may see this,' it declares, under crossed Union flags and the British coat of arms, 'that the bearer, Mr. X, aged about blank years, has been manumitted and no-one has a right to interfere with his liberty.'

Noble words: but as we noted earlier the real death warrant of Arabian slavery has not been signed by British power or Victorian morality, but by money.[1] And on the Trucial Coast, as elsewhere, money nowadays eats away like a cancer at the old life and all its institutions. It has not yet destroyed them, as it has done in Kuwait, or brought them near to paralysis, as in Bahrain; but it is lodged already in every vein and artery, and beginning to spread irresistibly now, and with speed. At first the money was measured only in tens of thousands of pounds, when the first oil companies began their explorations soon

[1] See above, p. 136.

194

after the Second World War. At that level the cancer was no bigger, so to speak, than a mole on a man's neck. Then, slowly, the figures began to grow and the money to circulate like cells of infection corrupting the ancient bloodstream. There were the wages remitted by tribesmen who were tempted from their homes for the first time to work in the new and booming oilfields farther up the Gulf. There was a British Government development fund, for £500,000, to set up the first few schools and clinics, and an agricultural research station. There was the Kuwait Government's first experiment in inter-Arab aid, supplying water-wells and teachers for the Trucial Shaikhdoms long before it began to pay protection money to its larger Arab neighbours. The Trucial Scouts helped to spread the cancer, creating security where there was none before, expanding its military headquarters in Sharjah, drawing a thousand weekly pay packets, starting a trade school for the men and an elementary school for their children. As the search for oil became more fevered, the exploration concessions changed hands at higher prices, and the cancer spread again. As India grew poorer and Muscat more troubled, the gold-smugglers and gun-runners of Dubai grew richer. By 1960, the flow of money along the Coast was already beginning to be measured in millions instead of thousands. And then, at last, oil was found. On Das Island in 1960, the Abu Dhabi Marine Areas — a subsidiary of British Petroleum and the Compagnie Française des Pétroles — announced a substantial discovery. Soon afterwards the Abu Dhabi Petroleum Company — a subsidiary of the Iraq Petroleum Company — announced a major find on the mainland. Twelve years after the I.P.C.'s representative had watched the last of the Trucial wars, eight years after Fujairah had been shaken from its total isolation, the commercial vultures began to gather over the Trucial Coast, for they knew that its old life was now as good as dead.

On a visit to the Gulf at the end of 1963, I met the first evidence of this accumulating wealth upon the Trucial Coast as far away as Baghdad, where a dozen baskets of trussed and hooded hunting hawks were loaded on to my aircraft. They were on their way to Dubai and Abu Dhabi, where — as I discovered — the hunting of the bustard and the desert hare, once pursued on foot with a few dogs and a local bird or two, was now accomplished with Land Rovers, Cadillacs and imported falcons by the score. So great was the new demand for birds that the price of a good falcon from Northern Syria had risen by 50 per cent in the previous eighteen months to £200 or more; and in the winter months, when the game was good, a single shaikh would take 50 or 100 birds on his hunting trips and think little of losing a score of them.

Indeed, while I was there, Shaikh Rashid, the Ruler of Dubai, left by sea for a hunting trip in southern Persia, taking more than thirty friends and retainers and something like £30,000 worth of birds on board his private dhow.

But there were far more solid signs of wealth upon the Coast than this. In the town of Dubai alone, where the oil concession had just changed hands again at a higher price than ever, there were four separate banks; in the village of Abu Dhabi, three. Gray, Mackenzie's 'light' was indistinguishable among the neon signs and street lamps that cast their nightly glow upon Dubai's narrow harbour. The boatmen who had heaved me across the creek six years earlier with choppy little strokes on their crude oars now sped me from side to side with outboard motors. The creek had been both bridged and dredged: the first by courtesy of the Ruler of Qatar, who had married Shaikh Rashid's daughter and built the bridge as a wedding gift; and the second through the co-operation of the local merchants, who were delighted to discover that the filthy accumulation of centuries which the dredgers and bulldozers deposited on the banks would fetch £10 a square foot as building land. The elegant wind-towers were disappearing — torn down, or hidden behind tall blocks of air-conditioned flats — and in the *suk* that had been so empty on my previous visit, the Swiss watch manufacturers had established yet another Arabian empire. In three minutes and forty-five seconds one morning I watched the secretary of the Ruler of Dubai, clad in a printed cotton skirt, double-breasted jacket and transparent plastic sandals, enter a shop where I happened to be buying a penknife, select eight gold and jewelled watches, to a total value of slightly over £1,000, and walk out with his booty slung into a string-bag with scarcely a word spoken. The shopkeeper took this remarkable transaction as calmly as the secretary. When it was finished, he turned to me with an amiable shrug: 'That happens once a month,' he said, 'and I'm not the only one who supplies the Palace.'

Dubai had already stolen much of the visitors' trade from The Fort at Sharjah by acquiring two hotels since my previous visit, and it was about to complete the process by opening its own international airport as well, with a glittering control tower of tinted glass and concrete and loud-speakers purring in the lounge. There would be no salt-water showers and hallucinated hangers-on there. Come to that, there was no longer much place for them in Sharjah, either. My poor, mad negro was dead, they told me. The Fort was surrounded by the permanent barracks and workshops of the Trucial Scouts, and taxis by the dozen were available to make the trip to Dubai. Everywhere along the Coast the British had multiplied: more police and army officers, more doctors, advisers, and bankers. Many of them were displaced officials from India, the Sudan and Africa, the last of the great diaspora of British imperial servants, now gathered here in this benighted corner of Arabia to perform the Empire's final office.

Most important of all, of course, there was the change in Abu Dhabi. Outwardly it was only a small and hesitant change as yet. There was a new hotel, with a Greek manager from Alexandria and a chef paid £300 a month, and in the unkempt, fly-blown alleys of the *suk*, beside the bales of gaudy Indian cloths and the sacks of sweet tobacco, there were new Pakistani restaurants in lean-to shacks of cardboard and a 'Repairing House for Electrical, Side of All Motor Vehicles'. But whereas Dubai had the air of a genuine boom town, Abu Dhabi was still essentially a village in appearance. At first sight this was surprising, for with barely 20,000 people scattered among its waste of lagoons, sandpits, desert and infrequent oasis, Abu Dhabi was already, in theory, one of the richest little countries in the world. Alas, however, Shaikh Shakhbut had none of the commercial confidence of Shaikh Rashid in Dubai. His life was too enmeshed in fear, suspicion and obstinacy. While Rashid probably learned the tricks of trading and smuggling at his father's knee, Shakhbut acquired little more than an acute sense of danger. In his line of desert hunters and warriors with its savage record of murder, trade was demeaning, finance a mystery and life itself an uncertain blessing to be guarded with knife-like cunning. He was credited with, and displayed, a quick intelligence; but it often seemed as though his thirty years of rule had left him with a manic view of the world — too jaundiced to permit hope, too eccentric to admit argument. Since the discovery of oil in his territory he had become even more difficult, and was described to me in an exasperated moment by no less a person than the Political Agent in Abu Dhabi, as 'just about the worst cross I've ever had to bear'. Admittedly the Agent, Colonel Sir Hugh Boustead, was never a man renowned for his patience. Sunny, energetic, and sometimes explosive, he had blazed a trail of endearing and usually effective eccentricity for the best part of fifty years from the army in the Sudan through advisory jobs in the Aden Protectorates and Muscat, to the verge of honoured retirement in Abu Dhabi, and it would have been agreeable and in keeping for him to have signed off with a flourish by winning Shakhbut to the rational, imperial, British way of progress. It was not to be. By the time Sir Hugh left in 1965, Shakhbut had made himself the oddest of all Britain's embarrassments in Arabia. Where other rulers might press for better deals and more money, and long to have untold oil riches to spend, Shakhbut not only refused to spend most of what he had but even declined to accept all the money that the oil companies wished to thrust upon him.

This was not a result of altruism or generosity. Briefly, and without the technicalities that veil the finances of the oil business from the puzzled eyes of laymen, what Shaikh Shakhbut lacked was an income tax law. With that he could have levied a tax on the income of the oil companies from their operations in his territory that would have taken his own share of the proceeds up to the standard level of 50 per cent, and probably more. Without it, he could not, and was forced to be content with a straightforward, and much lower, royalty on each ton of oil produced. As a result, although Abu Dhabi's production would have entitled him, under the normal oil agreements, to receive nearly £20 million a year by the end of 1964, Shakhbut was getting only about £6 million. For both the oil companies and the British Government, this strange impasse was a source of acute dyspepsia. The companies could not simply take the extra profit with a thankful heart: on the contrary, they were forced to reserve large sums in the knowledge that an eventual settlement would certainly be retrospective, and in the meantime they risked the disfavour of other Arab governments in the oil business for allegedly under-cutting them by their apparently discriminatory treatment of Shakhbut. The British Government, equally, did not wish it said that it was a party to the unscrupulous exploitation of Arab oil. Together, therefore, the companies and the Government produced Arab accountants and commercial lawyers for Shakhbut's edification, and presented him with a draft law for an income tax modelled on those of his richer cousins in Saudi Arabia and Kuwait. But neither argument nor assistance shifted Shakhbut, who seemed neither to understand the technicalities of oil finance himself — which was not surprising — nor to trust anyone else to help him.

To the British, who had seen it all before, the way ahead in Abu Dhabi was obvious and urgent — development, administration, organisation and all that. So they presented Shakhbut with a £25 millions plan for turning his scraggy little village of palm thatch huts and mud villas into a model town of the Gulf, with power and water supplies, hospitals and schools, shopping centres, recreation areas, industrial quarters and all the mod. cons. of the contemporary urban planner — a model of enlightenment for all to see. Like the draft law for the income tax, however, Shakhbut examined it and put it to one side. Stiff notes followed from the Resident in Bahrain. Angry exchanges ensued with the Agent in Abu Dhabi. But when Shakhbut acted at last it was only to turn to a Lebanese entrepreneur, who introduced a German firm, which did a few little jobs piecemeal on terms that Shakhbut disclosed to no-one, leaving the British spluttering with even more frustration than before.

Some saw malice in Shakhbut's strange actions. Some saw sheer meanness, some saw obstinacy, and nearly everyone saw fear. The fear that was rooted in his poverty-stricken past was strengthened by his experience of wealth. Until he became one of the world's potential multi-millionaires he had never had more money for his state than he could count for himself in an afternoon, and few foreigners had ever bothered to give him so much as the time of day. But when the cash was beyond all his calculations he was surrounded by business-men with propositions, officials with advice, consultants with plans, and journalists who would pick his bones for a story. Like a man who had won the football pools, he was learning that money makes no friends. Terrified of losing all contact with the life he knew, mistrustful of all who tried to lead him into new ways, he sat day after day in his crowded little *majlis*, nervous, withdrawn and stubborn, tapping at his shoes with a whippy camel stick and contemplating his inescapable dilemma. He might be extravagant, like the Saudis of old and the Shaikhs of Qatar, seeking to buy popularity today and raising envy and unrest tomorrow. He might be a miser, hoarding his millions, and hear the mutters of discontent among his people grow in a few years to a consuming roar. He might be diplomatic and enlightened, long-of-life and all-wise, and live to see — like the Ruler of Kuwait — his authority weakened and perhaps his very existence threatened by the turmoil of social and political change that his money and his wisdom would promote.

In the end, however, there was no choice, for it was all Lombard Street to a China orange that Shakhbut's oil income, even at its early levels, would transform Abu Dhabi in one short generation whatever he did or did not do. Indeed, in spite of his fear and obstinacy, the process had already begun when I last saw him in his palace at the end of 1963. The first shipment of oil had left Das Island a year earlier, and the first tanker to load at the mainland terminal was even then lying just offshore. Still Shakhbut rejected the long-term plans and rational laws that the British wanted him to adopt, but the sheer accumulating pressure of money was beginning to force him along paths whose end he hardly dared to contemplate. There were new schools, with teachers from Jordan; new clinics, with doctors from Pakistan; a new water supply, with engineers from Germany; and every day in the *majlis*, while his retainers whispered secret entreaties in his ear and their hawks clutched the frayed covers of the sofas round the walls, the sober-suited business-men bowed before him with yet another proposition from Birmingham or Beirut.

If no more oil is ever discovered in the Trucial Shaikhdoms, Abu Dhabi's riches alone seem enough to accelerate the social revolution in them all. From Buraimi to Fujairah, the pressures are gathering with increasing speed around more or less bewildered men who will be pitchforked out of their traditional world into a Piccadilly Circus of enterprise, envy and chicanery. The tribes will crumble under the impact of money and education, and Cairo's Arab nationalism will find eager listeners among a new generation. Probably these pressures are no great menace yet to shaikhly prestige or British power. They only hint at troubles that may come — in ten years' time, perhaps, when the new generation has grown to manhood. Until then, at least, the old Arabia may maintain its dominance here; but sentence of death has been passed upon it, and I suspect that Shaikh Shakhbut ibn Sultan knows it. Perhaps the fear that he harbours and the obstinacy he displays are the reactions of a man who, having cheated death for more than thirty years, now recognises an assassin he cannot escape; the cancer of the twentieth century.

15

Anatomy of a Dispute

————————∿∿∿∿∿ ❁ ∿∿∿∿∿∿————————

There seems nothing at first, or even second sight, to justify the place of the Buraimi oasis at the centre of an international dispute for a generation. From the air it looks like a collection of shabby green rugs thrown down upon a scarred and pitted pavement. On the ground it seems even more impoverished and diffuse, each green rug revealing itself as a chain of threadbare gardens with a sandy canvas showing through a thin embroidery of palm trees, and the surrounding waste of thorn, dune and gravel stretching to infinity in every direction. No oil is pumped from here, and the oil companies apparently have abandoned whatever hope they once had of finding any. The airstrip is no more than a roughly-levelled patch of stony desert between the thorn bushes, and the only military forces present are one company of the Trucial Oman Scouts in an absurdly romantic whitewashed fort that looks as if it had strayed from *Beau Geste*, and a smaller number of the Sultan of Muscat's army in another mud-walled compound a few miles away.

Yet both Britain and Saudi Arabia considered the place important enough to justify 'police actions' against each other here, and diplomatic relations between the two countries were severed for seven years because of their dispute. An international arbitration tribunal sat in Geneva for a year attempting, unsuccessfully, to settle their quarrel. A United Nations investigator was called in to examine it. Scholars and advocates on either side have produced formidable works about it. The Saudi Arabian Memorial prepared for the Geneva Tribunal, runs to three large volumes of description, history, maps and tax records. The British Memorial, presented on behalf of Abu Dhabi and Muscat, is equally impressive; and a British scholar, Dr. J. B. Kelly, working independently of either side, has produced still another closely argued volume about the dispute.[1] Never, the puzzled visitor may feel, as he

[1] *Eastern Arabian Frontiers*, Faber and Faber, London, 1964.

scuffles through the dusty gardens of Buraimi, was so much devoted by so many to so little. In fact, however, the Buraimi affair was far more significant than the appearance of the place suggests, for in the guise of an obscure frontier squabble about a few water wells and palm trees it contained several of the most crucial conflicts between the old Arabia and the new. It may be too much to call Buraimi a symbol, but it was — and to some extent still is — a sharp focus of those clashes whose effects we have traced elsewhere in Arabia between tribalism and the idea of the modern nation-state, between nomadism and fixed frontiers, ancient poverty and contemporary wealth, 'nationalism' and 'imperialism'. It is, therefore, one of the textbook cases of Arabia's growing pains.

Historically, Buraimi has always been important to the tribes of south-eastern Arabia as the principal oasis of Northern Oman, and the gateway from the southern deserts of the Hasa, in Saudi country, to the harbours of the Trucial Coast and the interior valleys of Oman, under the Sultan of Muscat's often exiguous sway. A three-cornered contest for the allegiance of its people and the use of its wells between the Saudis, the Sultan, and the Shaikhs of the Trucial Coast went on through most of the nineteenth century. The oasis then was rather like an island. The surrounding desert-sea 'belonged' effectively to no-one, although its caravan routes might be dominated by one ruler or another, much as British naval guns dominated the trade routes of the ocean. The oasis, on the other hand, having a stable nucleus of settled inhabitants, and seasonal influxes of wandering tribesmen from elsewhere, could be said to 'belong' to whichever distant overlord most effectively imposed his authority among its people. Occasionally, the dominant overlords were the Wahhabi predecessors of the modern Saudis, who sometimes compelled the Buraimi villagers to pay taxes to them. Often, and in this century fairly generally, it was the Sultans of Muscat or the Shaikhs of Abu Dhabi who exerted most authority.

This persistent ambiguity of allegiance was part of the familiar pattern of the desert, where fixed frontiers were pointless to nomadic tribesmen and the payment of feudal tribute was taken as the mark of sovereignty. But the demands of modern oil exploration and development froze this fluid order. Oil is related to territory, not to people. Its whereabouts are fixed, not moveable. Sovereign governments that wish to grant oil concessions must, therefore, have their national boundaries agreed and charted, so that the oil companies may know the territorial limits of their work. When the Buraimi dispute began, in 1949, the only such boundary of any consequence in eastern Arabia was that agreed under British supervision in 1922, dividing Kuwait, Iraq and Saudi Arabia. In south-eastern Arabia there were either no boundaries whatever or a succession of hypothetical lines on the map, resulting from a series of Saudi territorial claims over the previous 35 years, each a little wider than the last. None of these lines had been accepted by all parties, and none had been demarcated; and the last of them, proposed by the Saudis in 1935 and generally known as the Red Line, did not come within 100 miles of Buraimi. As far as the British and their local friends were concerned, in fact, the working frontier between Saudi Arabia and the British-protected shaikhdoms lay in the desert well westward of Buraimi along a slightly modified version of the Red Line, also dating from 1935 and known as the Riyadh Line. The oasis itself was assumed to be divided in its allegiance between the two British-supported rulers, as it had been, off and on, through much of the previous century. Of its total of eight small villages, two were subject to the Sultan of Muscat and six to Shaikh Shakhbut in Abu Dhabi.

By 1949, however, the discovery of rich oil resources in Qatar and intensified exploration in the Trucial Shaikhdoms persuaded the Saudis that a further territorial claim in the south-east might bring them handsome rewards. Accordingly, they proposed a new frontier, which sliced several miles into Qatar and enclosed four-fifths of Abu Dhabi territory and a substantial piece of Muscat and Oman, including the entire oasis of Buraimi. It is possible that they were encouraged to proceed with this expanded claim by the belief that the British were on the run, anyway. The British evacuation of Palestine the previous year, following hard upon the withdrawal from India, could well have suggested that British commitments in the Gulf would also be abandoned under pressure. It is likely also, that the increasing ill-health at that time of the old King, ibn Saud, enabled less scrupulous or more adventurous members of the royal family, and their advisers, to pursue a policy which in earlier days he might have discouraged. It is pretty certain that the need for a final and, if possible, generous definition of the concession area granted to the Arabian American Oil Company (ARAMCO) settled the precise timing of the claim, for it was in 1949 that ARAMCO was asked by the Saudi Government for the first time to surrender a proportion of its unexploited territory. Before the company could select rationally which parts it would relinquish, it had to be sure firstly, of the limits of the original concession which were set by the Saudi frontiers, and secondly, that it had done at least a preliminary geological survey of the whole of it. To be on the safe side or, as some would say, the greedy side, pending an agreement on the frontier, ARAMCO concentrated its survey teams in the disputed south-east where they several times found themselves prospecting the same areas as I.P.C. teams from Qatar or the Trucial Shaikhdoms, near or beyond the unmarked Riyadh and Red Lines.

There is little evidence that either of these oil companies officially pursued a policy of deliberate territorial expansion, and the picture that was sometimes drawn of the Buraimi dispute as a straightforward Anglo-American oil war was always too simple. For one thing, Standard Oil of New Jersey and Socony Mobil, two of the four shareholders in ARAMCO, are also among the shareholders in I.P.C., so that as far as they were concerned the dispute could not have been worth making much fuss about. On the other hand, both pragmatism and prejudice tended to drive the British and American Governments into opposing camps on the issue, and the Saudis were certainly encouraged to pursue their claims by the knowledge of Washington's tacit approval. The prejudice existed chiefly in the State Department, where a good many officials in the 1950's were anxious — often for honest enough reasons — to see the British Empire and all its works dismantled, and were not above giving the process a hearty shove whenever they could. In the Persian Gulf, and throughout Arabia, they seemed for a long time unaware of the extent to which the British presence probably saved the United States from herself assuming extra burdens. Instead, a tacit support of Saudi claims against the British-protected rulers seemed to them a logical extension of the vague American commitment to 'anti-colonialism', as well as a direct contribution to American commercial interests as represented by ARAMCO. Their attitude was appropriately embodied by the late John Foster Dulles, who — as Secretary of State — spoke openly at one stage of British 'aggression' in Buraimi and justified his remarks by referring, with blithe unreality, to something called 'public opinion' in Saudi Arabia.[1]

No doubt these American predispositions encouraged the Saudis not only to persist in their new claim, but also to put more pressure upon ARAMCO to support them than they might otherwise have dared to do. The Saudis were already making life uncomfortable for the company, through their demand for a partial surrender of the concession area, and they were about to go further in negotiating the first of the Middle East's 'fifty-fifty' agreements for sharing the profits of oil production. Without American Government backing, therefore, ARAMCO may have felt in no position to refuse, even had it wished to, the equipment and expertise which the Saudis repeatedly sought to aid their Buraimi campaign during the next few years. Pragmatism — or profits — com-

[1] *Full Circle*, The Memoirs of Sir Anthony Eden, pp. 334–5.

pelled the company to be, to some extent, a Saudi instrument. The pressures on I.P.C. were less direct. Neither the Sultan of Muscat nor the Shaikh of Abu Dhabi was as demanding as the Saudis, for they both depended on British support for their existence, and could hardly take a high-handed line with a partly British oil company. But the British Government was involved through its majority share-holding in British Petroleum, one of the major trading companies in I.P.C.; and in the absence of much knowledge of the remote Buraimi district among its own officials Whitehall was only too ready to use I.P.C.'s men-on-the-spot to assemble the British case. Hence, I.P.C. also was dragged in willy-nilly. While ARAMCO lorries carried Saudi arms and policemen into Buraimi, and Dr. George Rentz, an American Arabist on the company staff, supervised the preparation of the Saudi Memorial for the Geneva tribunal, the chief contributor to the British Memorial was Mr. Edward Henderson, then employed by I.P.C., who later joined the British Foreign Service.

The first stage of the Buraimi dispute was confined to talks. Acting on behalf of the Shaikh of Abu Dhabi by treaty, and for the Sultan of Muscat at his request, Britain dismissed the Saudi claim as being devoid of either historical or contemporary validity. This was perhaps an exaggeration. There had been Wahhabi influence in Buraimi in the previous century, a few Saudi merchants still lived there, and — although this was not something the Saudis wanted to trumpet abroad — Buraimi was a traditional centre of the slave trade in which Saudi dealers were by far the most active. There was also some unrest in the two Muscat villages at the time, chiefly owing to the Sultan of Muscat's refusal or inability to pay his local agents properly. Wilfred Thesiger, who visited Buraimi in 1948, described the Sultan's authority there as 'purely nominal';[1] and although British officials attempted to draw the Sultan's attention to the results of his neglect they were characteristically rebuffed by that proud, self-contained and penny-pinching little man, with the comment that he did not like interference in the administration of his kingdom.[2]

It was in the Sultan's villages that the second and more serious stage of the dispute opened in 1952, when the Saudis sent the Amir Turki ibn Utaishan to occupy them with 40 soldiers. He set up his headquarters in the village of Hamasa, next to the village of Buraimi from which the

[1] Wilfred Thesiger, *Arabian Sands*, Longmans Green & Co., London, 1960, pp. 216–17.

[2] In this and following passages, I am indebted for several details to certain persons directly involved in the events who have given me their own account of them.

oasis takes its name. This was where the Saudi slave traders lived, and with discontent already evident among some of their people these two settlements were a natural base from which to subvert the whole oasis. In their reply to this bold move, the British showed just the sort of hesitation that the Saudis probably expected. The reaction of British advisers in the Gulf was that the Saudis should be thrown out again immediately in a demonstration of the Sultan of Muscat's sovereignty, *de facto* as well as *de jure*. The first of the Trucial Oman Scouts had just then been recruited, and the Political Agent in Dubai advocated that they should be employed in the operation, together with the Sultan's forces, to present the Saudis with a united front. Both Whitehall and the Sultan agreed, and while a detachment of Scouts was sent to the Abu Dhabi side of the oasis, the Sultan assembled at Sohar, on the Muscat coast, an army of eight thousand tribesmen stiffened by his small, regular Field Force which was commanded by British mercenary officers. Among this army were many warriors from the Oman mountains, carrying the white flag of the Imamate of Oman which was to be raised against the Sultan only three years later, with Saudi support. Within a few weeks the two forces were ready to converge upon the Saudis in Buraimi.

In London, however, Sir Anthony Eden at the Foreign Office was under American pressure to do nothing rash. He demanded an assurance from British officials in the Gulf that the re-occupation of Buraimi could be achieved without bloodshed. They replied that they expected it would be, but they could not, in the nature of things, give an absolute guarantee; whereupon Eden, declaring bloodshed to be unthinkable, called off the operation. He was only just in time. The Trucial Scouts were easily reached by wireless and were stopped in their tracks with a week or more to spare, but the Sultan's forces at Sohar were about to begin their long march and were out of cable communication. The nearest Foreign Office man was Major Leslie Chauncey, the British Consul-General in Muscat, separated from Sohar by 150 miles of wretched tracks. To him the fateful message of cancellation went, with instructions to deliver it to the Sultan immediately. Critics of Major Chauncey have suggested to me that a more imaginative man might have hesitated, pondering the possibility of a 'diplomatic breakdown' on the way to Sohar, or rebelling at the thought of a hard and uncomfortable drive merely to cancel an operation to which he and the Sultan had devoted much time and effort in the expectation of praise, and perhaps reward. But if such rash initiatives could be contemplated by others, they were not much in Major Chauncey's line. He was a former officer of the Indian Army, stiff and straight and close-cropped, laconic and mistrustful of publicity, honest and dutiful — an old-fashioned man from an old-fashioned world. And in his dutiful, old-fashioned way he leaped into his car and drove like the wind, or as near to it as he could get, through the choking dust of the coastal date groves, to Sohar and the Sultan.

When Chauncey presented his message the Sultan drove a shrewd bargain with him. His men, said the Sultan in effect, were in a state of high and patriotic excitement, fitting to the proud mission to which he had called them. He could not now order them tamely to disperse without explanation. He therefore insisted that Major Chauncey should hand him the message in full view of his army and remain at his side while he read it to them, so that they would understand that the British Government, not the Sultan, was responsible for this cowardly withdrawal. Otherwise the operation would have to go forward. Chauncey could do nothing but agree. The Sultan publicly accepted the message and read it to his men, freeing himself of all blame. His soldiers went home, no doubt bewildered, and the Saudis continued to occupy Buraimi.

It is interesting now to speculate on the possible consequences of this remote little humiliation of the latter-day Raj. Probably, for a start, it suggested to the Omanis in the Sultan's forces that Britain's support of the Sultan was not a serious obstacle to their own ambitions, when these came to be expressed three years later. Probably, also, it encouraged the Americans to believe that Britain, in the last resort, would always respond to State Department pressure; and this in turn may have had a direct bearing on the deceptions and misunderstandings of the Suez operation four years afterwards, when, far from impressing the Americans with his determination to use force against President Nasser, Eden took pains to conceal his intentions from them, apparently in the belief that a *fait accompli* would be accepted in Washington whereas consultation would only lead to American threats and a British withdrawal. Inevitably, the Sohar incident must have confirmed the Saudis in their view that Britain was on the run and could be harried safely. And it is certain that the Sultan seized it as a stick with which to beat the British Government, and has never ceased to cite it since as an example of Britain's 'bad advice' in his affairs.

In retrospect, I think, it must be accepted that the advice was bad. Even if the wider, speculative consequences are discounted, the immediate practical consequence was to leave the Saudis in possession of Buraimi, able not only to continue their programme of subversion but also to suggest to an innocent world that they, and not the Sultan of Muscat, exercised sovereignty there. Having abandoned the threat of force, Britain had no choice eventually but to accept this invidious situation and go to arbitration; and in July 1954, an arbitration agreement was signed in Jeddah providing for the submission of the dispute to an international tribunal. Both sides were to withdraw their forces from the oasis to undisputed territory, and replace them only with police groups of up to 15 men each. Thus, as a condition of arbitration, the Saudis had established their right to share in the control of the oasis.

Arbitration was no more successful than the earlier talks in producing any settlement. The Saudis — quite reasonably in view of British hesitations — assumed that their own triumph was now inevitable, and used the period of arbitration, as they had used the years before it, to strengthen their grip on Buraimi. Although they withdrew Turki ibn Utaishan and his soldiers, they continued to smuggle arms into the oasis and to bribe the local shaikhs. They appointed as their supposedly independent representative on the tribunal the official of their government who was in charge of Saudi operations in Buraimi, and they even attempted to bribe other members of the tribunal — presumably in the belief that gold could achieve among international jurists as much as it had done among the beduin of Buraimi.[1] When, inevitably in the circumstances, the arbitration broke down, the British were back again at square one with the Saudis still in Buraimi and their own position weaker than before. This time, however, they took the decision they had funked three years earlier to throw the Saudis out. On October 26th, 1955, the Trucial Oman Scouts and the Sultan of Muscat's forces moved together into the village of Hamasa and the Saudi police commander surrendered with his 15 men. Henceforth, said Sir Anthony Eden, the Riyadh Line would be regarded as the Saudi frontier and no unauthorised crossings would be permitted.

Had this been done in 1952 it is possible — although I think not probable — that no more would have been heard of the matter. But by 1955 the dispute had been widened beyond its local implications. During their stay in Buraimi the Saudis had extended their influence and money to the neighbouring mountains of Oman, where the tribes who had rallied to the Sultan in 1952 were growing restive three years later — excited partly by Saudi money and partly by the distant prospect of oil discoveries in their territory which they hoped to keep to themselves. Barely were the Saudis expelled from Buraimi than the flag of rebellion was raised in Oman. At Christmas, 1955, the Sultan of Muscat hastened there in wrath and his tiny Field Force under its mercenary British officers hurried to his aid from its new base in

[1] Kelly, op. cit. pp. 202-5.

Buraimi. Twice within two months, therefore, British-controlled forces and British-protected rulers had taken military action; once against an independent Arab state and once against Arabs who claimed their independence. The rights and wrongs of these two matters needed no further arguing in Cairo or elsewhere in the Arab world. Britain stood convicted, as usual, of attempting to crush the Arab nationalist revolution. It mattered not that the Saudi regime was then among the most reactionary and profligate of any in Arabia, or that the Omani rebels were led by men at least as feudal as the Sultan of Muscat whose common ground with the nationalist revolutionaries in Cairo and Damascus was limited to say the least. Britain was involved, shots had been fired. The cry of 'imperialist aggression' — unhappily echoed by Mr. Dulles — united everyone. Moreover, the Saudis had already prepared the way for this development. During the years of negotiation and arbitration they had sought to bring pressure on Britain throughout the Middle East by financing opposition movements in Jordan, Iraq, Kuwait and elsewhere when the governments of those countries were still widely regarded as British puppets. In these years, indeed, Saudi money was as much the mainstay of the Arab nationalist movement as Egyptian propaganda or Nasser's political ability, and when the time came the nationalists were willing enough to provide the appropriate *quid pro quo* by shouting 'Hands off Buraimi!'

The re-occupation of the oasis in 1955 was not the end of the affair, therefore, but the start of a third and wider phase of the dispute in which the particular merits of the case on either side were submerged in the generalities of the power struggle throughout the Middle East. This phase gathered intensity after the Suez crisis, ten months later, when Saudi Arabia took the opportunity to break off diplomatic relations with Britain in support of Egypt and placed herself, for the moment, in the forefront of the 'anti-imperialist' Arab powers. By this time, Buraimi and the associated name of Oman had become part of the secondary vocabulary of the cold war, as the Soviet Union extended her diplomatic gains in the Arab world; and Britain's position as protector of Abu Dhabi and the ally of the Sultan of Muscat was threatening to involve her in repeated embarrassments far beyond the boundaries of Arabia.

That this phase more or less petered out without reaching the climax that once seemed likely was due to several factors. The Saudis themselves ran short of money, chiefly through their domestic extravagance, and had little to spare after 1957 for fomenting Arabian rebellions or financing Arab nationalism. As a result the local pressure eased fairly steadily after a second rebellion in Oman against the Sultan of Muscat had been suppressed in the summer of 1957. The collapse of any pretence of a united Arab front which followed President Nasser's apparent triumphs in 1958 also weakened the pressure on Britain, especially as the Saudis realised then that Nasser was almost as hostile towards them as he was towards the British. Finally, although almost unnoticed at first, there came a change in American attitudes. Once the Suez crisis was out of the way and the worst of its debris was cleared up, American and British policies in the Middle East began, fitfully and uncertainly, to converge. Partly, this was due to American disillusionment with the Saudis, whom they had tried for a time — and failed — to promote as a focus of Arab influence and power that would eclipse or rival Nasser. But chiefly, perhaps, it was the result of Britain's increasing weakness in the area and Russia's growing strength. By 1960, at all events, many of Washington's old reservations about British colonial attitudes in the Middle East seemed to have been overcome, and Britain's special position in the Persian Gulf in particular was accepted in principle as an essential part of world-wide western strategy.

In these shifting power patterns the spurious issue of nationalism versus imperialism that had threatened serious trouble over Buraimi was obscured, and the dispute gradually lost its fire. Once Britain and her protégés were in possession, the Saudi case languished; and it was the Saudis who now sought arbitration as a way of making the best of a bad job. The British Government refused to return to that position, but agreed instead that the United Nations Secretary-General should send a personal representative to look into the affair. The late Dag Hammarskjold chose Herbert de Ribbing as his man, the Swedish Ambassador to Spain, who was later to investigate the associated troubles in Oman as well. His report remained confidential, and failed to raise the dispute from its ashes. The Saudis continued to insist that an agreement to return to arbitration over Buraimi was their minimum condition for resuming diplomatic relations with Britain, and the British repeated that no good could come of putting back the clock again. Neither side, however, foresaw the *deus ex machina* which broke this stale old deadlock. This was the Yemen revolution in 1962, which encouraged Saudi Arabia to mend her fences with Britain as the only other power on the Arabian mainland which might challenge or contain the new Egyptian presence in the Yemen. Tacitly, and swiftly, after the revolution, the Saudis dropped their demand for a return to arbitration and re-opened diplomatic relations with Britain in January, 1963, with no more than a vague agreement that discussions should continue under the supervision of the U.N. Secretary-General.

Thus began the fourth — and so far the last — stage of the Buraimi dispute, fourteen years after the opening phase had started. This last phase constitutes a *de facto* but not a *de jure* settlement, in which Saudi Arabia officially reserves her position but all parties including the oil companies proceed in practice as if the matter were closed. When I last visited Buraimi at the end of 1963 this *de facto* settlement was clearly established. The British were busy delineating the first fixed frontier in the area, charting and patrolling the Riyadh Line far out in the desert, west of the oasis. ARAMCO and the I.P.C. had reached an informal understanding that their survey and drilling teams would not approach the line more closely than five miles from either side, leaving a ten-mile no-man's land to minimise the possibility of a clash of interest between them. And the oasis itself, formerly so isolated and impoverished, was undergoing the now familiar Arabian transformation by money.

Ten years earlier, Shaikh Shakhbut's chief representative in Buraimi — his brother, Shaikh Zaid — had been offered a bribe by the Saudis to induce him to transfer his loyalty, amounting, so it was said, to £30 million. But Zaid had sworn long ago to his mother to respect Shakhbut's life and rule (which may be one reason why Shakhbut has lasted so much longer than his predecessors as Ruler of Abu Dhabi) and he refused the Saudi temptation. Now he was reaping his more modest reward with a share in Shakhbut's new oil wealth. Full of popular esteem as the 'Lord of Buraimi', he was more generous and probably more wise than his suspicious brother, and most of the money he received seemed to be spent on genuine public welfare. Some of the results, to be sure, were a shade incongruous, like the electric street lamps on crude wooden poles which illuminated the dusty little oasis village of Al Ain, and the traffic policeman who stood twelve hours a day at its cross-roads directing a steady daily flow of a score of Land Rovers and a shaikhly Ford convertible or two. But already there was enough money in circulation to have attracted two British banks. Where, ten years earlier, there had been little but poverty and the Saudi slave market, there were now two young British managers competing amiably for business, inviting each other to modest little dinner parties and meeting every morning for a friendly and refreshing beer. The money they handled, and that Zaid disbursed, was just the fertiliser that Buraimi's gardens needed, and their green pile appeared, upon inspection, less threadbare than it looked at first sight. Repairs were being made to every decayed *falluj* — the ancient, underground irrigation channels that carried the water from the oasis springs to the date palms and vegetable plots. Public bathing pools and washing places had been scooped out and cemented here and there along their courses; and among the shoals of minnows that darted indefatigably in the cool, clear current, empty Tide and Rinso packets and old wrappers of Palmolive and Lux swirled about the bottom — sodden symbols of the new prosperity. Once, as I passed such a bathing pool, I heard feminine giggles and glimpsed two young girls peering at me over the top of a wall. As I looked, they vanished, but they left their clothes behind, hanging on a thorn bush. Beside two long, black gowns and two pairs of embroidered pantaloons, I saw two white nylon petticoats, two white brassieres, and two pairs of frilly, nylon pants. Affluence — relative perhaps, but undeniable — had arrived.

With the affluence came a firmer sense of government than Buraimi had ever had. Through Zaid's attentions and Shakhbut's money, Abu Dhabi was now firmly in command of its six oasis villages. Only on the Muscat side did Buraimi seem unchanged. The Saudi slave trade had been suppressed, of course, but no new oil money had filtered through to the Sultan's people, who displayed a faintly sullen, constipated air as they squatted listlessly among their decayed mud walls. Seeing the progress of their neighbours in Zaid's domain, they were asking, I was told, that the Sultan should sell them to Abu Dhabi. Only a year or two earlier he had given them the idea himself by disposing of an isolated crumb of his territory called Gwadar, on the barren coast of Baluchistan, by selling it to Pakistan for £3 million. They confidently expected that he could get as much for his two Buraimi villages from the newly-filled coffers of Shaikh Shakhbut; and they looked forward to being as well paid by Zaid for their new loyalty as some of them had been by the Saudis when they had sold themselves to those masters, ten years before. *Plus ça change . . . ?* Perhaps: yet soon the subjects of Muscat, too, may change their minds, for in 1964 new oil strikes were made in Oman which will provide money, eventually, to strengthen the Sultan's purse and hand. Then, if the Sultan is only half as shrewd as Zaid, his authority, too, will be stamped upon Buraimi more firmly than ever before. Money, it may seem then, will have fixed the shifting Arabian frontiers at last and the fourth stage of the Buraimi dispute will have proved to be the final one.

Unfortunately, the long-term future may not be so simple. A fifth stage in the dispute is implicit in the Saudi refusal to accept the present situation as final. Soon after diplomatic relations with Britain had been resumed, the Saudi Foreign Minister made it clear to me, in a private conversation in Jeddah, that his Government had not abandoned its claims in Buraimi or its belief in the independence of Oman; and in June, 1964, at about the time the new oil strikes in Oman were reported, it offered a small, but no doubt significant, reminder that these matters might be re-opened at its convenience when it sent a warning to the Abu Dhabi Petroleum Company (I.P.C.) that it was trespassing on Saudi territory.[1] Thus, for all the appearances to the contrary, the dispute is still unresolved, and whatever sense of stability may seem to accrue from the new riches of Shaikh Shakhbut and the Sultan, the British commitment to the protection of these rulers remains the only effective guarantee that the present *de facto* settlement can survive.

To replace that guarantee by another equally effective, or to secure a new and more satisfactory settlement of the frontier question in south-eastern Arabia, is the pre-requisite of an orderly British withdrawal from the area. Unhappily, as we have seen, such developments still seem remote. Here, therefore, as elsewhere on the Arab shores of the Persian Gulf, the present petrifaction may not be permanent; but as yet there is nothing to put in its place save the ancient, and now unworkable, flux.

[1] *Sunday Times*, July 26th, 1964.

16

The Long Sleep

————————~~~~~❀~~~~~————————

Officially in Muscat this is still the fourteenth century; and as the sun sinks behind the enfolding cliffs and the lanterns begin to flicker down the darkening alley-ways, it is easy to forget for a moment that this is only because Muscat uses the Muslim calendar. The twentieth century of Christian reckoning seems far enough away.

Since the revolution in the Yemen opened the gates of Sanaa and Taiz, Muscat has been the only capital left in Arabia whose folk are still locked within their town walls every night. Three hours after sunset an ancient cannon sounds from the battlements of Murani, one of a pair of Portuguese forts that stand high on either side of Muscat's narrow harbour, and while the roar echoes and re-echoes among the surrounding crags the guards at the town gates set aside their rifles and slowly heave shut the iron-bound doors in the mud wall. Inside they confine the representatives of the old order — the British Consul-General, musing on his verandah above the black waters of the harbour, the Sultan's police in their cramped quarters among the cannon of Fort Murani, the slaves in the Sultan's palace on the cramped waterfront. Outside they exclude the first, few harbingers of the new world — the taxi-drivers with their Land Rovers parked beside the gate, the young bank manager in his smart, new bachelor flat, the eager officers of the Sultan's expanding army in their neat little bungalows, five miles away. Thereafter, none may leave or enter Muscat until the gates are opened again at dawn, and anyone abroad within the walls must, by law, carry a lantern with a lighted flame.

In the towns of Saudi Arabia, as well as the Yemen, and even in some settlements of the Persian Gulf and the Aden Protectorates, a similar routine prevailed at night until only a generation or so ago. But revolution of some sort has overtaken all of them. Only in Muscat is the twentieth century still held more or less successfully at bay. Historically there is some irony in this, for the Sultanate of Muscat and Oman once was one of the richer and less-secluded corners of Arabia. Three and four hundred years ago, when the Portuguese dominated the eastern trade routes, they boasted of their trading settlement on the island of Hormuz, not far from the Muscat coast, that 'were the world a golden ring, Hormuz would be its diamond signet'. For 150 years they maintained a factory in Muscat itself, and they left several forts in the interior of Oman as well as on the cliffs overlooking Muscat harbour. When Portuguese strength declined, that of the Sultans of Muscat advanced. In the eighteenth and early nineteenth centuries Muscat could claim to be the greatest independent power in the peninsula. For a century its Sultans were the overlords of Zanzibar, Mombasa and Mogadishu in East Africa, while their agents gathered slaves and trade from Lake Victoria to China, and their navy contained 75 ships of the line. It is true that there is some doubt about how many of these noble vessels could actually put to sea. British observers of the day are on record as suggesting that their appearance was more impressive than their firepower. Yet it is possibly some measure of Muscat's old importance that in 1798 the reigning Sultan was the first Arabian ruler to be invited to sign a treaty with Britain. Through the agency of the East India Company, which hoped to enlist his aid against the pirates of the Persian Gulf, he was persuaded to side with Britain against France in the Napoleonic wars, and two years later he admitted the first resident British Political Agent in Arabia. Even as late as 1833 Muscat was still thought sufficiently important to be wooed by the distant government of the United States, which sent a mission to sign a treaty of friendship and commerce with the Sultan — the first formal agreement between America and any Middle Eastern power.

By then, however, the Sultanate had entered upon a long decline. At sea the British curtailment of the slave trade severed the sinews of its commerce and the use of the new steamers on the route to India diminished the number of vessels visiting its ports. Dynastic rivalries and naval weakness cut Zanzibar adrift, while inland, beyond the barrier of the Oman mountains, the growing power of the Wahhabis from central Arabia threatened the authority of the Sultans among the tribes. Thus impoverished and attacked, Muscat turned in upon itself like a hibernating tortoise and went quietly to sleep. Deep in slumber it has remained ever since. No colonial power, no great ruler, no sudden oil riches, have yet disturbed its peace. No overwhelming demands of trade or imperial strategy have shaken it back to life, nor has any political revolution so far enlivened its dormant rhythms. Wrapped in secretive and suffocating silence behind its rocky promontories, it has become one of the last Rip Van Winkles of Arabia.

It is curious how silence seems to characterise the town, as if its mud walls were sound-proofed against all rude intrusions. Voices are subdued, few motor vehicles ever pass through the gates to shatter the whispering peace, and the floury dust of the unpaved alleys muffles every footfall. In the steam heat of an afternoon the whole place lies as still as a corpse. Even the air feels dead. Trapped between the cliffs of the harbour and the barren hills behind, it is unnaturally free from breeze or breath and induces a sleep that is close to coma. Compounding this stale and inbred atmosphere, a puritanical Islam enforces its joyless prohibitions: no smoking in the streets, no music anywhere, and alcohol only for European Christians, to be obtained through the British Consul-General. Atrophied alike by the conventions and the heat, life in Muscat has but a feeble pulse. Now and then a ship will call on its way to or from the Persian Gulf, and a solitary launch will put out from the waterfront to meet it as the hoot of the siren echoes round the cliffs and the anchor chain drops like a rumble of thunder. In the evenings, when the sun's glare has passed from the rocks, Muscat's boys assemble for a fleet-footed game of hockey outside the walls, reminding you that India is only just across the water; and every other Monday at the social club Sayyid Abbas, an uncle of the Sultan, may be seen at his regular match at badminton, with his white shorts freshly laundered, his beard damp with sweat and a handkerchief soaked in Chanel No. 5 to wipe his glistening brow.

But these are short-lived moments — mere flickers of wakefulness in the town's long sleep. Silently and irresistibly at most other times the past exerts an hypnotic domination. The Portuguese forts tower in romantic splendour above the cove like magnificent galleons in full sail, and abandoned cannon, smooth and burnished with the passage of centuries, nuzzle the dust at unexpected street corners to remind the visitor of Muscat's vanished power. Intricately carved doors in sagging walls speak of the wealth that once accumulated here, and on the cliffs above the anchorage a few fading splatters of whitewash record the passage of an empire. 'My visitor's book,' the Sultan playfully calls those cliffs, where generations of sailors of the Royal Navy have been sent aloft with brush and bucket to paint the names of their vessels upon the rock. Legend and the Sultan have it that even Nelson did his stint up there when he visited Muscat as a midshipman at the dawn of his career. Certainly, many fine old naval names are still decipherable. H.M.S. *Teal* is there, and H.M.S. *Surprise*, H.M.S. *Wren* and H.M.S.

Bramble; but it is characteristic of the dominance of the past in Muscat that the more legible the whitewash the less evocative are the names, for Britain — like Muscat — has been going downhill a bit in recent years, and her ships are not as numerous nor their names as resounding as they used to be.

To some extent this domination of the past in Muscat is an accident of history and geography. But to some extent, also, it is a result of deliberate choice. Like many Arabian rulers, the present Sultan, Said bin Taimur al bu Said, thirteenth in his dynasty to rule Muscat and Oman, frankly distrusts the modern world and he has tried consciously and with some effect to close his country's doors against it, much as Muscat's town gates are closed against the traffic of the night. Profoundly conservative, penny-pinching and isolationist, the Sultan has become one of the most absolute of Arabia's remaining rulers, and his kingdom mirrors his prejudices as much as he reflects its ancient ways. It is the last place in Arabia where slavery is permitted. Its Koranic punishments seem harsh, its health standards are visibly dismal, its literacy rate is probably worse. By the standards of the modern, western world, the Sultan may seem neglectful, even contemptuous, of his people — yet by comparison with his own kind and contemporaries he is, on the whole, humane. He may have neither the vision nor the daring of the late ibn Saud, nor the quiet wisdom of Abdullah of Kuwait, but he is certainly no monster among Arabian despots. Not for him the head-choppings and hand-loppings of the old Imam Ahmad of the Yemen, or the dissolute personal life of the princes of Saud or Qatar. His justice is generally consistent and temperate, his habits are modest, and he exhibits — especially in private — an undeniably sharp intelligence and a disarmingly shy charm. He is even prepared to admit the necessity of change in a detached and intellectual way. 'Of course,' he once told me, 'it must come. But slowly,' he added, with typical caution, 'for in Muscat there is very much to do, and — as you say in English — more haste means less speed.'

It is in this fundamental, and in many ways understandable, conviction that change must come slowly to his kingdom that the Sultan has tried to keep the world at bay. Visitors from abroad are discouraged, and publicity for himself and his country is avoided stubbornly and with skill. Entry visas for Muscat are as hard for most foreigners to obtain as they used to be in the Yemen under the Imam Ahmad, and even when granted they confer no right to travel beyond the confines of the coastal towns. Alone among the independent territories of Arabia now, Muscat and Oman has neither transport nor accommodation for the ordinary traveller, and anyone who wants to see the interior of the country must either make himself a guest of the Sultan's army or enlist the aid of the oil companies prospecting in his domains. The activities of these two agencies as we shall see, have made certain that even this introspective corner of the peninsula is no longer virgin territory, but it is one of the Sultan's special concerns to see that they do not connive at the raping of it any faster than he can help. Accordingly, their aid is hard to obtain and their activities are mostly unobserved and unreported, conducted behind a screen of secrecy tighter than any now left in Arabia. In the last ten years, for example, not more than a dozen journalists have managed to get into Muscat and few of those have had more than unwilling co-operation from the Sultan. The first and most fortunate of them was Mr. James Morris, who was able to accompany the Sultan on behalf of *The Times* on a lightning sweep through the interior in 1955, when some of the Omani tribesmen rebelled against the Sultan's rule. Mr. Morris's subsequent chronicle of this stirring adventure contained the first general account of the Sultan's kingdom to appear in modern times, and made what looked like a decisive breach in Muscat's traditional defences.[1] Certainly, his journey marked a great advance on the experience, only seven years before, of Mr. Wilfred Thesiger, the last in the great tradition of Arabian explorers, who was turned back from Oman by hostile tribesmen; but the promise that it contained of Muscat's swift capitulation to the forces of worldly curiosity remained unfulfilled. Two years later, when the Oman rebellion was resumed more seriously, and British troops and aircraft were employed to suppress it, only Fleet Street's agitation, and some consequent representations from the British Government, persuaded the Sultan to admit a few reporters to see what was going on. I was among those who visited both Muscat and Oman on that occasion and, together with an American reporter, I was later granted the first orthodox press interview the Sultan had ever undertaken. Aside from its novelty, however, the interview was unremarkable, for the Sultan proved a natural master of the evasive answer; and all the efforts of my colleagues and myself in Muscat and Oman appeared only to strengthen his conviction that the press could have nothing but an unwelcome role to play in his scheme of things. When I wrote afterwards to his British Foreign Minister, asking permission to accompany the Sultan if and when he chose to revisit Oman, I received a friendly but firm reply:

'Not all the reporting was so felicitous, and all that came of ———'s visit [naming a magazine photographer who had taken the Sultan's

[1] James Morris, *Sultan in Oman*, Faber and Faber, London, 1957.

picture] was one rather grim photograph in Paris-Match captioned "Victoire pour le petit Sultan", and reproduced in a Cairo paper as "the traitor Sultan." It is not on the whole surprising that the Sultan is no more convinced of the necessity or desirability of press publicity to the Muscat way of life than he was before the recent spate of it. I cannot therefore hold out any hopes of your going up to the Interior with him. . . .'

It was five years before this chilly verdict was modified, and I again obtained permission to enter the Sultanate; and I know of only one other western journalist who was able to visit Muscat professionally during, or since, my long wait.

It is not only journalists that the Sultan keeps so obstinately at arm's length. Few people, Arab or European, are welcomed into his confidence. The British Government, which protects and aids him, is treated with suspicion. Requests that he should reveal the extent and nature of his financial resources, so that the British Government might decide for itself how much aid he really needs, have been studiously ignored. The British, in the Sultan's view, must make up their own minds how much he is worth to them; his money is his own affair. Most individual British officials in his pay are no closer to him. He frankly prefers them to their Arab counterparts because, so it seems, they are safer as well as tidier in administration. They can be sacked at will (and sometimes are) without local repercussions, and they are less likely to get ideas above their station and seek to depose him, as some of his native subjects conceivably might do if given their heads. But they are rarely trusted with any decision, however small, for the Sultan likes to retain absolute control. Characteristically, he has chosen to live in virtual exile within his own kingdom, cut off both from his officials and his people. He seldom visits Muscat and never stays there except in an emergency. His palace on the waterfront, where the Portuguese Governor once lived, is occupied only by his mother and a few retainers. The Sultan prefers the cooler comforts of Salalah, a tiny and dilapidated settlement in the province of Dhofar, 500 miles away, where he can look out from the windows of another palace upon the rollers of the Indian Ocean, swelling grandly from the southern horizon to break upon a long, white beach. Here, surrounded by a mere handful of his subjects and separated from the rest by the desert of the Empty Quarter, he is sheltered from the interruptions and importunings that might disturb his life in Muscat. Like Queen Victoria in retreat at Balmoral, he has turned his back upon the world.

The Sultan's barriers are designed not only to keep the world out of

Muscat but to keep Muscat out of the world. Although in law he is an independent ruler of a state considerably bigger than, say, Kuwait, he refuses even to consider joining the United Nations, and he looks upon the Arab League and most of his fellow-Arab rulers with undisguised contempt. In all international dealings he prefers to be represented by British spokesmen in total disregard of the resulting damage to his standing in the world. In spite of British hints that he might with advantage cultivate a few judiciously selected foreign friends, the only diplomatic representative he has chosen to admit to Muscat, besides the British Consul-General, is an Indian Consul whom he usually treats with the sort of superior indifference that a Maharajah might have accorded a box-wallah in the heyday of the Raj.

His own schooling at the Indian College of Princes under the Raj made him one of the best-educated of all Arabia's traditional rulers, yet he is loth to let even his immediate family enjoy the same advantages. His only son, Qabus, was nineteen before the Sultan was persuaded by the British to let him go abroad for the first time — initially to London for some much-needed cramming, and afterwards to the Military Academy at Sandhurst, where he proved an able cadet. The Sultan's brother, Tarik, a man of notable ability and wide horizons, speaking fluent German, French and Turkish, as well as Arabic and English, was similarly prevented from sending any of his children to school overseas until one day, frustrated beyond endurance, he fled the country with two of his sons and packed them off to Roberts College, an American foundation in Istanbul where he had begun his own education. It is tempting to see in the contrast between the two men an implicit comment on the defects of British education for an imperial ruling class, for while the Sultan has all the public hauteur and private charm of an aristocrat born and bred to rule, his brother displays — in conversation anyway — both a greater vision and a far more common touch. Yet in fairness to the Sultan it must be said that his responsibilities as ruler have never been easy. His kingdom is large, diffuse and sparsely populated, and his father, who abdicated in 1932, left him nothing as a young man but a pile of debts and an exiguous income from Customs dues. For most of his adult life, therefore, Sultan Said has dedicated himself of necessity to recouping the family fortunes with the thrift of an unregenerate Scrooge. No ruler in Arabia holds his purse-strings tighter. He divulges no figures, he produces no budget, he takes whatever he can get and spends only what he must. The traditional generosity of an Arab chieftain, which so often nowadays spills over into absurd ostentation, is utterly foreign to his nature. He shares with the eccentric Shaikh Shakhbut of Abu Dhabi a passion for counting the pennies. His frugality strengthens his aloofness, helping to persuade him that he is better out of the world than in it. It is, after all, cheaper to let the British represent him abroad for as long as they will and finance him at home for as long as they feel they must, whatever the cost to his international image, than to do either of these things for himself. It saves money to deny education to his family and his people, and it may even be thrifty to eschew the doubtful delights of Muscat in favour of a solitary life in Salalah. Far away across the desert there the Sultan is safe from the financial demands of his relatives and administrators. The only one of them who ever squeezed an extra penny out of him, so the gossips say in Muscat, was a forceful uncle who rode seventeen days on camel-back from Oman and so surprised his nephew by his unheralded arrival in Salalah that he was given £300 on the spot. As this was carefully calculated by the Sultan, however, to be just enough to pay him for the camels he had foundered on the trip, the expedition was never repeated.

Yet even in the Sultan's self-imposed seclusion the world cannot be entirely rejected or ignored. It presses in apace upon him and his kingdom, and neither walls nor convictions can any longer keep it out. In spite of all appearances to the contrary — the silence and suspicion and the dominance of the past — a new nexus of change has quietly established itself throughout the country in the last few years. Those symbols of the new world locked outside the gates of Muscat every night suggest some of its inevitable ingredients. The taxi-drivers, who represent better communications; the bank manager, who implies money; and the army officers, who signify the imposition of a new order, have been laying the foundations for several years for the next, quickening steps in Muscat's advance into the twentieth century. Three miles north along the coast from Muscat town you may see the process in blatant operation. There, in another little port called Mattrah, the illusion of the long sleep has already been dispelled. Superficially, Muscat and Mattrah are twin towns, as much in appearance as in proximity. Mattrah, like Muscat, is stranded at the head of a narrow anchorage, overlooked by a splendid Portuguese fort, and surrounded on the landward side by a large mud wall. But while Muscat still dozes, Mattrah has begun to throb with work. Both from land and sea Mattrah is a shade more accessible, and it has become the modern rendezvous for the date-growers and fishermen of the coast and the tribesmen who come down with their camel trains from the Oman mountains. Any day of the week you may find 50 or 100 camels tethered outside Mattrah's walls, coughing and groaning and spitting out their green bile, while their owners go among them, unloading the bags of charcoal burned from the mountain scrub, and the baskets of little yellow limes from the Oman valleys, and sometimes pressing an affectionate handful of gritty dates between the slimy, yellow fangs of their beasts. It is not, however, the camels and their commerce upon whose significance you should dwell, but the irrelevance of the town gate next to them. Massive, solemnly guarded, and locked every night, like the gates of Muscat, at three hours after sundown, Mattrah's gate stands astride the track like a true custodian of Arabia's ancient history ready to bar all new and foreign forces from the town. Alas, its custody is utterly unavailing, for at one side the wall has been knocked down, and with a twist of the wheel or a flick of the goad, the lorries and the laden camels, the Land Rovers and the busy donkeys go bustling past regardless, while the guards on the gate polish the silver chasing on their rifles and heave the great doors ceremoniously to and fro. Change, after all, waits for no man: not even for a Sultan in Muscat.

17

The Beginning of the End

The beginning of the end for the last bastion of traditional Arabia came, I suppose, in 1948, when Wilfred Thesiger reached to within sight of the heart of Oman but found it in the last resort 'more difficult for a European to penetrate . . . than it had been a hundred years before.'[1] At that time, Oman was one of the least-known inhabited regions of the world. Lieutenant Wellsted of the Indian Navy had crossed it as early as 1835, but since then only three other Europeans had ever got beyond its fringes and not more than half-a-dozen had even got that far. Its central massif, the Jebel Akhdar or Green Mountain, was a craggy and supposedly impregnable fortress, 9,000 feet high, around whose plateau summit and stern flanks one of Arabia's most fanatical sects had established a morbidly exclusive sway. They were the Ibadhis, of the Shiite branch of Islam — as puritanical as the Sunni Wahhabis and even more inbred. Cut off from the rest of Arabia by the great deserts of the Empty Quarter, secure in their solitary valleys and glens, their unyielding beliefs had survived untroubled by the temptations of a wider world. Not even in the Yemen was such a deliberate isolationism maintained as that of Ibadhi Oman in the century before Thesiger's arrival. Rejecting intercourse with others, the Ibadhis became notorious even in Arabia for being given overmuch to prayer and piety and for their distrust of strangers. The British traveller Bertram Thomas, who served for a time as Wazir to the present Sultan of Muscat's father, found them a tiresome lot when he visited the fringes of Oman in the 1930's, not merely prohibiting alcohol, tobacco and music, but even showing distress at the sound of drums during the burial of a negro slave.

' "God forgive them!" murmured the sanctimonious Omani at my side.

' "Drums aren't acceptable to you?" I questioned.

[1] Thesiger, *Arabian Sands*, p. 218.

' "No, nor pipes; but these are slaves and know no better."

' "Yet the Muqabil tribe in Oman have pipes?" I said.

' "Yes! But they are Sunnis. We are Ibadhis, and in Ibadhi Oman we forbid these instruments of the devil." '[1]

When Thesiger arrived, fifteen years later, the Ibadhi Imam was 'an old man, a fanatical reactionary, and bitterly hostile to the Sultan and to all Europeans;' and in the end, to the explorer's great chagrin, this sour old man's influence was sufficient to persuade the tribes to turn Thesiger back from central Oman, refusing him permission to enter the main town of Nizwa or to explore the Jebel Akhdar, on the grounds that 'if they allowed me to travel there at will I should be followed by other Christians in cars, looking for oil and intending to seize their land.'[2] Their fears were hardly fair to Thesiger, who was perhaps the most respectful of all the great Arabian explorers of the traditional ways of the peninsula that he so dearly loved; but in any case, to turn him away was almost the last traditional gesture that the world permitted them. Soon enough, the oilmen got there anyway in their Land Rovers, and within five years the Iraq Petroleum Company, under the title of Petroleum Development (Oman) Ltd., was drilling its first exploratory hole in the Fahud basin, between Oman and the Empty Quarter.

Thus began what soon was known as the Oman question, which became one of the hardiest perennials of pan-Arab politics and the occasion of the last significant extension of the *Pax Britannica* in Arabia. It is a question that has been obscured, alas, by more than its fair share of claptrap and misunderstanding. Week after week for a decade now, Cairo's *Voice of the Arabs* has rolled out its accusations against the spineless and/or brutal lackeys of Muscat who do Britain's nefarious will by suppressing what it calls the 'free and independent state of Oman'. Month after month the office of the Imamate of Oman in Cairo had issued detailed records of heroic victories won by freedom-fighters in 'colonialism's aggressive war against Oman'. Year after year Arab delegates to the United Nations have urged upon a puzzled General Assembly the cause of their 'progressive and freedom-loving Omani brothers' held in submission to a 'reactionary Sultan of Muscat' only by the 'savage and overwhelming use of British armed force'. Abstruse points of Omani history, and even of Omani 'constitutional law' have been bandied about with apparent conviction. So-called scholars and orientalists have been called to witness this fancy or that; and an extensive apparatus of 'Free Oman' propaganda has been created,

[1] Bertram Thomas, *Arabia Felix*, Jonathan Cape, London, 1938, pp. 29–30.
[2] Thesiger, op. cit. pp. 218 and 258.

ramifying from its inevitable centre in Cairo through most of the Arab capitals and throwing up a bizarre branch in London where, in a seedy little office near King's Cross Station — sandwiched between the Movement for Colonial Freedom and the League for Democracy in Greece — the Committee for the Rights of Oman tries to arouse the conscience of the British people about 'national misdeeds' in south-eastern Arabia.

Fortunately, most of this nonsense has been discredited by its own absurdity — like the notorious claims about British soldiers killed or injured by the freedom-fighters, which amounted to some thousands by the end of 1964. In fact, total British casualties in Oman over the previous seven years were eight dead and two injured, with an extra handful of Arab soldiers killed or injured in the Sultan's own forces. The only time the casualties approached those repeatedly claimed by the 'Free Omanis' was when 236 civilians were killed, drowned or burned to death in the sinking of the British cargo-liner *Dara* in the Persian Gulf in 1961, apparently as a result of Omani sabotage. Even at the United Nations, where so many lost or foolish causes have found a sympathetic hearing, Omani propaganda has fallen pretty flat. Indeed, perhaps the biggest blow to the Omani cause was administered by U Thant's special envoy, Mr. Herbert de Ribbing, who visited Muscat and Oman on a mission of inquiry in 1963. Mr. de Ribbing uncovered a few signs of discontent here and there in the Sultan's kingdom, and evidently found the Sultan stubborn, as others have done before and since. He also confessed with disarming honesty his inability always to evaluate the evidence he collected. But the principal claims of the 'Free Omanis' about the size and nature of 'the war', the legal and historical independence of the 'Oman State', and the existence of a 'British military occupation', received no support from him at all.[1]

The truth is that Oman is not at war; and what is more, in recent years it never has been, except for three small campaigns and some sporadic banditry. At no time have the Omani rebels numbered more than five or six hundred men in action — although more may have sympathised with them from a distance — and never, except in those three campaigns, has any regular unit of the British Army served in Oman. The first of the campaigns, in December, 1955, saw the Sultan enter unopposed the little town of Nizwa in central Oman, asserting — or, as he would say, re-asserting — his authority in the region after a small-scale tribal uprising. The only soldiers of the British Army

[1] U.N. General Assembly, *Report of the Special Representative of the Secretary-General on his visit to Oman*, October 8th, 1963.

who were employed, excluding a few British mercenaries who commanded the Sultan's Field Force, were members of a solitary wireless communications unit lent to the Sultan for the occasion. According to Mr. Peter Fleming, who accompanied the Field Force into Nizwa before the Sultan's arrival, 'The only shot in a bloodless campaign was fired at, or more probably in the general direction of, a Land Rover which had me on board.'[1] The second and biggest campaign, part of which I witnessed myself, followed in the summer of 1957, when the rebels declared themselves again in greater force. In less than a month of occasional shooting, daily air attacks and minimal bloodshed, some 500 British soldiers subdued the rebel villages and then, promptly, were withdrawn. Thirdly, in January 1959, 200 men of the Special Air Services arrived fresh from anti-guerrilla operations in the jungles of Malaya to winkle out the last of the rebels from isolated strongholds on the summit of the Jebel Akhdar, around which the rebellion had continued to flicker. Since then the peace of Oman has not been disturbed by more than the laying of a few mines and ambushes and the constant rumbles of propaganda from abroad.

To assert that there is no war, however, does not prove there is no trouble. On the contrary, there has usually been trouble between Muscat and Oman much as there used to be between England and Scotland, and as there still is between Kurds and Arabs in Iraq, or between Zaidis and Shafiis in the Yemen, and townsmen and tribesmen in South Arabia. The Sultan's domains have never rested easily beneath his or anyone else's rule, for there are only tenuous bonds of interest to hold them together against the natural divisions of geography, tribes, race and religion. The basic division, as the name of the Sultanate implies, is that between Muscat and Oman. Muscat is more than just the nominal capital and seat of the Sultan. It represents most of the coastal strip stretching almost from the Straits of Hormuz to the tip of Arabia at Ras al-Hadd, where the last frail sandspits curl south-westwards into the Indian Ocean, towards the shores of the province of Dhofar. North of Muscat town is the coast of Batina, a long bootlace of date palm groves laid between a sandy beach and the gravel outwash from the Oman mountains, with palm-thatch villages and mud forts scattered freely among the groves like ribbon development along a suburban highway. South of Muscat the mountains close in towards the sea in a precipitous jumble of red cliffs and dark coves. This is a treacherous, squally part of the coast, with only rare settlements tucked under the cliffs until you come to the old, and half-abandoned port of Sur, standing like a for-

[1] Introduction to *Sultan in Oman*, by James Morris.

gotten Venice on its wide, unexpected lagoon. Like Venetians, the people of all this coast look to the sea for their lives — to India, Persia and the monsoon trade routes that carried the Portuguese to Hormuz and the Sultan's ancestors to Zanzibar. They are a seacoast amalgam of Baluch and Persian, Arab, Indian and Negro, their faiths are mixed, and in spite of some efforts by the Sultan to reform them in the image of his own, somewhat modified, Ibadhi creed, their ways are a little lax by puritanical standards, as seafarer's ways are apt to be.

Oman, on the other hand, is mountainous and land-locked, pastoral and agricultural wherever a spring sprouts from the rocks, barren and empty wherever the water fails. Its people are Arab to the bone, and from their severe and pure-minded heights they look down upon the corruptions of the coast with undisguised contempt. In the conflict between these two regions, between the seafarers and the landlubbers, the highlanders and lowlanders, Arabs and mongrels, puritans and worldly-wise, the history of this corner of Arabia has been shaped in a constant drum-fire of tribal battle and truce. Sometimes, as through the eighteenth and some of the nineteenth century, the Sultans of Muscat have been acknowledged as leaders, or Imams, in Oman as well. Sometimes Sultanate and Imamate have existed separately, sometimes there has been no Imam at all. It was the Omanis who threw the Portuguese out of Muscat in 1650, establishing the supremacy of the mountains over the coast long enough to enable them to found the present ruling house of Muscat and endow it with their own Ibadhi faith. But since the eighteenth century Oman has rarely been able to throw off Muscat's ultimate authority, in spite of periodic efforts, partly because the coast offered to the mountains their only contact with the rest of the world and partly because the Sultan — as the visible and accessible power on the coast — was generally recognised and supported by Britain and other foreign states.

Oman's weakness was compounded by the internal divisions of its people. Two tribal federations, the Ghafiri and the Hinawi, were generally the arbiters of power. Divided as they usually were, they tended to accept the Sultan's authority by default, if not by choice. United, as they were only on rare occasions, they asserted some regional autonomy. After the strength of the Sultans declined in the nineteenth century, the two federations came together briefly during the First World War and took advantage of the weakness of the present Sultan's father to secure from him acknowledgement of their power in the so-called 'Treaty of Sib'. This agreement, which was signed in 1920 at the little coastal town of Sib, is put forward by the 'Free Omanis' today as their formal title to independence, but the only available text fails to bear them out.[1] Instead, it appears to have given them a form of Home Rule, with the right to administer their own local affairs and to elect their own Imam in place of the Sultan of Muscat, who had held both titles until then for over 100 years. At best, therefore, Oman's autonomy was tribal and religious, without the characteristics of an independent state. In law, the Sultan of Muscat never relinquished his sovereignty.

For 30 years after the Agreement of Sib little more was heard or known of Oman, except for the fragmentary reports brought back by men like Thomas and Thesiger. But the arrival of the oil prospectors hard on Thesiger's heels ended its antique isolation and inflamed old resentments with a new sense of avarice. To the traditional discontent with the Sultan's rule, and the religious disapproval of the strict Ibadhis for the Christian interlopers, was added a suggestion that the Omanis were about to lose the hitherto untold riches of their land to the Sultan's skinflint purse. Why not, some of their more alert and crafty minds began to ask, reject the Sultan finally and forever and reap the rewards of oil discovery for themselves?

Even in 1948 this had been in the mind of their most powerful tribal ruler, Suliman bin Himyar, the strongest figure in the Ghafiri federation and paramount shaikh of the Beni Ryam tribe who controlled the Jebel Akhdar. Professing friendship for Thesiger, he had attempted then to double-cross both the Sultan and the fanatical old Imam by proposing that Thesiger should obtain for him the British Government's recognition as the independent ruler of the Jebel Akhdar with a status similar to that of the shaikhs of the Trucial Coast.[2] Thesiger refused, but by 1954 Suliman's notion had gained ground, not only through the actual arrival of the oil prospectors and the apparently greater imminence of riches, but also because of the death of the old Imam and the emergence (reputedly by dubious means) of his former secretary, Ghalib, as his successor. Ghalib, it seems, was no fanatic. Unlike his curmudgeonly predecessor, he was ready to co-operate with the foreigner, especially if there was money in it, and he had a forceful and ambitious brother, Talib, who was eager to support his claim to do so as an independent ruler. Joining forces with Suliman, they prepared for rebellion.

Now Ghalib and Talib belonged to the Hinawi federation, and their alliance with Suliman re-united Oman's two chief tribal groupings. This in itself announced danger for the Sultan, as the events culminating in the Agreement of Sib had shown, forty years before. Yet it is

[1] See Appendix III. [2] Thesiger, op. cit., pp. 261–2.

unlikely that they could have achieved much against the Sultan's forces in the 1950's without the help of outside powers; and what distinguished their uprising from its precursors in Oman was that for the first time the rebels were able to get such help. The Saudis, who had already been rebuffed in their attempt to occupy the Buraimi oasis on Oman's northern border, now saw a chance of outflanking the Sultan's position there by supporting a rebellion in Oman with arms and money. No sooner had the Buraimi arbitration broken down in 1955 and the Sultan's villages in the oasis been re-occupied, than trouble began in the Oman mountains. At first it was suppressed by the Sultan's prompt response in December of that year, when, as James Morris recounted afterwards, Suliman came down from the Jebel Akhdar to make his peace, driving an American convertible with a negro slave riding postilion on the boot. The Sultan was conciliatory, promising the Omani leaders in Nizwa that he would not interfere with their traditional way of life, and upholding the Ibadhi faith by banning public smoking in Muscat thereafter, in order to show that his capital could be as much a model of Koranic discipline as anywhere in Oman. Ghalib was permitted to stay in his native village on promises of good behaviour, but Talib fled to Saudi Arabia to enlist more help in fostering a new rebellion.

It took two years to get the rebellion off the ground again, but when it was resumed in the summer of 1957 it had acquired a wider significance. In those two years the position of the western powers in general and Britain in particular had been challenged more seriously than ever before throughout the Arab world. The Russian arms agreements with Syria, Egypt and the Yemen, and the Suez crisis and its humiliation of Britain had transformed the Middle Eastern balance of power. Once more, as in 1949 when the Saudis first advanced their Buraimi claim, it looked as if Britain was on the run; and this time the leaders of Oman joined hands with those of Egypt as well as Saudi Arabia to turn Britain's new weakness to their own advantage. Talib recruited an army of three or four hundred men, paid and trained by the Saudis in Dammam; Suliman bin Himyar had visiting cards printed in uncertain English entitling himself 'Ruller of the Green Mountain'; the Voice of the Arabs adopted the rebel cause; and the Arab League was easily persuaded that the Omanis were valiant fighters for progressive Arabism against the filthy British and the feudal Sultan. In a rational world, one might suppose, the spectacle of an avowedly revolutionary regime in Cairo supporting such a plainly reactionary tribal and religious movement in Oman in harness with the despotic and profligate Saudis, whom the Egyptians affected to despise, would scarcely have seemed the most convincing demonstration of progressive Arabism at work. But there is more than one kind of rationality, and it was enough for most Arabs to be reminded again that 'the enemy of my enemy is my friend, and the friend of my enemy is my enemy'. The British, demonstrably, were the enemies of all progressive Arabs. The Sultan of Muscat was a friend of the British. Therefore he was an enemy of progressive Arabs. Therefore all who opposed him were progressive Arabs. Q.E.D. Thus, the Egyptian desire to harass Britain, and the Saudi wish to revenge themselves for their defeat in Buraimi were allied to Omani tribalism, isolationism and greed in one of Arabia's most characteristic post-war feuds.

Inevitably on this second occasion the British Government had to bear a greater burden of action. Without sacrificing at one stroke most of the principle and a good deal of the practice behind their position in Arabia, and perhaps elsewhere, they could not ignore the Sultan's predicament. The short-lived success of his first attempt to subdue the rebels, and the Omanis' acquisition in the meantime of full pan-Arab patronage, had revealed the futility of relying on the Sultan to maintain his rule unaided. By treaty and precedent Britain was committed to his support, and the Government believed, with some justice, that to be dilatory in fulfilling this obligation would wreck Britain's credit not only in Muscat but throughout the British-protected states of the Gulf on whose oil supplies Britain's industry and finances depended. Coming so soon after the débâcle of Suez, any vacillation might also confirm, from Cyprus to Singapore, that Britain was now ready to surrender to every challenge. No real choice existed, therefore, but to extend the *Pax Britannica* for the first time, faded and threadbare though it might seem, beyond the coasts of Muscat into the mountains of Oman. Accordingly, in the years after 1957, while the Saudis and Egyptians fought the Omanis' battles from a distance, the British fought the good fight for the Sultan on the spot. They withdrew their own soldiers as swiftly as they had sent them — but they trained, led, armed and paid the Sultan's. They supplied officials for the Sultan's Government and argued his case in the United Nations. They educated his only son and tried to persuade the Sultan to educate the sons of other people. In short, at last — and almost in spite of themselves — they began in Muscat and Oman some of the imperial tasks they had virtually completed throughout the rest of their disappearing Empire. And in beginning them, they heralded the inescapable fall of this last traditional bastion of Arabia.

18

Things to Come

———————————∿∿∿∿∿ ❀ ∿∿∿∿∿———————————

'... The Vicars of Bray seemed to have made their new peace all over Oman today. Brigadier Robertson went out from his field headquarters between Firq and Nizwa and toured some of the last remaining villages of the dissident area, accepting formal surrender from the elders of Tanuf and Bakhla.

'Your Correspondent was one of a small party flown to his camp today. Colonel Campbell, the commander of the Cameronians detachment, said that the last seen of the rebels was a party of 30 or 40 fleeing into the hills. Only three villages of any importance remained which had not yet offered formal surrender, but no difficulty was expected with them. . . . Most of the people appeared to have found the rebels "damned nuisances", who ate their food and spoiled the date harvest.

'Our own welcome in the alleys of Nizwa was not what you would call abandoned. Some trap-jawed older worthies peered in silence from the shade of their favourite trees, but whether in contempt or only half-blind puzzlement it was hard to say. The younger ones pressed forward with tentative smiles, occasional handshakes, and a few self-conscious English mutterings of "Hello!" "Goodbye!" and "Okay!" Overhead a couple of Venom jet fighters buzzed the town and the little crowd looked up, unafraid and mildly curious, used by now to these wonders.'

(From a dispatch to *The Times* by the author,
dated Bahrain, August 13th, 1957.)

In such hum-drum ways do eras end — and others begin. Less than ten years before I filed that message the greatest living Arabian explorer had been unable to set foot in Nizwa. Yet that morning I had arrived in a four-engined aeroplane, with half-a-dozen other journalists, to join 100 men of the Cameronian Regiment encamped in the scrub before Nizwa, where they were shattering the ancient quiet of Oman with the songs and cries of their native Glasgow as they bathed in the crystal stream that descended from the Jebel Akhdar. 'I belong to Glasgae, dear old Glasgae toon': the chorus that rose from the banks of the stream tolled an ironic bell for Muscat and Oman.

Our stay in Nizwa was brief. We climbed to the roof of the great round tower in the town's massive old Portuguese fort to inspect the puny damage inflicted there by aerial rockets from the jet fighters. We wandered through the *suk* and found it empty — destitute, apparently, of goods or money. We watched a negro slave having his head shaved — the laughing centre of a delighted crowd as an American cameraman recorded his indignity for the television screens of the world — and were ourselves watched by a populace that revealed every emotion about our presence from sullen resentment to girlish flirtatiousness. That evening we flew out again to Bahrain, and within two weeks the last of the British troops followed us leaving the Sultan of Muscat to consolidate the authority they had won for him in Oman. 'There is no intention to become permanently involved,' said a British spokesman at the time. The troops had merely responded to a temporary call for help.

But the British, and the world they represented, could not enjoy so short a stay. More than five years later, when I saw Nizwa again, a shiny new barracks for the Sultan of Muscat's Army had been built with British money where the Cameronians had squatted in the scrub, and a permanent airstrip had been prepared by British engineers where I had landed on the first occasion in a cloud of dust and whirling gravel. From that airstrip I took off again in November 1962, with a British pilot in one of the British aircraft of the Sultan's new Air Force, to fly over the Jebel Akhdar. Until 1957 not a single European had penetrated the mountain for over 100 years. Now, as we circled its rocky flank, laboriously gaining height to cross the summit, we saw swinging close beneath us the immense clefts and gorges which had helped to preserve the mountain's secrecy. On their sides were tiny, flat-topped houses and villages, clinging to the rock amid terraces of astounding green, like a vision of Shangri-La. Wellsted had visited some of them in 1835, and described them in his *Explorations in Oman*:

'By means of steps we descended the steep side of a narrow glen, about four hundred feet in depth, passing in our progress several houses perched on crags or other acclivities, their walls built up in some places so as to appear but a continuation of the precipice. These small, snug, compact-looking dwellings have been erected by the natives one above the other, so that their appearance from the bottom of the glen, hanging as it were in mid-air, affords to the spectator a most novel and interesting picture.'

From above the picture was as novel and interesting as ever, and as far as I could see, utterly unchanged. But on the plateau summit of the Jebel the new world had planted its symbols: an airstrip was laid out, with a few huts to one side, where a British officer of the Sultan's forces waved to us as we made a couple of passes overhead and tumbled out through the door of our aircraft two or three bags of mail and supplies for his men. Then we roared on, cork-screwing perilously down one of the gorges on the other side, to land at another new airstrip and visit another new army camp.

This is now the pattern of government in the Sultanate. Since 1957 the Sultan's Armed Forces have become the core of his country, and inevitably the burden of making them so has been borne by the British Government, which could only withdraw its own troops successfully by creating an effective local substitute for them. This modern and belated extension of the *Pax Britannica* has cost the British Government nearly £1 million a year since 1960 in direct subsidies to the Sultan of Muscat. Besides paying for the new army camps and airstrips, the money has financed new roads and wireless communications. It has helped to restore crumbling village forts all over the country, patching up their old walls and battlements more as tokens of the Sultan's authority than for practical purposes of defence. It has enabled the Sultan's Army to change its character, size and duties. In the old days of the Sultan's Field Force most of the soldiers were Baluchis from the Batina coast whose working language was Urdu. They were not more than a few hundred strong, their officers were only a handful of British mercenaries mostly retired from the Indian Army, and they rarely showed their faces beyond Muscat's coastal strip. Now Arab tribesmen are recruited in equal numbers and Arabic has become the army's principal language. Its strength is well over 2,000 men and half its 50 or 60 British officers are seconded from regular positions in the British Army. It is better equipped and more professional, and by keeping detachments stationed permanently throughout the country it has established a new peace in every corner of the Sultanate.

At first glance this may seem a purely reactionary programme, calculated to provoke just those criticisms of 'British occupation' and 'military aggression' with which Cairo Radio and the 'Free Omanis' make such exaggerated play. In fact, it is nothing of the sort. As in Saudi Arabia under ibn Saud, in the Yemen under the Imam Ahmad, in South Arabia under the British, or anywhere else where a central authority has begun to impose some modern order upon an old tribal society, the assertion of the Sultan's law throughout the land is revolutionary, promoting social change both by the fact and the manner of its accomplishment. In dozens of remote villages and hundreds of tribal families, the money spent on restoring old forts and paying new recruits has opened a window on the world for the first time. Many an Omani or Dhofari has learned to read and write in the army, and perhaps to repair a motor engine, as well as to advance his family's well-being with his soldier's pay. The Sandhurst principles of the British Army officer, absorbed in person by Qabus, the Sultan's son, have been extended at second-hand to others of less exalted birth through the training and example of the British officers in the Sultan's Army. When I was last in Muscat a dozen local officers had already been commissioned and more were on the way. There may not yet be a budding Nasser among them, nor even an Abdullah Sallal, for the most ambitious young officer can hardly regard an army of 2,000 men as an adequate springboard for political revolution in a society still dominated by tribal ways. But it is not fanciful to foresee the day when the Sultan could find his authority challenged by the sort of self-assertion among his new officers that heralded King Saud's ultimate downfall after the Yemen revolution in 1962.

There are other channels besides the army through which the twentieth century has begun its remorseless seepage. These, too, are often of British origin or inspiration, pressed upon the Sultan either by the private advisers he has hired from Britain or by official representatives of Her Majesty's Government. They are, indeed, the necessary accompaniment of military pacification — the other face of the latter-day Raj. Better internal security, for instance, has enabled a stagnant economy to be stirred into its first attempts at self-improvement for more than 100 years, reversing the history of Muscat's long decline. What might be called the case of the returning peasants may serve as an illustration of the process. When Lieutenant Wellsted climbed the Jebel Akhdar he was able to do so partly because the reigning Sultan of his day was still the beneficiary of the proceeds of the slave trade and was able, in consequence, to extend his writ through most of the interior of Oman. Because of the greater reach of the Sultan's purse and sword, Oman was comparatively prosperous and Wellsted found every sign of a flourishing agriculture there. Many trees and fruits were growing on the Jebel Akhdar — 'pomegranates, citrons, almonds, nutmegs and walnuts, with coffee bushes and vines.' But the decline of the slave trade and the weakening of the Sultan's power left Oman isolated and rebellious and destroyed much of this prosperity. Many Omanis migrated to the coast or to Zanzibar, and the irrigation channels which had brought water and fertility to much of the Jebel Akhdar and its neighbourhood began to collapse in disuse. Their destruction was completed in the air raids which accompanied the expulsion of the last of the rebels from the summit of the Jebel in 1959, and the remaining villagers on the mountain prepared then to abandon their homes for good. The British Government, however, sent an officer of the Royal Engineers together with their chief agricultural adviser in the Middle East — a burly and sardonic gentleman named Jack Eyre — to see whether the channels could be restored and the villagers persuaded to return home. They decided that restoration was possible, indeed, and stayed on the Jebel for several months to supervise the job. Afterwards they distributed diesel pumps to the villages to improve the water flow, and as a final gesture of rehabilitation Eyre opened an agricultural research station in Nizwa, under a Pakistani director, to act as a permanent source of local experiment, advice and example. By the end of 1962 three things had happened as a result. First, the villages on the Jebel had been re-populated. Secondly, Omani exiles as far away as Zanzibar had heard of the improvements and were inquiring whether they could return to cultivate their ancient family plots again. And thirdly, in an inspired importation of alien custom, the research station had held the first recorded vegetable show in Nizwa, to which hundreds of villagers from miles around had brought their own exhibits. Small beer, perhaps, in the modern story of Arabia, but full of the authentic taste of the peninsula's transformation.

Less happily, so far, the schools of Muscat and Oman have not advanced, for the Sultan remains profoundly suspicious of education as the principal cause of uneasy minds and disloyal sentiments. It took many centuries in Britain, he told me once, to create a people who were both educated and content: how, he asked, could he be expected to do the same thing in a generation? Adamantly, he has refused to try. Teacher-training scholarships have been dangled before him unavailingly, secondary schooling and university places have been offered without success. There were only three modern schools in the country when I was last there, and the suggestion that the Sultan might open a national radio station which could combine education with propaganda had been frustrated by his suspicion that it would only be the thin end of a subversive wedge.

Yet the wedge of knowledge is being inserted in spite of all his caution. Nobody nowadays need be marooned in Muscat and Oman if he really wants to get away, and in the last few years at least a score of the Sultan's subjects who could gain no support from him in their quest for an education abroad are believed to have found their way to communist countries. More important, literally thousands of the best and brightest of his people, lacking opportunity at home, have sought work and money in the oil-fields further north in the Persian Gulf. In some of the villages of the Batina coast there is hardly a man left between youth and old age: they are all in Bahrain, Kuwait, Dhahran or Qatar, sampling the fruits of the new Arabia. From there it is a short step for some of them to Cairo or Baghdad, where they learn the ideas of a new world and a new century. Few of them will return to Muscat as friends of the Sultan.

Upon those who stay behind the *Voice of the Arabs* works its strenuous charms without need of education. You do not have to read or write to respond to its urgent broadcast calls for freedom, justice and the triumph of Arabism, even if you are only vaguely aware of what those terms are supposed to mean. 'O, Arabs!' says the familiar voice, magically emerging from the air, 'Why do you not rise against the British imperialists? Let us cast out the foreign dogs and all who are traitors to Arabism!' And many an Omani, sitting under a thorn bush with the transistor radio his cousin or his nephew brought back from Kuwait, may listen — and be tempted to agree.

It would be absurd to suggest that such changes had sunk very far into the traditional life of either Oman or Muscat. The Sultanate is still a land where tribalism and feudalism are overwhelmingly important, where horizons are limited, administration minimal and the laws of the Koran are supreme. To visitors its blemishes often seem appalling. They shudder at reports of a drunken uncle of the Sultan beating the prisoners in Muscat gaol, with — so the local whisper has it — the Koran in one hand and a forbidden brandy bottle in the other. They are exasperated by the Sultan's isolation and his secrecy, and they recoil from the sanctimonious viciousness of some of the old Ibadhi leaders. They are horrified by the pervading sickness of the Sultan's subjects. In the villages of Oman there is often not a single healthy inhabitant in sight. Trachoma, tuberculosis, malaria, rheumatism and decaying teeth, on top of years of self-imposed in-breeding and involuntary under-feeding, have made the Omanis as poor an advertisement for the life of the noble savage as any I have seen; and it was no surprise to anyone who knew the district that Jack Eyre and his army companion both contracted tuberculosis themselves when they were working on the Jebel Akhdar. To the raddled and wall-eyed villagers of Oman they must have seemed not merely strangers but physical freaks until they did.

The point is, however, not that the modern world has suddenly triumphed in the Sultanate, or even that it is anywhere more than faintly visible yet, but that it has, in so many small and sometimes subtle ways, arrived. And as we have seen in nearly every territory in Arabia now, once that happens the changes that result are apt to feed upon each other, so that the graph of transformation follows a sharply rising curve. Muscat and Oman will be no exception to this general rule. If there ever was any chance of the Sultan greatly restraining the pace of change once the British began their belated intervention, it was destroyed in November 1964. That was when the event to which the British intervention had always pointed was announced at last. The Shell Oil Company, as successors to Petroleum Development (Oman) Ltd. in the exploration of the Sultan's territory, confirmed the rumours that had been buzzing in the Mattrah *suk* for a year or more of a substantial commercial strike of oil in Oman. A pipeline would be constructed from the interior to a terminal on the coast near Muscat, the company added, and by the end of 1967 they hoped to be exporting oil at the rate of six or seven million tons a year.

With this announcement, the fateful acceleration of change has begun in Muscat and Oman. From abroad we may expect the Egyptians, and possibly the Saudis too, to increase their political pressure upon the Sultan, and from within the new oil money and the new oil jobs must quicken the penetration of Muscat and Oman by the ideas and emotions of the outside world. This is likely to complete the eclipse of the 'Free Omanis' as much as it ultimately threatens the Sultan's rule, for both of them are representatives of the Arabian past. The indigenous question of the Imamate of Oman and its dubious independence is dying now, if it is not yet dead. For a few more years it may serve as a stick with which to beat the Sultan, but the long-term threat to his position does not lie there. Instead, it is in the incipient revolution of rising expectations that will be carried forward on the backs of the oil industry and the *Pax Britannica*. Unlike the rebellion in Oman, this cannot be suppressed: it can only be channelled, with luck and skill, to more hopeful ends.

In this process, Britain may be called to account as much as the Sultan. By custom and treaty she is his friend and protector, and in the rush of development that is about to descend upon his kingdom British help will be needed more than ever, and British protection may be sought more often. There will be roads as well as pipelines, canteens and office blocks as well as military camps and airstrips to build. There will be native labour to train and an administration to be created. There will be unprecedented sums in the Sultan's treasury and the jealousy of his neighbours will be correspondingly deepened. Nominally, of course, the Sultan will remain independent, but in practice for the next few years at least, he may be more than ever a dependent of the latter-day Raj. Far from not being permanently involved, as the British spokesman said in 1957, Britain will be entwined more firmly than before in all the affairs of the Sultanate — until one day she will have helped so much to change the face of the country that she can either go gracefully, or be kicked out, when the political revolution succeeds the economic and social changes that have begun.

Thus the last rape of the old Arabia will take its course. It is still only thirty years, let us remember, since Freya Stark risked her life to enter the Hadhramaut, only half that time since Thesiger was turned away from Nizwa, and not a decade yet since the world still looked upon the Yemen as the kingdom of silence. Now, with the violation of Muscat and Oman's solitude there is scarcely a virgin corner left. Everywhere in the peninsula the old world is pregnant with the new.

Whether the changes that will result will be altogether for the better is a judgement I do not care to make. Some, certainly, say that they will not be; that all that is replacing a once coherent civilisation is the bastard child of the old Arabia and the new West, in whom arrogance conquers nobility, greed overcomes generosity, and the slow, reserved courtesies of the desert are brushed aside by the ill-mannered deceptions of a commercial culture. No-one who has seen Kuwait or Jeddah, Qatar or even Aden can whole-heartedly disagree with this pessimistic verdict. Nor is it possible in the light of the recent travail of the Yemen to be optimistic about the outcome of early political revolution in Arabia. On the other hand, it strains all reason to see any merit in the murderous and fratricidal strife that prevailed only yesterday upon the Trucial Coast, or the religious schisms and fanaticisms that have racked so much of Arabian history, or the sheer, physical ill-health that still besets many of its people. All the past was not noble or romantic, nor will all the future be as ruinous as the pessimists make out.

In the end, however, neither pessimism nor optimism is strictly relevant. For better or worse, what has happened has happened; and the shape of the Arabian future is already implicit in the Arabian past. All that remains is to say farewell to innocence and gird ourselves to understand the shape of things to come.

Epilogue

A few months after I had finished writing the foregoing chapters I was back in Arabia again. The occasion was the suspension of the Aden constitution in the autumn of 1965, after many months of nationalist terrorism in the town. Once again, it seemed, Britain was playing the Arabian reactionary, restoring direct rule to her old colony after a decade of fitful approach to independence. And once again the Aden nationalists were up in arms. As I surveyed the narrow streets of Crater from the security of a British Army lorry it was as if nothing had changed these ten years — except to get worse. The schoolboys were chanting 'Gamal Abdul Nasser!' at every British soldier. Sullen groups of demonstrators were being rounded up into Army compounds. A fierce tang of tear-gas hung in the air, and the streets were littered with crude barricades, burned-out cars and broken glass. As I was standing at a corner amid the wreckage for a moment, a man dashed up to me and thrust an envelope into my hand. A colleague with frightening memories of wars and rebellions elsewhere cried 'Careful!' and knocked it to the ground. It might, she explained, contain an explosive booby trap. In fact, as we discovered after cautious experiment, it held nothing worse than an appeal in Arabic for the British to get out of Arabia, in the name of God. How often, I thought then, I had been here before, in flesh and in weary spirit as well.

Yet in reality things had changed, and were continuing to change, far more than was apparent at first sight. Within a few months of that incident in Aden, the British Government acknowledged as much when it announced, in February 1966, that it would abandon the Aden military base by 1968, as soon as the Federation of South Arabia became independent. There would not even be a treaty of defence or protection for the shaikhs who had sheltered under Britain's wing for so long. True, the nationalists in Aden and their friends in Cairo professed to be unconvinced; and Conservative Party spokesmen in Britain — all their old Suez hackles rising — gave them some grounds for suspicion by making rash election promises to retain the Aden base, after all, if they were returned to power. But in effect the proposal was final. Once it was

239

announced, no British Government could go back on it without provoking more trouble than the base could possibly be worth. After more
than a century-and-a-half of uneasy paramountcy in the peninsula,
Britain had embarked irrevocably upon her own farewell to Arabia.

This is only one of the many changes that have overtaken Arabia in
the nine months that have now elapsed since the previous chapters were
completed. None of them has especially dismayed me, however, or
caused me to wish that I might revise substantially anything I have
written. Only one seemed to me to be unexpected, and that one, fortunately, had more symbolic than practical significance. That was the
deposition in 1965, with British help, of the Ruler of the little Trucial
Shaikhdom of Sharjah, who promptly resorted to Cairo, in the usual
manner of Arab political exiles, and afforded the Egyptian propagandists some light relief as the latest martyr in the cause of Arabism and the
nationalist revolution. One or two events were ultimately unavoidable,
like the death of Shaikh Abdullah, the wise old Ruler of Kuwait. Most
were, in some sense, predictable; and at least some of them were actually
foreseen in earlier pages — like the appearance of women on the television screens of Saudi Arabia; Shaikh Shakhbut's tardy acceptance of
a 'Fifty-Fifty' oil agreement in Abu Dhabi, to hasten the spread of the
contemporary cancer along the Trucial Coast; the student riots in
Bahrain, which resulted in several deaths in the spring of 1965; and the
open clash between Iraq and Iran which disturbed the outlook in the
Persian Gulf in the closing months of that year.

Two other developments of 1965 and early 1966, however, although
also in some respects foreseen, seem to me to belong to a different order
of importance, and to deserve a final comment. They are President
Nasser's continuing difficulties in the Yemen, and the clearer emergence
of Saudi Arabia as the likeliest heir to British influence in the Persian
Gulf. Obviously, these two are closely linked. President Nasser's failure
is King Faisal's gain, for it is precisely because Nasser has been unable
to defeat the royalists in the Yemen that Faisal is now seen as the most
powerful influence in Arabia. Under his leadership the traditionalists,
apparently, have overcome the revolutionary challenge; and, as I write,
hopeful conservatives both in the Middle East and Britain are gathering
beneath Faisal's banner as the revolutionary Arab nationalists once
gathered under Nasser's. History, they are convinced, is now on their
side. Tribalism and Islam have defeated republicanism and socialism,
and the Arab revolution has spent its strength. Moreover, they see the
same pattern taking shape throughout the world, for revolution in the
middle 1960's is almost everywhere out of fashion. The golden 'fifties

of positive neutralism, when Russia and America vied for the favours of any petty potentate, and newly independent states came trooping into the limelight ten by ten, have been overcast by the dull sobriety of recent years. Russia is now as much concerned about China as about America, and is almost as eager to keep the peace in the world as to stir up more trouble. From Ghana to Indonesia, the *avant garde* of revolution is in retreat, as the hard, grey facts of life take their toll of rosy dreams. In this world-wide movement, events in Arabia must take their place, it is argued, responding to pressures that the peninsula's inhabitants are only dimly, if at all, aware of.

Up to a point, all this is true, for the Arab revolution — like so many others — has been overtaken by its own successes. We have only to look back ten years to see how sweeping these have been. The British prised loose from most of their old positions in the Middle East, right-wing governments overthrown, monarchical regimes forced into new moulds, the tremors of revolution reverberating even in the remotest corners of Arabia — after so much success in so little time, a pause for breath is almost inevitable. It may even prove to be a lengthy pause, for it seems unlikely that Nasser can ever recapture the first fine rapture of his post-Suez years, or that the movement towards Arab unity can regain the impetus it once seemed to possess. Nasser is older, and probably wiser, and Arab unity manifestly lies in ruins. Yet it would be a mistake to write off either as a spent force. Certainly President Nasser is no longer the irresistible power that he once seemed to be, but as an elder states-man he retains great influence. He is the head of the biggest and, historically, the most stable Middle Eastern country. He has resources of industry and education at his disposal that are unrivalled in the Arab world. It is not just for propaganda purposes that Egyptian school-teachers are scattered throughout the Persian Gulf, for example; they are there because no other Arab country can provide so many qualified men and women. Cairo's radio, television, press and film industries operate on a scale far beyond the reach of any of Nasser's rivals. And the President's personal record, although far from unblemished by mistaken judgements and abandoned policies, is one in which many Arabs still take pride, even when they have come to disagree — some-times violently, as is the Arab way — with his contemporary actions. Even the Yemeni tribesmen fighting for the Imam against Egyptian troops are said to keep Nasser's picture pasted to the walls of their mountain caves, for they know him to be the man who has shown the way not only to revolution but to Arab self-respect, after centuries of humiliation and subservience. He remains, therefore, much more than first among equals in Arab eyes. He pre-empts the centre of the Arab stage; and although he cannot impose his own policies as easily as he used to, he can still dispose of other people's more effectively than anyone else.

Similarly, although Arab political unity may be as far away as ever, Arabism as a spiritual force seems to survive every setback. Essentially, it is a feeling for a common language and a common tenor of life. Colloquial Arabic is spoken by perhaps 80 million people in the Arab lands between the Atlantic Ocean and the Persian Gulf; and although its forms differ more widely than all the spoken English dialects, from the Appalachian hillbilly to the Durham miner, it is always recognisably the same language. Above all, it is the holy language of Islam, and specifically — in its classical form — the language of the Koran. Its meanings and symbols are woven into the entire fabric of Arab life, providing, as it were, a common nervous system through a complex inheritance of linguistic and religious cross-references. From this system great leaders may still evoke great things.

I have pointed out before how easily Arab movements can be reversed — how quickly they are apt to splinter at the touch of success, yet how they may re-form and rise again from the depths of apparent failure. Nothing induces such reversals more swiftly than the sense of an external challenge to the concept of Arabism. Such a challenge still exists in Arabia. The British are withdrawing from Aden, at last, but they are not yet departing from the Persian Gulf. Indeed, one of the consequences of their abandonment of Aden will be the strengthening of their military and political presence in the Gulf, with more troops in Bahrain, closer supervision of the Trucial Coast and — no doubt — an increased involvement in the Sultanate of Muscat and Oman. Thus, the coincidence of Arabian traditionalism and foreign domination which created such a powerful nationalist ferment in southern Arabia in the last ten years, could easily be repeated in the Gulf shaikhdoms over the next decade. Just as easily, then, the old spirit of nationalist revolution may be rekindled, and Nasser and the new Arabia will be once more at the throats of Britain, King Faisal, and the old.

But even if neither Nasser nor Britain were involved at all there would still be a clash between the old and the new Arabia in which the new would be bound to triumph. As modern wealth and communications increase in the peninsula, so do modern ambitions; and it is the everlasting irony of history that the traditionalists can only effectively combat these things by assuming modern weapons. The Yemeni royalists have only resisted the republicans so successfully by adopting half their tenets, and Faisal has only established his present ascendancy because he had the wit to accept some of the reforms in Saudi Arabia that Nasser's supporters have always demanded.

The notion that history is now on the side of tradition in Arabia is therefore a temporary illusion. Tribalism, to be sure, will put up a stout resistance to change. The fight of the faithful will be prolonged. It may even, from time to time, be successful. But it will never, in the long run, be more than a rearguard action. At every new post on the dusty road of retreat it may seem to the participants — as it seemed to me in Aden, not long ago — that they have all been there before. But no sooner will the weary thought form in their minds, than they will discover that they have not. The sands will have shifted, the contours changed again — and almost before they know it they will be rushing on regardless towards the next crumbling redoubt. That is the way of the world.

London, March 1966

Appendix I

ADEN PROTECTORATE TREATIES

The following is the text of the Protectorate Treaty between Britain and the Sharif of Baihan, in the Aden Protectorate, concluded in 1903. In all important respects it is typical of the Protectorate Treaties negotiated by Britain in the nineteenth and early twentieth centuries with other traditional rulers of the Aden Protectorate.

The British Government and Sharif Ahmad-am-Mohsin of Behan-al-Kasab being desirous of maintaining and strengthening the relations of peace and friendship existing between them:

The British Government have named and appointed Major-General Pelham James Maitland, C.B., Political Resident at Aden, to conclude a treaty for this purpose.

The said Major-General Pelham James Maitland, C.B., and Sharif Ahmad-am-Mohsin aforesaid have agreed upon and concluded the following Articles:

I

In compliance with the wish of the aforesaid Sharif Ahmad-am-Mohsin the British Government hereby undertakes to extend to the territory of Behan-al-Kasab and its dependencies, being under the authority and jurisdiction of the said Sharif, the gracious favour and protection of His Majesty the King-Emperor.

II

The said Sharif Ahmad-am-Mohsin hereby agrees, on behalf of himself, his heirs and successors, and of the people of Behan-al-Kasab under his jurisdiction, to refrain from entering into any correspondence, agreement or treaty, with any foreign nation or power; and further promises to give immediate notice to the Resident at Aden or other British officer, of the attempt of any Power to interfere with the territory of Behan-al-Kasab or its dependencies.

III

The said Sharif Ahmad-am-Mohsin of Behan-al-Kasab hereby binds himself, his heirs and successors, for ever, that they will not cede, sell, mortgage, lease, hire, or give, or otherwise dispose of, the territory of Behan-al-Kasab, or its dependencies under his jurisdiction, or any part of the same, at any time, to any Power other than the British Government.

IV

The above treaty shall have effect from this date, in witness thereof the undersigned have affixed their signatures or seals at Aden this twenty-ninth day of December one thousand nine hundred and three.

P. J. Maitland, Major-General,
Political Resident at Aden.

Mark of
Sharif Ahmad-am-Mohsin

CURZON
Viceroy and Governor-General of India

This treaty was ratified by the Viceroy and Governor-General of India in Council at Backergunge on 24th February 1904.

Louis W. Dane,
Secretary to the Government of India
Foreign Department

Appendix II

ADEN ADVISORY TREATIES

The Advisory Treaties signed by Britain and the traditional rulers of the Aden Protectorate date from just before the Second World War in the Eastern Protectorate and mostly from just after the War in the Western Protectorate. In general the Eastern Advisory Treaties leave more to the discretion of the rulers than do the Western Treaties. The following is the text of the first Advisory Treaty negotiated in the Western Protectorate, between the Sharif of Baihan and the British Government, dated 1944. It is characteristic of all the succeeding Western Advisory Treaties, and except for the qualification already noted, follows fairly closely the pattern established by the Eastern Treaties.

IN THE NAME OF GOD, THE MERCIFUL COMPASSIONATE.

TREATY BETWEEN HIS MAJESTY'S GOVERNMENT IN THE UNITED KINGDOM AND THE SHARIF OF BEIHAN

WHEREAS His Majesty's Government in the United Kingdom and Sharif Husein bin Ahmed al Habili, Regent to Sharif Saleh bin Husein bin Ahmed al Habili, Sharif of Beihan and its Dependencies, are desirous of reaffirming their Treaty obligations and of strengthening the friendly relations which have for long existed between His Majesty's Government and the Sharifs of Beihan. And whereas Sharif Husein bin Ahmed al Habili, Regent to Sharif Saleh bin Husein bin Ahmed al Habili, Sharif of Beihan, is desirous of developing and improving the Territory of Beihan and its Dependencies and of declaring his intention of ruling wisely and justly and His Majesty's Government are prepared to assist him with their advice.

His Majesty's Government in the United Kingdom have named and appointed Sir John Hathorn Hall, Knight Commander of the Most Distinguished Order of Saint Michael and Saint George, Companion of the Distinguished Service Order, Officer of the Most Excellent Order of the British Empire upon whom has been conferred the decoration of the Military Cross, Governor and Commander-in-Chief of the Protectorate of Aden, to conclude a Treaty for this purpose.

APPENDIX II

Sharif Husein bin Ahmed al Habili therefore undertakes solemnly and faithfully on behalf of Sharif Saleh bin Husein bin Ahmed al Habili, Sharif of Beihan, and his heirs and successors:

Article 1

That he will abide by all Treaties, Agreements and Promises entered into by himself or his predecessors with His Majesty's Government or their Representative.

Article 2

That he will at all times co-operate fully with and accept the advice of the Governor of Aden in all matters connected with the welfare and development of the territory of Beihan and its Dependencies.

Article 3

That, being desirous of participating in the Cost of agricultural, social and security services in the territory of Beihan and its Dependencies, he will accept as a proper charge upon his revenue such allocation therefrom for these purposes as shall be determined annually by the Governor of Aden in consultation with him.

Article 4

And His Majesty's Government likewise undertake to abide by all Treaties, Agreements and Promises entered into by the British Government or their Representative with Sharif Husein bin Ahmed al Habili, Regent to Sharif Saleh bin Husein bin Ahmed al Habili, Sharif of Beihan, or his predecessors and to assist him and his heirs and successors with advice for the purpose herein before stated.

Article 5

The present treaty has been drawn up in English and Arabic. Both texts shall be of equal validity; but in case of any divergency in the interpretation of any part of the treaty the English text shall prevail.

For and on behalf of His Majesty's Government in the United Kingdom and subject to their confirmation and approval

(Signed) J. HATHORN HALL
Governor and Commander-in-Chief of the Protectorate of Aden

On behalf of Sharif Saleh bin Husein bin Ahmed
al Habili, Sharif of Beihan and his heirs and successors

(Signed) Sharif Husein bin Ahmed al Habili
Regent to the Sharif of Beihan.

Appendix III

Unofficial version of the Treaty (Agreement) of Sib of 25 September 1920, as quoted in 'The New York Times' of 13 August 1957, and reproduced in the report of the Special Representative of the Secretary General of the United Nations October 8, 1963

In the name of God, the Compassionate, the Merciful.

This is the peace agreed upon between the Government of the Sultan, Taimuribn Faisal, and Sheikh Isa ibn Salih ibn Ali on behalf of the people of Oman whose names are signed hereto, through the mediation of Mr. Wingate, I.C.S., political agent and consul for Great Britain in Muscat, who is empowered by his Government in this respect and to be an intermediary between them. Of the conditions set forth below, four pertain to the Government of the Sultan and four pertain to the people of Oman.

Those pertaining to the people of Oman are:

1. Not more than 5 per cent shall be taken from anyone, no matter what his race, coming from Oman to Muscat or Mattrah or Sur or the rest of the towns of the coast.

2. All the people of Oman shall enjoy security and freedom in all the towns of the coast.

3. All restrictions upon everyone entering and leaving Muscat and Mattrah and all the towns shall be removed.

4. The Government of the Sultan shall not grant asylum to any criminal fleeing from the justice of the people of Oman. It shall return him to them if they request it to do so. It shall not interfere in their internal affairs.

The four conditions pertaining to the Government of the Sultan are:

1. All the tribes and sheikhs shall be of peace with the Sultan. They shall not attack the towns of the coast and shall not interfere in his Government.

2. All those going to Oman on lawful business and for commercial affairs shall be free. There shall be no restrictions on commerce, and they shall enjoy security.

3. They shall expel and grant no asylum to any wrongdoer or criminal fleeing to them.

4. The claims of merchants and others against the people of Oman shall be heard and decided on the basis of justice according to the law of Islam.

Written on 11 Muharram 1339, corresponding to 25 September 1920.

Appendix IV

A LAST WORD ON WORDS

One problem that besets all western writers on Arabia is how best to reproduce in their own language the manifold signs and sounds of Arabic. Should they write of the Prophet as Mohammed or Muhammad, Mahomet or Mehemet? When might a shaikh, or a sheik, better be a sheikh? And is not the proper form of Gamal Abdul Nasser something more like Gamal Abd-un Nasr? To some extent the answer depends on the writer's nationality. The French, for example, have devised a characteristically ruthless system of transliteration which bears very little resemblance to most forms of Arabic but has the merit of a fine Gallic consistency. The English, on the other hand, muddling along as usual, permit an infinity of popular permutations while their scholars draft Anglicised forms so faithful to the original Arabic as to be almost unintelligible to the layman.

Parallel difficulties often arise over the use and meaning of certain names and titles. Some of these have been touched on in the text of this book — the confusion over the meaning of shaikh, for example, (see page 31) and the possible significance to be attached to the name of the Yemen (page 33). There is even a problem about the common noun, *abd*, incorporated in the name Abdul (or Abd-el, Abd-al, Abd-un). Strictly speaking, this means a slave or a servant, and Abdul means 'slave (or servant) of' someone or something — usually one of the ninety-nine Arabic incarnations of God. But because most slaves were negroes *abd* has come also to signify a negro, whether or not a negro is, in fact, a slave. In Arabia, where slavery was until so recently a widespread and accepted feature of society, this has sometimes led to embarrassing confusions. The Ruler of Dubai, I believe, surprised a western visitor not long ago by announcing that on a recent trip to America he had seen more slaves in Washington D.C. than anywhere in his life before. What he meant, less surprisingly, was that he had seen more negroes.

There are also, sometimes, political difficulties about nomenclature. The Arabs have claimed in recent years that the stretch of shallow water between Arabia and Iran should be called the Arab Gulf. The Iranians insist — perhaps a trifle illogically by their own standards — that it is the Persian Gulf. And then, of course, there is a trap for the unwary in the name of the United Arab Republic. This name was adopted in 1958 to describe the new state created in February of that year by the union of Egypt and Syria. It has remained, however, the official title of Egypt alone, ever since Syria seceded from the union three-and-a-half years later. Thus Egypt and the U.A.R. have become synonymous, but so also have Egypt-and-Syria and the U.A.R. Yet Egypt alone is a very different political creature from Egypt-and-Syria.

To all such Gordian knots of Arabia I have taken the blunt instrument of personal preference. It is far from a consistent weapon, being conditioned partly by a desire for as much accuracy as possible and partly by the wish not to disconcert the reader with too many unfamiliar terms and spellings. Mohammed, Mahomet and Mehemet, for instance, have generally become Muhammad throughout because I happen to think this form is both easily recognisable and also nearer than the others to the sort of noise most Arabs make when they utter the name. Mehemet Ali, the Egyptian ruler, remains, however, Mehemet Ali because it is unthinkable to envisage him as anything else (except, perhaps, Mahomet Ali). Nothing but personal preference dictated my choice of Ahmad for Ahmed, Husain for Hussein, amir for emir and shaikh instead of sheikh. On the other hand, while I have used *suk* instead of *suq* and Kassem instead of Qassem (still less Qasim) I have stuck to the commonly recognisable form of Qatar instead of the theoretically possible Katar. Qatr, or Gutr — which is what the name often sounds like on the spot — were too outlandish to be considered.

To the problems of Persia and the Persian Gulf, and Egypt and the U.A.R., I have tried to apply rules compounded of history and common-sense. With respect to my Arab friends, there is, if anything, less justification for calling the Persian Gulf the Arab Gulf than vice-versa; and in English useage there is no justification for a change at all. The Persian Gulf, therefore, it has remained. On the other hand, I could not join with those who continue to apply the ancient name of Persia to the modern state of Iran. Wherever the modern state is in question, therefore, I have called it Iran. Wherever historical references demanded, I have used the name of Persia. The U.A.R./Egypt confusion was more difficult to resolve, but in the interests of clarity it seemed best to revive the name Egypt for the present state over which President Nasser rules. As far as I am concerned, therefore, the title, United Arab Republic, refers only to the state which was brought into being so briefly by the accession of Syria to Egypt, between 1958 and 1961.

Finally, there is the little matter of that typographical pet of the Arabic scholars, the ' which represents the Arabic consonant *ain* and which is sounded like a sort of glottal stop. I have cast it out without mercy. No doubt Sanaa should properly be Sana'a, Saud should be Sa'ud, and Qataba should be Qa'taba, and we should all be clicking our palates over them like broody hens. But not here. Except for quotations from other writers whose idiosyncrasies I have left intact, there should not be an *ain*, or an ', in this book. What it has lost, as a result, in scholarly appearance, I hope it may have gained in general appeal.

Books

There is an extensive literature in English about Arabia, but most of it, in the nature of things, deals with the old world rather than the new. The following is a mere skeleton list of the books I have found most useful for information or insight.

GENERAL BACKGROUND

Bullard, Sir Reader, *Britain and the Middle East* (Hutchinson's University Library, London, 1951)

Gibb, H. A. R., *Mohammedanism* (Oxford University Press, London, 1949)

Guillaume, Alfred, *Islam* (Penguin Books, 1954)

Hartshorn, J. E., *Oil Companies and Governments* (Faber & Faber, London, 1962)

Kirk, G. E., *A Short History of the Middle East* (Methuen & Co., London, 1948)

Monroe, Elizabeth, *Britain's Moment in the Middle East* (Chatto & Windus, London, 1963)

Royal Institute of International Affairs, *The Middle East* (Oxford University Press, London, 3rd ed. 1958)

Royal Institute of International Affairs, *British Interests in the Mediterranean and Middle East* (Oxford University Press, London, 1958)

Sanger, R. H., *Arabian Peninsula* (Cornell University Press, Ithaca, N.Y., 1954)

HISTORY, TRAVEL AND EXPLORATION

Doughty, C. N., *Wanderings in Arabia* (Duckworth, London, 1908 — an abridgement by Edward Garnett of Doughty's *Travels in Arabia Deserta*)

Hansen, Thorkild, *Arabia Felix* (Collins, London, 1964)

Lawrence, T. E., *Seven Pillars of Wisdom* (Jonathan Cape, London 1935)

Scott, Hugh, *In the High Yemen* (John Murray, London, 1942)

Stark, Freya, *The Southern Gates of Arabia* (John Murray, London, 1936)

Taylor, Bayard (Ed.) *Travels in Arabia* (Charles Scribner's Sons, New York, 1881 — an anthology of nineteenth-century exploration)

BOOKS

Thesiger, Wilfred, *Arabian Sands* (Longmans Green, London, 1960)

Thomas, Bertram, *Arabia Felix* (Jonathan Cape, London, 1938)

MEMOIRS

Belgrave, Sir Charles, *Personal Column* (Hutchinson, London, 1960)

Ingrams, Harold, *Arabia and the Isles* (John Murray, London, 1942)

Johnston, Sir Charles, *The View from Steamer Point* (Collins, London, 1964)

Van der Meulen, D., *The Wells of Ibn Sa'ud* (John Murray, London, 1957)

REGIONAL STUDIES AND CURRENT AFFAIRS

Ingrams, Harold, *The Yemen* (John Murray, London, 1963)

Kelly, J. B., *Eastern Arabian Frontiers* (Faber & Faber, London, 1964)

King, Gillian, *Imperial Outpost — Aden* (Royal Institute of International Affairs, London, 1964)

Memorial of the Government of Saudi Arabia submitted to the international arbitration tribunal on the Buraimi dispute, 1955. (3 vols.)

Morris, James, *Sultan in Oman* (Faber & Faber, London, 1957)

Philby, H. St. J., *Sa'udi Arabia* (Ernest Benn Ltd., London, 1955)

Reilly, Sir Bernard, *Aden and the Yemen* (H.M.S.O. London, 1960)

Western Arabia and the Red Sea (Compiled by the Naval Intelligence Division of Her Majesty's Government, London, 1940–45, for the Geographical Handbook Series. This volume has never been published but is available through secondhand booksellers and for consultation in British Government offices)

There are also standard guide-books for Aden, Kuwait and Bahrain which offer much useful information in small compass.

Acknowledgements

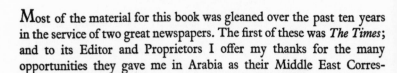

Most of the material for this book was gleaned over the past ten years in the service of two great newspapers. The first of these was *The Times*; and to its Editor and Proprietors I offer my thanks for the many opportunities they gave me in Arabia as their Middle East Correspondent between 1956 and 1960. They have also kindly permitted me to reproduce a passage from one of my dispatches of those years.

Secondly, I am grateful to the Editor of *The Guardian*, who enabled me to make several more visits to Arabia in the following four years, and to whose generous understanding I owe the fact that I found time to write this book.

I have also to thank Mr. M. B. Yeats, and Messrs. Macmillan & Co. Ltd., publishers of the Collected Poems of W. B. Yeats, for their permission to reproduce the poem entitled 'The Great Day'.

Many other people and organisations have placed me in their debt with kindness, information or hospitality over the years. I can only mention a few. The British Army and the Royal Air Force have often enabled me to visit parts of Arabia that I would never otherwise have seen. Officials of the British Foreign Office and of the Colonial Service have been prodigal of their time and explanations. My friends Dino and Michael Athanassacopoulos in Aden, Ronald Codrai of the Iraq Petroleum Company, and Bill Clark in Abu Dhabi are only four of the many individuals to whom I owe much. Another is my old friend and colleague, James Morris, whose persistent encouragement persuaded me to start this book. And, of course, there is my wife, who has borne the writing of it with patience and good humour and brought a ruthlessly professional eye, as well, to the selection of the photographs. I say thank-you to all of them; and add that although many others are unnamed, they are unforgotten.

D. H.

Index

INDEX

INDEX

Beni Ryam tribe (Ghafiri federation, Oman), 228

Besse & Co. in Crater, Aden, 23

Boustead, Sir Hugh, political agent in Abu Dhabi, 197

Britain, *see* Aden; attitude of to Yemen revolt, 58, 63, 97, 106; Arab interests of, affected by her leaving India, 148; as guardian of small Arab states, in 1947, 148–9; and Bahrain, *see* Bahrain; intervention of, Trucial coast, 184–8; and Egypt, *see* Nasser; and Nasser's 1964 threats, 172; role of in the Muscat-Oman struggle, 218, 224–32; future of, in Muscat, 237–8; and Saudi Arabia, 208 seqq., *see* Buraimi; in Persian Gulf territories, 141–50; established on Arabian shore of Gulf, early 19th century, 145; choice left to, in Gulf, 151–62; *for historical details, see* Nasser, Saud, Suez, *also named countries and regions, esp.* Bahrain, Baihan, Buraimi, Iraq, Jordan, Kuwait, Muscat, Oman, Persian Gulf, Qatar, Saudi Arabia, Trucial Coast, Yemen; final farewell to Arabia, 240, 241

British Government's February 1966 Aden decision, 239–40

British Military co-ordinating Committee for the Persian Gulf, 142

British Petroleum Company, 195; Aden refinery of, after blocking of Suez Canal, 19; and the Buraimi dispute, 205

Buraimi oasis: Saudi Arabia's claim to, 154; Saudi slave traders in, in 1950s, 135–6; Britain expels Saudis from, 1955, 188; Oman rebellion follows 1955 arbitration breakdown, 229; the 1955 reoccupation of, 209; aspects of the dispute, 60, 119, 155, 185n, 201–13; improved conditions in, 211–12; Trucial Scouts in, 193; as a symbol, 202

Bushire, East India Company established in, 143

Busi tribe, Britain's 1954 protectorate treaty with, 30

Byblos, 18

Cairo, the Saudi princes in, 119; *see* Egypt, 'Voice of the Arabs'

Cameronian regiment at Nizwa, 231, 232

Central Treaty Organisation, and Gulf affairs, 157

Chamoun, President (Lebanon), downfall of, 45

Chauncey, Major Leslie, British Consul-general in Muscat, at time of Buraimi dispute, 206–7

Chinese: in the Yemen, by end of 1958, 91, 92; Chinese build road from Sanaa to Hodaida, 100, 104

Codrai, Ronald, quoted on Dubai-Sharjah war of 1948, 186; in Fujairah, 187

Committee for the Rights of Oman, in London, 225

Communism in the Arab peninsula, 131; Kassem's support of, against Iraqi nationalists, 170

Compagnie Française des Pétroles, 195

Condé, B. A. de Bourbon (an American in Taiz, Yemen), 73, 74, 79, 82–3, 83n

Council of Rulers on the Trucial Coast, 157–8

Crater (Aden), 23–4, 51, 57, 239

Crescent Hotel, Aden, 17, 20, 21, 55, 64, 72

Curzon, Lord, first Viceroy of India to visit Persian Gulf (1903), 146, 175, 178; quoted, 149, 186

Cyprus bases: and Port Said 'interventions', 41; Aden important to maintenance of, 44

Damascus agreement (Yemen and United Arab Republic), 91

Dammam, first oil well in Saudi Arabia, 129; the modern village at, 131

Das Island, oil discovery at, Persian Gulf, 184, 195, 199

Dhahran (ARAMCO) oil town, 122, 130, 131; as challenge to the old Arabia, 129–39; and Saudi liquor laws, 127–8; 'Dhahran Standard Time', 124

Dhala amirate (Aden), 76, 79

Dhofar, 226; Dhofar uplands, 18, 29, 38

Dinshaw, Cowasjee, Parsee trader in Crater, Aden, 23

'Dissidence', 49, 66; *see* Yemen

Djibouti (Radio), 107

Doha, Turkish garrison withdrawn from, 1916, 147

Doughty, C. N., *Arabia Deserta*, 11, 12, 249; on the Arab character, 47

Douglas-Home, Sir Alec, on extent of Britain's support for Imam in Yemen, 62

Dubai (Trucial Coast principality), 184; at war with Sharjah and Abu Dhabi, 186; in 1957, 190–1; gold smuggling from, 191–2, hunting in,

INDEX

INDEX

Medina (*see also* Mecca), 117, 119, 128, 134

Mehemet Ali, of Egypt, fails to penetrate Arabian heartland, 11–12

Memorial of the Government of Saudi Arabia, 185n

Mocha, Red Sea coffee port, Yemen, 70; America builds road from, to Taiz, 104

Mogadishu, old Muscat overlordship of, 215

Mombasa, old Muscat overlordship of, 215

Monteith, W., British Chargé d'Affaires in Taiz, Yemen, 74

Morris, James, *Sultan in Oman*, 218, 226 and ns, 229

Muhammad Ali al Jifri, leader of South Arabian League, 23; *see* South Arabian League

Muhammad al-Badr, Crown Prince, later Imam, of the Yemen, 83; communist contacts of, 41, 57, 71, 95; as admirer of Nasser, 57, 88, 93; visits Russia, 90, 91; character and appearance of, 89, 112; errors made by, in 1959, 88–9, 93; as reformer, 93–5; supporters of (opponents of Ahmad and Hassan), 90–1, 97; becomes Imam Badr, 94; loses throne, 56, 57, 94–5; conditions after overthrow of, 104–5; remains royalist leader in spite of Saudi dislike of him, 108; signs charter of United Arab States on father's behalf, 121; lesson of, for Faisal as reformer, 139; reasons making feasible Britain's and Federation's support for, 58

Mukalla, a port of Aden, Eastern Protectorate, 37, 39, 40

Murban oil wells (Abu Dhabi), 184

Musandam peninsula, Trucial Coast, 187; tribal warfare continuing in mountains of, 191

Muscat (and Oman): Portuguese in, 12, 215; still holding 20th century at bay, 212–22, 235–7; Nelson said to have visited Muscat, 216; Muscat as Britain's ally against Napoleon, 13; outside Ibn Saud's control, 118; Sultanate of, 141–3; territory described, 226–7; British Consul-general at M., 142; slavery in M., 144, 193, 194, 217; oil agreement with Britain, 1923, 147; oil discoveries of 1960s in, 148; extent of British influence in, 149; Oman rebellion, *see* Oman; forces of M. at Buraimi oasis, 201; Saudi extend claims against (Buraimi), 202 seqq.;

Britain supports, 205; and Sohar operation, 206–7; British aid M. in Oman revolt, 208–9; discontent in after Abu Dhabi's new oil prosperity, 212; the 1798 treaty with Britain, 215; curtailment of slave trade as beginning of decline of, 215; difficulties of penetrating M. and O., 217–19; M. refuses to consider joining U.N., 220; Sultan styled 'friend of Britain' by enemies, 230; M. triumphs in Oman, 232

'Naib' defined, 31

Najd family, of Saudi Arabia, 117

Najran: point of Yemen and Saudi conflict of aims, 74

Napalm bombs, Egyptians use in Yemen, 110

Napoleon, *see* Muscat

Nasariyeh Palace, Riyadh, 119, 132

Nasser, Gamal Abdul, President, 20, 69; and the Aden 'old hands', 24, 25, 55; the British-French-Israeli attempt to overthrow, 1956, 23; 1958 successes of, 45; and Saudi Arabia, 45, 119, 120–1, 131–2; supports Saud against Faisal, 1964, 133; lacking knowledge of Saudi Arabia, 138–9; supports republicans against Imam in the Yemen, 49, 58 seqq.; the Imam's 1956 friendship pact with, 71; Britain's negotiations with, after Yemen revolution, 59, 60–3; Aden as major obstacle to better relations with Britain, 64; Muhammad al-Badr's attitude to, 88–90, 91; creates United Arab Republic, 91; embarrassed by Yemen's membership of United Arab States, 92; Yemen foothold as his first in Arabia, 99; favours aspirations of 'Free Yemenis', supports Sallal, 93, 97, 99; relationship of with subordinates, 102–3; dissolves U.A.S., 94; America's attitude to, over Yemen affairs, 106–8; sees impossibility of military solution in Yemen, 111; and Britain, in Persian Gulf, 151, 152; dispute with Iran since 1960, 154; Kuwait's attitude to, after Suez crisis, 163; Kassem's quarrel with, 170; agents of, in Kuwait, 171–2; and Bonn's intention to recognize Israel, 1965, 172; arms agreement of, with Russia, affecting Bahrain, 180–1; continuing difficulties of, in Yemen, 241; as 'elder statesman', 241; *The Philosophy of the Revolution*, 172; a possible future role of,

INDEX

possible pooling with Bahrain's for Trucial Coast development, 158; frictions with Bahrain, 159; Saudi Arabia's claims on, 160; nationalism in, 160, 190; linked (through a marriage) with Dubai, 196; 1949 oil discoveries in increase Saudi Arabia's claims, 203

Qishn and Socotra, Sultans of, 30, 40

Radfan engagement, involved background to, 48–9; prospects of subduing such tribal territories, 65

Raj, supersession of, 141–50

Rahida, Yemen frontier village, 70

Ras al Khaima, Trucial Coast shaikhdom, 159, 184; duped Mecca pilgrims at, 192

Ras Tanura, ARAMCO refinery at, 129

Rashids of Hail (Saudi house), rivals to Najd, 117

Rashid, Shaikh, ruler of Dubai, 159; as falconer, 196

'Red Line', see Saudi Arabia

Rentz, Dr George, role of in settlement of Buraimi dispute (Saudi Geneva Memorial), 205

de Ribbing, Herbert, U.N. investigator (Muscat, Oman, Buraimi) 1963, 210, 225 and n

Riyadh (Saudi Arabia), 106, 107, 117, 122, 124, 138; King ibn Saud's palace in (Nasariyeh), 119, 132; the Riyadh Line (Buraimi) regarded as Saudi frontier, modifying 'Red Line', 203, 204, 208, 211; press conferences at R. (Faisal's), 134; 'King Saud University' at R., of 1958, 119; the Riyadh-Dammam railway, Persian Gulf, 119

Riyan airfield, association of with Aden, 43

Russia: aids Yemen, 41–2, 71, 90, 91; arms agreements of with Syria, Egypt, Yemen, 229; sends *Askold* to Persian Gulf in 1903, 146; restoring sphere of influence from Turkey to Pakistan, 153; opens embassy in Kuwait, 153; growing strength of, in Middle East, 209, 210; today's attitude of, 241; see also Ahmad, Imam

Said bin Taimur al bu Said, Sultan of Muscat, 217, 219, 220; economic outlook of, 220, 221; see Muscat *and* Oman

St Helena, Bahrain exiles in, in 1956, 180–1

Salalah, province of Dhofar, Sultan of Muscat chooses as residence, 219, 221; airfield of, 43

Salif, a Yemen port, 42, 71

Sallal, see Abdullah Sallal

Sanaa, a Yemen capital town, 57, 59, 62, 63, 105; in important negotiations, 34, 76; and the Western Protectorate agreements, 34, 71, 76; the 'Yemen Arab Republic' declared at, 56; Saud's standing at time of Sanaa coup of 1962, 132; opponents of Imam in, 90, 99; shelling of his palace in, 95; China's motor road to, 91, 92

Saud, Abdul Aziz ibn, rise to power, 117; as modernizer, 118; secures succession for eldest son, Saud, 118; attitude to slavery, 135; as British protégé, 147; and the Buraimi crisis, 203 seqq.; *for chief events see* Saudi Arabia

Saud, King, son of Abdul Aziz ibn Saud, threats to his position, 45, 91, 120, 131 seqq; surrenders power to Faisal, 105, 120, 131 seqq.; extravagance of, 118–19; friendship pact with Nasser and Imam of Yemen, 71; as guardian of Islam's holy places, 119; plot against Nasser's life, 121

Saudi Arabia, 116–39, Chapters 8 and 9, *see also under* Buraimi, Dhahran, Jeddah, Mecca, Riyadh etc; emergence as a modern state, 14, 16, 116 seqq.; early impact on Aden Protectorate, 37; forays by, into Eastern Protectorate, 41; commercial influence in Hadhramaut, 40; upheavals in 1958, 45–6, 120–1; severs diplomatic relations with Britain after Suez, 60; resumes relations with Britain, 210; supports Imamate against Yemeni rebels, 60–3, 132; America brings pressure to bear on, 63; as spearpoint of Arab opposition to Nasser's plans, 99; Egypt bombs territory of, 106; America changes attitude to, 106; easily beats Egypt in financial contest, 111; strength of Wahhabi Muslims in, 116–18; descriptions of, 116–20; grants first oil concession, 117; disputes with Britain over Buraimi and Oman begin, 119; economic mismanagement in, 119–120; 'religious police' in, 125–6; first genuine budget in, 1958, 120; Saudi Arabs trained by ARAMCO, 130–1; first commercial law in, replacing *sharia*, 135; Faisal

INDEX

Sukhne (near Red Sea coast, location of Imam's palace), 76, 80, 83, 84, 86

Suliman bin Himyar of Oman (Ghafiri), paramount chief of Beni Ryam tribe, 228, 229

Sulman, Shaikh (Bahrain), son of Hamid bin Isa, 177–8, 179

Sultanates of Aden Protectorate, 30–1

Sunni Wahhabis of Oman, 223; *see also* Wahhabis

Sur (town and port, Muscat), 226–7, 244

Syria: with Egypt, as United Arab Republic, 45; Egyptian troops in, before 1961, 99–100; secedes from U.A.R., Sept. 1961, 94, 156; Saudi Arabia's opposition to alliance of with Egypt, 121; results of Egypt's failure in, 170

Taimur ibn Faisal, father of Sultan Said of Muscat, 220, 244–5

Taiz, a main town of the Yemen, 57, 72–3, 78, 80, 81, 82, 105; fruits, etc., of region, 81; opposition to Imam Ahmad in, 86, 89, 90; American road from, to Mocha, 104; Egyptians in, 99

Talib, leader of rebellion in Oman, 1955 and 1957, 228–9

Tarik, brother of Sultan of Muscat, Said bin Taimur, 220

Tarim, old town of Hadhramaut valley, 40

Thesiger, Wilfred (*Arabian Sands*), 11, 205 and n, 224 and n, 228, 250; is turned away from Nizwa (Oman), 218, 223 and n, 238; on Ibadhi Imam of Oman, 224; on Muscat influence in Buraimi in 1948, 205

Thomas, Bertram, Wazir to previous Sultan of Muscat (*Arabia Felix*), 223–4, 228

Tiger Bay, Cardiff, Yemeni from, 82

Tihama coastal desert, 74, 84

Time, measurement of, in Saudi Arabia, 123–4

Treaty of Maritime Peace, Persian Gulf, 1853, 144

Trucial Coast (of Oman), Persian Gulf, 184–200; Britain's present role in, 155; need for sweeping changes in, 238; Trucial System, 143–4; Bahrain as centre of, 176; Kuwait as excluded from, 158; seven minor shaikhdoms of, 142; oil discovered in, 1960s (Das Island), 148, 195; resents modernity, 154, 238; Saudi Arabia claims interest in, 160; internal divisions of, making co-

operation impossible, 157; young nationalists in, 160; oil developments hampered by tribal jealousies, 184; oil agreements of 1920s, and settlement of shaikhdom, 186–8; poverty and backwardness of, 190–192; slave traffic survivals in, 193–4; compared with Bahrain and Kuwait as wealthy region, 194; Trucial Council, and Shakhbut's attitude to, 189

Trucial Oman Levies, 188; Trucial Oman Scouts (developed from former Levies), 191–2; in Sharjah, 196; at Buraimi oasis, 201; in field against Saudi at Buraimi, 206; with Muscat forces, expel Saudis from Hamasa, 208

Turki ibn Utaishan, Amir, representing Saudi Arabia in Buraimi, 205, 208

Turks: in first World War, 147; as early invaders of Arabia, 12, 75; in Aden in 1915, 32, 33; *see* Ottoman empire

Umm al Qawain, Persian Gulf shaikhdom, 159, 184

Union of Democratic Forces in the Arabian Peninsula, 131

United Arab Republic of 1958, 45; Yemen joins, 45, 46; for Syria's role, *see* Syria; Sultan Ali Abdul Karim of Lahej joins, 46; later dissensions in, 46–7; presents a name problem, 247; Saudi Arabia's attitude to, 120

United Arab States, 45, 91; Yemen joins, 91; short life of, 92

United Nations, and Arab problems: Gulf affairs generally, 157; and future of Gulf, 162; Dec. 1963 Resolution on South Arabia's 'nationalist manifesto for independence', 66; and Egypt-Saudi Arabia engagement in the Yemen, 108; and Muscat-Oman disputes, 210, 220, 224–5

United States of America, *see* America, ARAMCO

Upper Yafai (Aden Protectorate), 30, 65

U.S.S.R., *see* Russia

Vasco da Gama, in story of Aden's decline, 18

'Voice of the Arabs' broadcasts, Cairo Radio, 24, 36, 43, 51, 64, 94, 224, 229, 233, 236

Wahhabi Muslims (*see also* Saudi Arabia), backwardness of, 135, 145; Britain's struggles with, early 19th

DATE DUE